WITHDRAWN
Italy

'The authors have produced an intelligent, well-informed and student-friendly introduction to contemporary Italian politics which covers the sweeping changes which have taken place in recent years.'

Richard Dunphy, *University of Dundee*

This textbook has been designed to provide students with an up-to-date and accessible introduction to the complexities of Italian politics of the 1990s. It will equip students with a sound understanding of the basics of Italian politics and government, and will provide clear and simple insights into the intricacies of Italian political behaviour.

The comprehensive coverage includes:

- an introduction to contemporary history, political geography and economic issues, as well as Italian political values and attitudes;
- a section on political behaviour which explores political parties, interest groups and the electoral earthquakes of the 1990s;
- a section on government institutions and their roles, including discussion of the executive, the legislature, the judiciary and sub-national government;
- analysis of Italy's often stormy relationship with the European Union;
- an exploration of recent events, such as attempts at institutional reform.

The authors, both experienced teachers of Italian politics, emphasize throughout the book those 'special' problems that have plagued Italy in the 1990s, such as corruption, bureaucracy, political deadlock, terrorism and organized crime.

Sondra Z. Koff is Professor Emerita at the State University of New York at Binghamton. **Stephen P. Koff** is Professor Emeritus at Syracuse University.

Italy

From the First to the Second
Republic

**Sondra Z. Koff
and Stephen P. Koff**

London and New York

Contents

Preface

This is a book about politics and political behaviour in Italy. It has not been written for political scientists, but rather for students and others interested in Italian political life. In Italy, one finds many good books on law and institutions or politics. However, few combine the two fields. The goal of this book is to do just that, to emphasize political behaviour within the context of the legal and institutional setting.

There are some books in English which cover parts of what is presented here. However, almost all of them are dated. Dealing with Italian politics brings with it the problem of frequent change. In fact, studies of all political systems pose this difficulty. However, among the democratic regimes, excessive kaleidoscopic and rapid change has been the mark of many aspects of Italian politics. This volume has endeavoured to present a balance between the events and political behaviour of the years from 1948 to 1998 and the great change in 1994. In other words, we speak of the First Republic, the transition years and the Second Republic, recognizing that in some ways the transition between the Republics is continuing. We fully recognize that the rapid political change will continue for some time. It is our hope that this book will provide the foundation for understanding many of these changes.

A book like this one could only be produced with the help and influence of many people. For the past thirty years and more, Italian friends have led us through the intricacies and delicate nuances of politics in their country. We learned from them much of what we could not obtain from books, articles and newspapers. First and foremost, we must mention Franca Toraldo di Francia, a friend and co-worker without whose aid this volume would not have been produced. She taught us much about Italy, especially its cultural life, which cannot be separated from its political life. Her friendship and affection over the years are highly valued. Guglielmo Negri also was a key figure in our political education. He opened doors for us, as he has done for so many foreign scholars, which enabled us to speak to key governmental and political leaders. Furthermore he read some of the manuscript, especially the chapter on the Parliament, and offered constructive criticism.

Several people who are now deceased offered us important interpretations of politics in their country. Among these were Giuliano Abbozzo, Enzo Enriques-

Agnoletti, Tristano Codignola, Carlo and Maria Francovich, Giuliano Innamorati, Gianni Meucci, Elsa Miele, and Elisa, Dino and Piero Moggi. Running the risk of omitting helpful people, we would like to cite persons who directly influenced this book. We hope they recognize their importance to us. Listed in alphabetical order they are: Laura Abbozzo, John Clarke Adams, Paolo and Lia Barile, Anna Maria Biondo, Rosanna Codignola, the Farina family, the Foa family, Paola and Lando Landolfi, Francesco and Lydia Melani, Anna Meucci, Giovanni Miele, Luca and Ada Moggi, Andrea and Monica Orsi-Battaglini and Alberto Predieri. We are also appreciative of the helpful comments offered by the Routledge reviewers. In addition, the staff at the following Florentine libraries were most helpful: the Biblioteca Nazionale, the libraries of the Faculties of Law and Political Science at the University of Florence and the library of the European Institute. Mention must also be made of Lila Shah, a former student who helped prepare English materials for the chapter on the judiciary.

Our children, to whom this book is dedicated, all have Italian names and are Italophiles like their parents. At times this book interfered with family activities. We thank them for their forbearance, interest and support. Our son, Vittorio, who in his own right is an Italianist, offered important insights.

In spite of all the help we received, of course, the authors take full responsibility for what is written here.

Abbreviations

ACI	Italian Catholic Action
AN	National Alliance
BR	Red Brigades
CCD	Christian Democratic Centre
CDU	Christian United Democrats
CGIL	Italian General Confederation of Labour
CISL	Italian Confederation of Workers' Unions
CORBAS	Rank and file committees
COREL	Committee for the Referendum on Electoral Laws
CSM	High Council of the Judiciary
DC	Christian Democratic Party
EC	European Community
EEC	European Economic Community
ENI	National Hydrocarbons Agency
EP	European Parliament
EU	European Union
EURATOM	European Atomic Energy Community
FI	Forza Italia
IRI	Institute for Industrial Reconstruction
MSFT	Italian Social Movement – Tri-Colour Flame
MSI	Italian Social Movement
NATO	North Atlantic Treaty Organization
P2	Propaganda 2 Masonic Lodge
PCI	Italian Communist Party
PDS	Democratic Party of the Left
PLI	Italian Liberal Party
PPI	Italian Popular Party
PR	proportional representation
PRC	Communist Refoundation Party
PRI	Italian Republican Party
PSDI	Italian Social Democratic Party
PSI	Italian Socialist Party
SIFAR	Italian counterintelligence agency
UDR	Democratic Union for the Republic
UIL	Italian Union of Labour

decline of the threat of communism came extensive scandals that severely tarnished the reputation of the traditional governing parties and their leaders. In 1992, corruption in Italy became a serious political problem. A seemingly isolated incident – the arrest of the administrator of a retirement facility in Milan, who was too slow in flushing down the toilet cash he had just received as a bribe – had momentous consequences and exposed the exceptional extent of public corruption. This led to a string of scandals, known as *Tangentopoli* (Kickback City), which transformed the political arena. In this case, every contract issued was subject to a *tangente* or kickback. It was revealed that the practice was common throughout Milan and other cities according to a specific formula. The coffers of major political parties and the bank accounts of politicians were swollen with bribes from the business community competing for public contracts. Such payments, considered a normal business expense, were linked directly to specific favours, such as a contract or the bending of a regulation (Cazzola 1992b; Della Porta 1992). A prosecuting magistrate now turned politician, Antonio Di Pietro, spearheaded the judicial campaign to remoralize public life, labelled *Mani Pulite* (Clean Hands).

The investigation spread throughout the peninsula and up the political ladder to the highest rungs. Estimates vary as to the number of suspects involved, but run as high as 5,000 persons representing a cross-section of Italy's political, social and economic elite. These were no ordinary scandals. They involved the foremost companies in Italy, and some foreign ones, that had paid bribes to political parties in order to gain public contracts. This led to suicides and imprisonment of some of the biggest names in the commercial world. It has been estimated that payments for large government contracts throughout the 1980s were around 6.5 trillion lire (approximately 4 billion dollars) a year. There was concern that, with so many businessmen involved, the management of top firms would be irrevocably damaged. The activities of the leaders of political parties seemed more dramatic. The number of people involved was greater, and included former prime ministers, parliamentarians and local party leaders. At one point, over half the members of Parliament were under indictment. More than 400 city and town councils were dissolved because of corruption charges. There was a difference in the nature of *Tangentopoli* in northern and southern Italy: in the North the political parties were in complete control of bribery, while in the South they worked with criminal organizations. The *Tangentopoli* scandals struck at the heart of the clientelist network.

It was obvious that bribery was the rule, not the exception. Corruption was a collective phenomenon, and although its specifics were unknown to the populace at large, they were known within restricted circles (Magatti 1996). Clientelism was systemic and tolerated throughout the First Republic. *Tangentopoli* erupted when the Republic encountered difficulties with increasing demands, a depletion of resources and growing bitter internal conflict. Coupled with the fall of the Berlin Wall, *Tangentopoli* set the stage for a generalized protest movement focusing on political corruption. The 'moral question' was critical to the emergence of new political actors. Italy experienced a legitimacy crisis. Within a span of two years, political corruption produced a massive de-legitimation process that obliterated not only an entire political elite, but the system which had governed the country for almost fifty years.

Tangentopoli relates to a contradiction in Italian society: the existence of many strict rules to govern the conduct of public officials so that the public interest will prevail, and the universal practice of clientelistic behaviour. It remains a critical element in Italian politics.

Other events and problems also paved the way for change. The spread of the Mafia beyond its traditional base in Sicily to all parts of Italy was accompanied by the increased use of violence by criminal organizations. The spiral of government spending seemed out of control and this, coupled with a huge public debt, threatened the economy. Long-term problems such as unemployment, inefficient social services and an unsatisfactory education system appeared to be worsening. An obsolete bureaucracy, the part of the government which the people encountered most frequently, remained inefficient, overstaffed and arrogant. Involving 6–7 per cent of the workforce, the Italian bureaucracy is per capita the largest in size of any western democracy. A comment often made in the 1980s was that Italy was not governable. Italians, especially the younger generations, demanded change. The traditional parties and the usual way of doing political business were rejected overwhelmingly by the electorate. It became clear that people no longer had confidence in the government. It should be noted that in the First Republic there was no rotation of power, in sharp contrast to the other western democracies.

Political geography: the North–South dimension

Although Italy can be divided into a number of geographical divisions, for purposes of simplicity, a generally recognized dichotomy is that between the North and South, with the divide being the capital city, Rome (Coppola 1997). This division has given rise to the Southern Question, the core of which is the striking social, economic, political and cultural differences between the two parts of the nation. This dichotomy, the basis of which existed prior to unification of the country in 1861, has been central to all facets of Italian development. Reasons for this diversity include late unification, excessive centralization and events identified with Fascism and the Resistance movement. The North has been dominant throughout Italian history.

From unification, the most prominent facet of the duality has been economic. The South, because of its poverty of resources, its lack of vital links to international markets, its feudal structure which was reinforced after unification, its harsh climate and topography and its restricted entrepreneurial class, has always had an economic status inferior to that of the North. This situation was also heavily influenced by the illiteracy rate, which was in any case high compared to other European countries, but in the South it was two to three times greater than in the North (Cafagna 1994). Clientelism pervaded the southern social and political fabric immediately after unification, with the advent of a national ruling coalition of the southern aristocracy and the conservative bourgeoisie of the North. The South lacked a new middle class capable of governing and representing the public interest in the new state. Its ruling class consisted of the old landowners who, representing themselves and their own parochial interests, served as a screen between the masses and the government (Bevilacqua 1993).

In the international framework, both North and South were politically subordinate and economically marginalized. They only began to count for something in Europe and beyond after unification. The birth of the Italian state guaranteed development of the peninsula (Pescosolido 1998). However, this development was not evenly distributed throughout the various regions and classes. Part of the duality between North and South relates to separateness, not only in terms of distance in kilometres. North and South did not have much contact. They were like separate countries. In the middle of the 1800s, the seeds of industrialization were planted in the North. A healthy banking industry invested in agriculture as well as industry. However, none, or very little, of what was in the North existed in the South. In the latter, commercialization and urbanization were superimposed on a traditional agrarian economic base. The lack of industrialization and modernization and rationalization of agriculture was an obstacle to the formation of stable and homogeneous social classes in the South. The unsound trade, fiscal and industrial policies of the government allowed the ruling class to reinforce its power. Given the predatory ruling class, a fragile administrative structure, an antiquated and clientelistic banking system, an inadequate infrastructure and brigandage, among other negative elements, what the South accomplished was almost miraculous. However, the gap between the two Italies continued to widen.

Under the heel of fascism, the Southern Question worsened. It has been identified as 'the single most serious failure of the Fascist regime' (Cafagna 1994: 64). A mistaken agricultural policy which damaged the soil, structural unemployment, the halt of political and economic development and the Second World War all added to the problems of the South. Reconstruction efforts in the postwar South, which experienced greater destruction than the North, were late and slow. *Laissez-faire* policies also worked to the disadvantage of the area. It was not until 1950 that the state assumed responsibility for southern development through a variety of agencies and programmes. Efforts focused on transferring payments and making investment decisions with the objective of developing the southern economy, especially its industrial sector. This approach ignored the absence of entrepreneurial initiative and an unskilled workforce in the South. Rather than encouraging endogenous initiatives, it discouraged them. This formula produced negative consequences. Government programmes exacerbated the South's dependency on central government intervention and perpetuated personal, clientelistic linkages and a huge well-oiled patronage machine. Efforts have been dysfunctional and the costs excessive (Mutti 1996; Nanetti 1988).

During the First Republic the infrastructure of the South improved, but hundreds of years of history are not easily overturned. The movement of people from the South to the North or other parts of Europe, the introduction of new industries in the South, the creation of an efficient road system which helped to integrate the nation, national radio and television networks and other factors wrought considerable change. However, extreme poverty can still be found in many southern areas. The way of life in a number of small villages has changed little over the years. On the other hand, in sharp contrast, the accoutrements of life in an advanced nation, ranging from better education to mod fashions and the availability of changed opportunities, are evident among a good portion of the young people in these areas.

In spite of many efforts, the South is still a consistent underperformer. Recent statistics underscore the existence of two Italies. In the North, the average per capita income is 18,715,000 lire; in the South it is 11,934,000 lire, and the gap is increasing. Thirty-six per cent of the population resides in the South, but its contribution to the gross national product is 25 per cent and to exports is 9 per cent. Moreover, only 36 per cent of public funds have flowed to the southern part of the country. In the 1990s, five million lire have been spent on each southern resident, while 5,200,000 lire have been expended on each northern resident. Lesser amounts of public funds are dispensed in the area of greatest need. Southern social services, public facilities and services are of low quality. Over a thirty-nine-year period from 1950 to 1989, the government spent 0.7 per cent of the budget to develop the South; it spent much larger sums to cover the deficit of the national railroad system (Marro 1992).

A recent regional industrialization index demonstrates the superiority of the North. The first ten places are occupied by northern regions, and the industrialization rate of the North is three times that of the South. The dramatic circumstances of the South are confirmed in the last census (1991) and more recently by the fact that the unemployment rate in the South is more than triple that of the North. This tremendous economic cleavage still persists after a decade in which Italian economic growth outdistanced that of all other member-states of the European Union (EU) (Cecchini 1995; Manca 1995). On the other hand, in terms of personal consumption and accumulation the South is modern and compares favourably with the North. This dichotomy between southern trends in consumption and production has been attributed to the breadth and depth of government intervention. Consumption levels have been maintained via a wide variety of social and economic policies (Leonardi 1995).

Regional development policies have stressed the role of the state and a centralized administrative–political decision-making apparatus. This strategy has not reduced the distance between North and South in terms of productivity. Enhancing Southern dependence on public funds, it has prevented self-sustained development (D'Antone 1996). Pressures related to the Single Market of the EU and reduction of the nation's deficit also reduced the utility of this approach. The government led by Romano Prodi has undertaken a serious commitment to the Southern Question, especially its high rate of unemployment. It has adopted a new strategy based on decentralization, fiscal federalism, centre–periphery relations with new financial mechanisms and controls congruent with EU policies, industrial and technological innovations, and new systems of professional training. The programme emphasizes a detailed plan for development of the infrastructure, area contracts, territorial pacts, incentives to firms and utilization of EU funds.

A new posture towards development is nurtured by state contributions linked to obligations, including financial ones, which a southern community undertakes. This 'negotiated planning' is critical to the creation of new relationships related to development. This is the rationale behind the area contracts and territorial pacts which involve partnerships between northern and southern provinces and industrialists for collaboration in development efforts. Partnerships are based on 'programme contracts' initiated by a strong northern district which, through a large financial incentive for the development of new installations, becomes linked with a southern one. Emphasis is not on the capacity of the districts to provide new factories with the latest technology, but rather on the acquisition of knowledge and skills which will eventually allow the weaker partner to compete meaningfully with the stronger one. Guidelines for this endeavour were developed jointly by government, business and trade unions. Such collaboration is important.

In another effort, the government is paying a bonus to firms that hire unemployed persons, especially youth. The longer the individual has been unemployed, the larger the bonus and the longer it lasts. A new development in training programmes is the payment of a fixed sum to young southerners who go to the North for a specified period to learn skills and agree to return to the South. This is a type of internship. The government has also reached an agreement with sub-national units of government on Agenda 2000, a new EU funding programme. The EU Single Market Plan is also important to the South. There is an expectation that with its commitment to help poor peripheral regions in the EU, it will provide considerable aid to southern Italy. However, many observers believe that regions such as the South are destined to fall further behind the more successful European nations. Historic corrupt practices, patronage politics, clientelism, the activities of the Mafia and other criminal organizations and similar ills continue to mark this part of the country. Reforms have been promised and initiated many times, but achievements have been limited. The efforts of the Prodi Government represent good intentions; what is important is the fact that they are being turned into deeds. Time is of the essence. Today the South is what it is because politicians wanted it that way: 'it is like Vesuvio: a volcano which only seemingly sleeps and which from one moment to the next can explode' (Fiammeri 1998: 7).

The North–South divide is also of significance in terms of political power, which in the First and Second Republics clearly resides in the northern part of the nation. This political pre-eminence is related to the North's economic position. Political decisions made in the capital often are fashioned by the prevailing economic interests of the North. What is good for the North has been frequently considered to be good for the nation. In terms of the number of persons having a significant role in the decision-making process, the North takes the lead; persons of northern origin occupy most of the important political party and governmental positions. As far as the former are concerned, northerners account for approximately 63 per cent of the offices; in the case of the latter, over the past decade they have occupied almost 60 per cent of the posts. On the other hand, southerners have dominated the bureaucracy, the police and the judiciary (Coldagelli 1992; N.A. 1997). This has hardened northern attitudes against southerners.

The economy

In postwar Italy, economic development has been impressive and tumultuous. The nation is now one of the top five or six most industrialized systems in the world; within the confines of the EU, it ranks third after France and Germany and before Great Britain. Dualism in the economy is very obvious. Different approaches demonstrate several dualistic characteristics. In spite of tremendous economic growth as the march towards the European monetary union progressed, Italy was a prime candidate for second-class membership. The economic system is a capitalist one with considerable state intervention. Although agriculture is central, commerce and industry have overtaken it. In spite of large-scale industrial growth, small firms continue to have an important role. They have been the backbone of the most recent economic development.

Agriculture was for a long time the dominant element in the economy, particularly in the South. While farming is still important, it has changed radically in nature. The introduction of scientific and mechanized agriculture has increased crop yields even as a large part of the workforce left the land. The number of young people engaged in agriculture has declined, while the percentage of women, immigrants and older people has increased. Marginal lands have been abandoned. Italy has become a major exporter of agricultural products.

Although Italy is described as an industrial state, as noted above, the astonishing economic development has not blessed all parts of the nation in equal fashion. Not only has the structure of southern industry been out of phase with efforts concentrating on industrial development, but public policies have not been successful in counteracting the tendency to focus efforts on regions where the industrial base has been and is more secure. This pattern in turn has impacted on regional relationships, which have become more delicate because of uneven economic development. There are also intra-regional variations. Although there has been industrial growth in certain parts of the South, such progress contrasts with the underdevelopment of other areas in this part of the country. The same may be said in reference to the development pattern in the North (Baldassarri 1993; D'Antonio 1993).

There is a high concentration of large-scale industry in the northern third of the nation. It is not only traditional heavy industry, such as automobiles, machine tools and farm machines, that marks industrial growth; the success of modern technology in fields like telecommunications, robotics, and energy, has been impressive. These high-technology industries, along with the fashion and design industries, have been an important source of foreign trade. Within the framework of international economic and monetary union, this new industrial specialization and increased activity abroad present both opportunities and risks, as evidenced from the new prospects resulting from changes in East–West relations and the contrast between the northern and southern hemispheres.

When dealing with the Italian economy, the dichotomy between the public and the private sectors must be noted. Per capita, Italy has the largest public sector among all of the nations of Europe. The economy has been characterized by vast government holding companies, which penetrate almost all aspects of economic life and cause political competition for key roles in the various units. There is a sharp contrast between the organization, operation and efficiency of the productive systems of the public and private sectors, with the latter recording a more favourable performance (Baldassarri 1994). In addition, there have been many debates concerning privatization, which has been slower in occurring than hoped, even though all governments of the Second Republic have emphasized privatization. Evaluations of the Italian economic system manifest dualistic characteristics as well. In spite of predictions of inevitable crises and decline, unexpected achievements regularly occur and come almost as a surprise. Persistent economic cycle crises are counteracted with very positive long-term performance.

Unemployment is a critical problem. The current job shortage is similar to that experienced in other Western European nations. However, the problem becomes more significant when coupled with the problem of the South and its lack of development. The two problems together '...have formed a giant knot which is becoming increasingly tangled...[and] as a consequence regional disparities are accentuated, and solutions become more difficult and complex' (Baldassarri 1993: 5). Official statistics do not tell the entire story about unemployment. There are two workforces in Italy. One includes those people who work in the very large public sector, the professions, industry and commerce, and agriculture, and who hold positions which are officially recognized and for which all taxes and benefits are paid. The second group consists of what is frequently referred to as the 'black market' labour force. The exact size of this force is not known, but it is estimated at millions of people. Twenty-seven per cent of the gross national product is attributed to their efforts (Sivo 1998). The reason for the large size of this group is that taxes for social services are very high, and by using workers who are not officially recognized, an employer can avoid paying these costs. The Italian worker is among the best protected in the world in terms of health, unemployment and other benefits. Usually the people in the 'black market' workforce are in either service or cottage industries. Workers can be either full-time or part-time, and for some this employment involves a second job. This 'black market' workforce is a very sensitive political issue. Trade unions and other interest groups and political parties, which are normally advocates for protection of workers, accept the situation. They fear a negative reaction not only from the unofficial workers but also from many people who support them.

It is clear that Italy has become a consumer society. As a result of industrial development, changes in the class structure are evident with the children of working-class parents moving into the lower middle class. This and other factors have reduced the power of trade unions, a development similar to that of most other nations in the Western world. Also of note is the decline in the size of the industrial workforce. As plants become more efficient and auto-mated, the number of workers needed declines. This has sapped some of the strength of the trade unions and has reduced worker militancy. Italy has a long history of severe conflict between owners and managers on the one hand and workers on the other. However, with the decline of trade unionism industrial relations have changed, and this in turn has impacted on politics and political behaviour.

Another duality, a surprising one, exists in terms of the Italian population. The historic problems of overpopulation and resultant unemployment no longer prevail in the same way they did for centuries. Where only a few years ago a rapidly growing population and a concomitant shortage of work caused many Italians to emigrate to the United States, Canada, Australia, Argentina and more recently to other Western European countries, this is no longer the case. Many observers were surprised when, in 1992, Italy reached a zero population growth rate and in 1994 a negative one. Although Italy was long marked by ethnic homogeneity, at a time when the nation is no longer exporting people it has become a haven for immigrants, principally from Africa, Albania, the former Yugoslavia and China. This influx of people, especially from the developing world, has led to considerable friction and many Italians have been charged with racist attitudes. In part, the newcomers are seen as competitors for jobs in the future.

Historical baggage

The history of the Italian peninsula goes back thousands of years. As one travels about the nation, the remains of ancient civilizations are encountered. Among these, the best-known is the Etruscan, but evidence of Greek colonies can be observed and the influence of North Africa and the Middle East can be found. The stark contrast between ancient and modern Italy is striking. Reviewing early Italian history is beyond the scope of this book, but some mention must be made of modern historical development.

In the second half of the nineteenth century, a modern unified Italy was born. Developments in the nation were part of an age of nationalism. Modern Germany was created contemporaneously with Italy in the period 1860–70. The Italian national unification movement is known as the *Risorgimento*, which means the rebirth of the nation, or the reawakening. Three foremost national heroes are identified with the creation of the new country: Giuseppe Mazzini, a political writer and activist; Giuseppe Garibaldi, an adventurer and military leader; and

Count Camillo Cavour, a diplomat and statesman. They have been described as the soul, the sword and the brain of Italian unification, respectively.

Mazzini, an ardent nationalist, wrote about and worked for a united independent Italy. Forced to live for many years in exile and frequently pursued by the police, his ideas and activities inspired interest in politics among many Italians, especially the youth. Garibaldi, a colourful and legendary man who travelled widely and had dramatic adventures in distant places, became the most visible of the three leaders. He led a red-shirted army, described as 'The Thousand', which gained support among local people as it marched across Sicily and up the peninsula. In many respects, Cavour was the true architect of the national unification. A statesman from Piedmont, one of Italy's most northern regions, it was he who took advantage of the rapidly changing face of Europe. He helped establish a constitutional monarchy for the new nation, and set the constitution in place. The king was Victor Emanuel II, the reigning monarch of Piedmont, and the constitution was the *Statuto*, which had been the basic document of the same state. As with any successful revolution, the *Risorgimento* became a central part of the nation's myth system. Yet for all of its heroes and victories in battle, a careful analysis shows that it provided an uncertain foundation for a modern democratic state.

It has been frequently argued that one of the major reasons why Italy and Germany fell prey to fascist dictators was that both countries were unified very late. Furthermore, neither nation had experienced a truly successful liberal revolution, and both had very limited experience with democracy. The Italy which was born during the *Risorgimento* began life with many difficulties. First and foremost was the alienation of the Catholic Church, which believed that a unified nation was against its own interests. It did not recognize the Italian state until 1929. Second, after long years of fragmented political arrangements with many people living under foreign domination, a new national identity did not develop easily. After the *Risorgimento*, Massimo D'Azeglio, a prominent statesman, said: 'We have made Italy. Now we must make Italians.' The royal House of Savoy based in Piedmont, and the first Prime Minister of Italy, Cavour, seemed alien to many Italians. The lifestyle of the Piedmontese was different from other regions, and to many their dialect was like a foreign language.

In an attempt to enhance national unity and standards, a process which came to be known as 'Piedmontization' was introduced. Borrowed from the French, it involved a highly centralized administrative state. A prefect, an official representing and responsible to the national government, was appointed to each province, a sub-national unit of government. To many, these officials seemed almost to be powerful foreign emissaries, and this system further alienated many Italians. It was deemed necessary, however, because the political elite believed that a strong and centralized administrative model would destroy the essentially feudal juridical and political structures of the old regime.

When it was unified, Italy was far behind northern Europe in terms of industrialization. The middle class was nationalistic, but it could not be described as a strong force for progressive change. The nobility was in a period of sharp decline and opposed most change. Some merchants, intellectuals and students were in the forefront of the progressive forces. The peasants, who were most numerous, were overwhelmingly illiterate. They had little part in the *Risorgimento* and they disassociated themselves from the other classes, which were often in conflict. Suffrage was extremely limited, and hence participation in the political system was meagre.

Italians use the phrase 'political class' to describe their political leaders. Immediately after the *Risorgimento*, a small group ran the country and the political arena was characterized by *trasformismo* (transformism), a strategy whereby opposition deputies were persuaded to support the government. A parliamentary majority to sustain the executive was not assured, and in addition to a manipulation of the vote, the administrative machine was used for purposes of political exchanges. Skilful premiers, and even the king himself, 'transformed' opposition Members of Parliament into government supporters by use of personal rewards, political patronage and government contracts. Governments were not products of political agreements based on principles, but of the variable and casual fluctuations of groups and personalities. Although coalitions were described as governments of the Right or of the Left, there was very little difference between them. Many of the same men served as ministers in governments of different political hues. The political process was devoid of issues and rotation of power, an important part of democracy, did not occur. Also, it should be remembered that in the early years of the unified nation, the growing working class had no true representatives in the legislature. Subsequently, around the turn of the century, it elected some representatives who were, for the most part, moderates. This situation resulted in much extra-parliamentary activity by the working class (Rebuffa 1995).

To overcome some of the noted difficulties and to enhance national unity and the nation's international standing, many political leaders believed that imperialistic adventures would be useful. Activities in East Africa aimed to give Italy a foothold on the continent and a reputation as an imperial power. The results of these activities were disastrous. Even as the right of suffrage was extended to more citizens, things changed little and the public did not develop confidence in political institutions. Corruption was extensive. The prefect worked in illegal ways to return preferred candidates to Parliament. Over one-third of the public budget was devoted to the military, even though generally a large part of this spending was seen as unnecessary and much of it was wasted or siphoned off illegally. The tax system favoured the wealthy. The treatment of the peasants and the workers, especially those affiliated with the nascent trade union movement, was harsh. There were violent uprisings and protests, but they achieved little. The end of the nineteenth century and the beginning of the twentieth century was the period of massive emigration as many Italians, especially those from the South, fled the nation because they were unable to find work and had no faith in the political system.

When the First World War began, Italy was neutral, but in 1916 the nation entered the war on the side of the Allies. Government leaders anticipated a short war with a minimum of casualties. Instead, Italy faced over two years of war with many devastating battles and large numbers of people killed and injured. When hostilities ceased, leaders expected territorial gains as one of the victor nations. The Versailles Peace Conference brought disappointment. Wilsonian principles of self-determination set the tone, and the country's gains were minimal. With disappointment came frustration, especially among nationalists and former soldiers. A few years later many of these people supported Mussolini.

Following the war, Italy entered a period of considerable instability. In addition to protests by the nationalists who were frustrated by the war settlement, there was the period known as Red Week when workers seized numerous factories. Violence in the streets occurred as leftists battled with a new element in politics, local right-wing groups. These organizations became the foundation of the National Fascist Party. Of the southern European nations, Italy was the only one to have a well-organized right-wing mass party in existence prior to the establishment of the authoritarian regime (Kurth 1993). The Italian middle class had become increasingly uneasy, especially after the birth of the Communist Party (PCI) in 1921, which was created by radical elements of the Socialist Party (PSI). The situation was ripe for the rise of a right-wing political party. Also to be noted is that in 1919 the Popular Party, a forerunner to the post-Second World War Christian Democratic Party (DC), was born. It was dedicated to protection of Catholic interests, and would not have dealings with other political parties because of their materialistic orientation. This further rigidified the political system.

In October 1922, the Fascist Party seized power in a *coup d'état*. The democratic regime collapsed under the threats of Fascist black shirts and increasingly violent street action. While major participants in this violence, the Fascists claimed to favour law and order. They offered themselves as the saviours of the nation from Socialists and Bolsheviks. The Italian people were not totally aware of what to expect from a Fascist government because there had never been anything like it in the Western European experience. A leadership state was created in which the dictator went unchallenged. Formally he was still responsible to the king, but this meant little. Free elections were eliminated and Parliament was marginalized. Elected local government was abolished, as was the free media. The judiciary lost its independence. Italy became a police state. All opposition parties were soon outlawed and many of their leaders were imprisoned, or fled abroad. This was a brutal dictatorship, a fact that is sometime lost sight of when Fascist Italy is compared to Nazi Germany with its enormous crimes committed against humanity.

Probably the best-known development associated with Italian fascism was the corporate state, which was organized on the basis of syndicates embracing government, owners, managers and workers. Its goals were to enhance labour harmony and to improve production in the service of the Fascist state. Free trade unions and the right to strike were abolished. Behind the subterfuge of labour harmony, the real wages of workers were reduced (Salvemini 1936). In its early years, some foreign political leaders were very impressed with the corporate state, but when clearer pictures emerged its achievements seemed meagre. Big business obtained rewards and corruption marked the system.

Mussolini saw himself as the leader of a new Roman Empire. He wanted world recognition, and to further this goal Italy invaded Abysinnia and conquered it in 1935–6, albeit with difficulty. The invasion flouted the League of Nations and demonstrated the weakness of that body, which had unsuccessfully applied sanctions against Italy. In the early part of the Second World War, Nazi victories and the seeming ease with which they were achieved led Mussolini to enter the conflict. He thought that participation in the war would entitle him to greater rewards in the peace settlement. Mussolini expected a short war, and the Italian military was not well prepared for a long and difficult conflict. Military actions proved disastrous; in most cases, the Nazis had to rescue the Italians.

Mussolini's dictatorship was a decade older than that of Hitler. In the years immediately after Hitler came to power in 1933, Mussolini saw himself as the senior partner in the relationship between the two leaders. However, in 1938 this perception changed quickly with Hitler's invasion of Austria, which was considered to be in the Italian sphere of influence. Soon after this Mussolini introduced racial laws, seemingly to impress Hitler. In addition to rescuing the Italian armies overseas during the Second World War, the Nazi forces virtually took over the defence of Italy after the Allies invaded the peninsula in the South. As the Allied armies moved northward, Mussolini's fate was sealed. In July 1943 his own top officials, working with the king, removed him from office in a surprisingly easy action. Although he was imprisoned, Hitler was able to rescue him. The German dictator provided the Duce with a puppet regime based in Salò in northern Italy. The Salò Republic, as it was called, was run by the Nazis and it was short-lived. In an attempt to flee to Switzerland in the face of the arrival of the Allied armies, Mussolini was captured by Resistance fighters, shot and hung upside down in a public square in Milan.

Unlike Germany, which demonstrated very little resistance to the Nazi dictatorship within the country, in Italy the resistance to fascism was extremely important. In the early years of the dictatorship it was somewhat limited to intellectuals and left-wing politicians. In the 1930s its base was broadened, and after Italy entered the war it was formidable, both psychologically and militarily. Involving Catholics, Communists, Socialists, Liberals and others, it was an important disruptive force to the Nazis and the Fascists. Resistance fighters demonstrated to their own people and the world that a significant number of Italians did not support the Fascist regime. After the fall of Mussolini and a period with a military-led government, the parties involved in the Resistance, the newly formed DC, the PCI, the PSI, the Republicans and a progressive group called the Action Party, formed a National Liberation Committee. This body took responsibility for governing. While facing a very difficult situation, it provided the anti-Fascist sentiment which was to dominate when the war was over and the new democratic regime was being created. Italy emerged from the Second World War with considerable physical destruction and political, social and economic dislocation as well as moral and psychological exhaustion. The spirit of the Resistance and the presence of Allied troops provided a positive environment for the creation of a new democratic system. While it was inevitable that there would be some support for Fascism, especially among those who had received considerable benefits from the dictatorship, the degree of this support was surprisingly low. During its twenty-year life, Mussolini's government seemed to have broad support, but this dissolved quickly with the fall of the regime.

The political history of postwar Italy can be divided into several relatively distinct periods (Rescigno 1994). The first ran from 1948 with the introduction of the Constitution until 1953. The First Republic took form under the leadership of the DC, headed by Alcide De Gasperi, who must be considered the most important leader of its early years. In this period, the full impact of the Cold War was felt and the Left was excluded from the government. The years 1953–62, generally known as the era of centrism, were marked by instability. This was a time of considerable economic expansion and the beginning of major social change, when giant holding companies expanded rapidly and a kind of centrist or centre-right Keynesian philosophy developed. In reaction to government instability, a new governing formula emerged in 1962. This was called 'centre-left', and was important to Italian governmental life for most of the remaining years of the First Republic. It brought the PSI into the governing circle with the DC and the small centre and centre-left parties. It enabled the DC to continue to dominate all governments of the First Republic, while the Socialists, a source of some reforms, were legitimized as coalition partners.

The next period, which encompassed the years 1968–72, was one of new patterns of unconventional politics. Political participation, mostly through protest movements, was broadened with some extremists becoming violent. The same thing was happening elsewhere in Europe, but with the exception of France, this phenomenon was most intense in Italy. Protesters believed the governing system was unresponsive and rigid. They felt the only way they could influence the system was to go outside the usual channels. In this period the government did bring about important reforms, including the actuation of the regions called for in the Constitution and the passage of a divorce law. Conservative forces also attempted a counteroffensive. Their desire to move back in time was typified by a referendum to abrogate the divorce law. However, the overwhelming rejection of the attempt to reverse this important and symbolic law marked, to a significant degree, the end of this type of conservative reaction. As a result of all this ferment, there was a sharp change in Italian political life, especially during the period from 1974 to 1979. An agreement was reached between the governing parties, led by DC Secretary Aldo Moro: in return for its support of the government coalition, the PCI was given a say in policy making. Even though the Communists remained outside the government, it was generally believed they would join the coalition in the near future. However, the murder of Moro by the Red Brigades destroyed this possibility. Even so, the achievements of this period were considerable. In terms of the passage of important legislation, this era of collaboration between the PCI and DC was the most productive in the history of the First Republic.

The period from 1980 to 1992 saw some efforts to redevelop a formula whereby the communists would support reform of the government, but this was not achieved. Moreover, there was increasing stress among the governing parties. The underlying consensus reflecting Marxism, Catholicism and Liberalism which was at the basis of the Constitution seemed to be at risk. Although considerable dissatisfaction with existing government institutions was manifest, there was little agreement as to how they should be changed. The clamour for institutional reform increased, however, and it appeared that change would come in one form or another. Yet, in spite of the great social and economic transformation during the First Republic, the political order stagnated. Conditions were ripe for change in the political system.

The Constitution of 1948 was written for a very different society and circumstances, by an intellectual and political elite. The people never had the opportunity to approve it in a referendum, and hence from the outset it lacked a certain legitimacy. As the economy expanded in a way that few people expected and the standard of living improved markedly, the populace seemed content with its fundamental law. Some scholars, such as Joseph LaPalombara (1987), argue that the criticism of the Constitution and its political system was too harsh. They indicate that in spite of the apparent poor performance of the government, economic and social modernization did take place; this could not have occurred if the political system was a barrier. They further assert that a close look at government instability would demonstrate that although the cabinet positions may differ, the same people have dominated governments for many years. Events at the beginning of the 1990s made these arguments moot.

When the consensus about the Constitution began to seriously break down, the Constitution itself seemed inapplicable to the new society as the whole environment had changed. Not only was the standard of living higher than in the three decades following the war, but the population was much better educated. A new middle-class outlook brought widespread calls for reform, and the Constitution seemed somewhat anachronistic for the new society. Also, *Tangentopoli* engendered a new and pragmatic focus on the issue of reform. While institutional change continued to be important, the old political party system seemed to be at the foundation of the nation's political ills. Some argued that it was the Constitution itself, which brought about the corrupt, self-serving parties, which in turn rigidified the entire political system. The parties assured that there was no alternation of power and no real oversight of governmental behaviour. It was almost as if the Constitution gained its only legitimacy through the political parties. They became the operative aspects of the myth system, and the institutions became only the accoutrements of their power. In the early 1990s, the continuation of the fall of communism and the political party scandals intensified the demand for change not only of the institutions, but also of the electoral law and the party system. Soon the old parties were all but wiped out.

Different ones replaced them, and in 1994 the people went to the polls under a new electoral law. The initiation of the Second Republic was evident.

2 Italian political culture

Diverse threads

Introduction

Fundamental to an understanding of any political system is knowledge of its institutions and groups, their operation, and the formal rules of the political game. Equally important are the feelings and outlooks of the citizens as well as their basic beliefs and values, or their culture. Political scientists, being concerned with the political world, use the term 'political culture' to refer to orientations towards the political system and its components, plus attitudes towards the role of the individual in the system. What distinguishes one political culture from another is the existence of a particular pattern of orientations. Each nation has certain political cultural characteristics, which aid in an explanation of its unique style, manner and substance of politics. Some aspects of political culture involve citizens' awareness of and knowledge about the political system and their judgements as to what kind of political order is most appropriate, the performance of the government, what role citizens should play in the political arena, their ability to influence public policy and to obtain their due from governmental agencies and whether decision makers and fellow citizens are to be trusted.

Political culture furnishes the framework in which political structures operate and serves as a control *vis-à-vis* the system of political interactions. It determines the guidelines as to what is appropriate in the political arena, the role of the public and private sectors and the viability of policy alternatives. It aids in explaining political conflict and it shapes the behaviour of citizens and decision makers. It is important to the stability and effectiveness of a system, and it accounts for change in a nation's political history. Political cultural factors also provide a lens through which citizens evaluate the political system.

The Italian political culture, like that of other Mediterranean political systems, is a fragmented one permeated by extensive cleavages, each of which recognizes important distinctions among groups of people in different circumstances. The population fragments into a network of subcultures, each wed to its own unique orientations. Geography, social class, economics, religion, disagreements about the regime, ideology, gender and age are some of the forces which have provided a basis for the existence of potent subcultures. Italian political culture thus provides a study of contradictions (Schiavone 1998).

Political cultural characteristics

Interpersonal trust

Interpersonal trust is important to the construction of a democratic political system and its stability. The significance of this orientation derives from the fact that it is essential to the formation of secondary associations and the smooth operation of a political system. In Italy, identification with one's fellow citizens has been weak and this is the reason widespread voluntary associations were slow in developing. In some respects, Italians are individualists, generally suspicious of others and usually reticent to speak openly and freely about their personal affairs and political opinions (Sani 1980). They are fearful that such information, which has been important in terms of employment and the granting of material and other rewards, will be used in a negative way.

In a seminal work, Banfield (1967) demonstrated that this low level of inter-personal trust was especially acute in southern Italy, where no moral obligations or any other ties were felt towards anyone outside the family. This situation has been attributed to the intense and extensive poverty identified with the area and historical factors, such as foreign domination and exploitation. This distrust of other individuals has been translated into distrust of authority, the state and its agencies, criminality, political stagnation and the lack of a sense of citizenship (Bevilacqua 1993; Cartocci 1994). It is reflected in relations with non-European Union immigrants. Persons coming from Africa and Asia began to become a significant force in Italian society in the early to mid-1980s. According to official statistics, they number over a million. This figure, not taking illegal immigration into account, varies by as much as 20 per cent. Reactions to this immigration have not been positive. Distrust and hostility have been intensified by the nature of Italy's emigrant history. Most Italian emigrants have been southerners. They ask: 'If the situation here is so bad that people have had to leave, why should we give what little we have to these invaders?' The immigrants represent cultures which are strikingly different from that of Italy, and much social disequilibrium has resulted, including severe acts of violence and even deaths. Public opinion polls indicate that Italians are not racists *per se*, but they are definitely in favour of limiting the entry of foreigners, especially those from outside the confines of the European Union (Koff 1993).

Although there is some evidence that this extreme distrust has been somewhat tempered, as indicated by the increase in the number of interest groups and the formation of new types of associations, the fact remains that interpersonal trust has not been and is not a feature of Italian political culture. Its absence helps account for divisions within the community. Distrust fosters isolation and alienation. The frequent outbreaks of violent behaviour that have coloured modern Italian history can be traced to these elements.

Class

Although there have been various nuances in the class composition of Italian society, throughout Italian history the social fabric has been characterized by rigid stratification. Historically, one was born into a class and rarely exited from it. The ascriptive values of the society automatically placed a person in a class. There has been little social mobility and intense class antagonisms and militancy. This lack of social harmony can be related to the deficiency in interpersonal trust. The class division, which was important to the development of the political party system, parallels and reinforces the geographic cleavage. Once again, the South can be singled out because class stratification has been particularly acute in that area.

Modernization was responsible for a considerable transformation in the class structure. In addition to the enhancement of individualism, one of its most important consequences was a dramatic development in the middle class. Italian society, especially in the South, has been noted for its lack of a middle class (Pasquino 1992). Although it consists of many groups competing for political and social resources, this class is becoming the dominant force in Italy. The different classes have viewed each other and the state with enmity. The latter is perceived as not having appropriately represented or responded to specific class interests and demands, even though the 1991 census indicates that the standard of living for all sectors of society has been constantly improving.

Religion

Religious groupings affect political viewpoints. The moral guidelines provided by their teachings serve as a lens through which individuals view the political arena. Moreover, religious beliefs impact on community-supportive values. Although the Vatican is a separate sovereign state, it is considered a part of Rome as well as of Italy; thus Italy has served as the home of the Roman Catholic Church, which was the state church. This has had implications for the political scene, and religion has had a great impact on Italian politics. Like class, it helped fashion the multi-party system. Further, from before the *Risorgimento*, religion has been a divisive element. Focusing primarily on the role of the church in the new state, the struggle between it and the secular ruling elite initiated the clerical–anticlerical cleavage in Italian political culture.

In terms of religion, Italian society in the postwar era has experienced major transformations. The role of the church, its organization and its relationships with the political system have changed drastically. Since the 1960s, Italian society has become less religious and more secular. The church, reflecting this secularization, does not have the hold over the Italian people it once possessed. Its history demonstrates its gradual, although not total, withdrawal from political power and status. As a result of its new role, Pope John Paul II is a foreigner in many ways other than his national origin (Nanetti *et al.* 1988). As the line of action of the church changed, so did its structure: at the dawn of the First Republic it was highly centralized, whereas now it is pluralistic. The importance of certain mass organizations has also varied over time.

Agreements signed by Mussolini and the Vatican in 1929 regulated relations between the church and the Italian state. Known as the Lateran Pacts, these documents included a concordat which established Catholicism as the state religion and defined the respective spheres of church and state. Unique among its European neighbours, Italy became a confessional state. In addition, priests were prohibited from joining or working with any political party. The church was committed to neutrality in party politics. Organizations related to *Azione Cattolica Italiana* (Italian Catholic Action) (ACI), an entity devoted to the spreading and realization of Catholic principles, were recognized by the state on the condition they remained under the direct control of the church hierarchy. This provision was politically significant. It guaranteed that a limited sector of Italian organized public life would be immune from Fascist influence. If ACI had not been protected in this manner any semblance of a future Christian Democratic movement undoubtedly would have been obliterated by the Fascists. The Concordat sheltered the future possibility of a Catholic party. Both instruments – the Concordat, which after a bitter battle was incorporated into the postwar Constitution, and the party – were utilized by the Papacy. Enjoying direct access to the party, the Papacy was able to exert extensive influence on Italian politics.

Thus in the immediate postwar period, the Holy See's intervention in and influence over Italian affairs was considerable. The long conservative reign of Pius XII (1939–58) stressed Catholicism, pro-Americanism and anti-communism. This message was enunciated to the DC via the Vatican's ancillary organizations, of which the principal one was ACI. This organization, with its multi-faceted structure, penetrated all aspects of Italian society. By using its own organization or controlling that of others, it was able to influence the political, labour, economic, social, cultural and religious activities of the heterogeneous Catholic population. It was through the support of the church and ACI that the DC was able to reach the faithful of all social classes.

Other Catholic organizations working alongside ACI were the Civic Committees, which were important in the early years of the First Republic. They were responsible for generating militant Catholic political activism, and at election time they served as the key mobilizing agencies of the Catholic vote. They had an important role in the Pope's and the DC's anti-communism campaigns. Also lodged in the Catholic world were a network of cooperatives and educational, welfare, health and institutions caring for the elderly. The web of the church's organizations was formidable. Though not belonging to the DC, many associations were associated with it and became known as 'collateral organizations'. These Catholic groups have used three, often conflicting, reference points for their activities: the church hierarchy, the political party and their own autonomous needs as a group. This complex network of organizations which developed in various areas of the Catholic world served to enhance the Catholic subculture. In the first years after the war, clerical control over this myriad world of Catholic associationism was effective and extensive.

The Holy See's intervention in and influence over Italian politics began its decline in 1958 under Pope John XXIII. Although he was Pope for only five years, and in spite of his traditionalism, in some areas he gave a new direction to the Papacy. A part of this was enunciated in his encyclical of May 1961, entitled *Mater et Magistra* (Mother and Teacher). This major statement of theology and policy introduced an optimistic tone into Catholic social thought, and called for wider government intervention. Attacking the concept of *laissez-faire*, it questioned the church's support of capitalism and noted the need for greater social justice and the integration of the underclass into the social and political order. This encyclical was issued in the midst of discussions concerning the creation of a centre-left coalition involving collaboration between Catholics and Socialists. Previously, the official church hierarchy had explicitly condemned such an experiment. In enunciating a search for new ideals and a different stance for the church, Pope John XXIII issued a critical re-evaluation of church teachings and practices. It was quite clear that, as opposed to his fellow clerics, he was sympathetic to the centre-left coalition and its basic tenets. He lifted the Vatican veto of the DC approach to the Socialists. He insisted that the church abandon the blatant interventionist role it had developed under his predecessor. The Civic Committees faded out of existence and the activities of ACI were severely circumscribed, turning to focus on the social and spiritual realms.

Another courageous act of Pope John XXIII, which gave impetus to the ecumenical movement, was the convening of the Vatican Council, known as Vatican II (the first Council sat in 1870). In an address to the delegates, the Pope emphasized that the church must meet the needs of the day and demonstrate the continuing validity of its doctrine. He established the need for it to modernize, develop better relations with other religions and face the problems of modern society. The Council exposed the relationships within the Catholic subculture. The result was a set of documents which were to give the church a new orientation. These included a number of liturgical innovations, a denunciation of anti-Semitism, and the principle of collegiality by which the Pope shared power with the bishops in specific clerical governing units.

In another encyclical, *Pacem in Terris* (Peace on Earth), Pope John called for international conciliation based on the neutrality of the church. A hand was extended in friendship to non-believers and dialogue was encouraged between people of different philosophical persuasions, which in practical terms meant approval of a dialogue between the Catholic and Marxist worlds. In addition, he cited the necessity for enhanced social and economic development of the working classes, the access of women to public life and anti-colonial struggles in lesser-developed nations. After this encyclical, papal documents began to express political and economic concerns in the language of human rights. The papacy of John XXIII signalled a new era in the history of the relations between church and society in Italy. Church activities were more often based on spiritual and pastoral functions, rather than on anti-communist, political and proselytizing roles.

Added impetus to transformation was provided by the growth in the latter part of the 1960s of grassroots evangelical groups of Catholics based on local communities and labelled *comunità di base* (base communities). Their mission was to reinterpret the social and religious meaning of the Gospels. A new alternative church, a church of the people, challenged the traditional ecclesiastical establishment. Having been identified with a bureaucratic structure which reinforced the status quo, these groups envisioned the exact opposite, a church that would be a real community or '...the human community seen in its religious aspect...' (Hebblethwaite 1987: 26–7). Obedience was no longer considered a virtue; acts of authority were no longer glorified. Rather, the charismatic gifts given to God's children were singled out for attention. The phrase 'charismatic disobedience' came into vogue and upset the peace of ecclesiastical institutions. In these base communities, the priesthood did represent a distinct class. Following the French model, worker-priests were established. Celibacy was questioned and there were cases where it was violated. Like most Italian phenomena, these communities were regional in terms of their geographical development. Coupled with the outcome of Vatican II and Pope John's new social doctrine, they resulted in the church passing a new message to the DC, along with a new type of influence.

Since Vatican II the church has de-emphasized its temporal status and privileges. Politics was also de-emphasized, though not eliminated, in favour of the church's religious mission. The new strategy, known as religious choice, reflected the decline of the religious cleavage as a prime mover of Italian social discourse. It signalled the death of collateralism and the primacy of the church over civil society and the state. It also meant the near collapse of ACI. The link between adherence to the church and support for the DC was ruptured. Religion and politics were to be separated. Moreover, it was recognized that the DC failed to provide a vehicle for the realization of a new Christianity. The divorce referendum of 1974, indicating a clear margin of victory for the forces wishing to uphold divorce, demonstrated this decline of the Catholic world and the erosion of the Catholic tradition. In 1981, the increasingly secular nature of Italian society was again reflected with the legalization of abortion which, like divorce, was upheld in a referendum. These two ballots indicated that the church could no longer be the prime actor in the determination of social policy.

Pope John Paul II, who became Pope in 1978, initially intensified his predecessor's efforts to discourage direct church intervention in Italian politics. Believing that religious responses to contemporary issues, as opposed to political ones, should be provided, the DC was again given a signal that it could not take church support for granted. The same held true for other Catholic associations. However, John Paul II created a furore in 1985 when he suggested that the faithful create an electoral bloc around the DC in the name of the 'unitary tradition' of Italian Catholics. He has always made it clear that not all political choices are compatible with faith and the Catholic vision of people and society. His suggestion of an electoral bloc pitted the Pope and his supporters against the bishops, the parishes, the religious personnel and ACI. The Pope had touched on a sensitive issue. Such a proposal indicated a possible return of the church to collateralism with the DC; and it established the isolation of the Pope. The latter was reaffirmed at the 1992 National Assembly of ACI, when delegates rejected collateralism and sanctioned education related to the social and political realms, but not to specific political party support.

John Paul II requested a new agreement between church and state be expedited. Not being congruent with reality, the Concordat was no longer valid. Church–state relations entered a new phase with the revision of the concordat in 1984. With this revision Italy was no longer a confessional state. Religious instruction in the schools became voluntary. Separation of church and state was evident in a provision which terminated the financial responsibilities of the state *vis-à-vis* the clergy. The tax exemptions of the church were restricted. The revised Concordat reflected the new lesser status of the church.

There are two facets to John Paul's papacy. On the one hand, he is seen as an advocate for peace, human rights, social justice and capitalism with a human face. It is this role which is appealing to progressives. On the other hand, he is known as an opponent of contraception, female clerics, marriage for priests, divorce, abortion and euthanasia. Conservatives appreciate such a stance.

Internal migration has also been a principal contributing factor to the secularization of Italian society. A consequence of the movement away from the land to the cities was a major decrease in the influence of the church. Migration from the South to the North was also important. Secularization certainly accounts for a decline in the DC's share of the vote during the First Republic. A survey undertaken by Catholic sponsors indicated that an overwhelming percentage of the respondents favoured an open vote for Catholics and opposed a preferential relationship with a Catholic political party (Zuccolini 1991). The electoral fortunes of the DC have reflected this attitude. The populace is now less willing to use the church's teachings as guidelines for making decisions related to issues of personal conscience. As the theologian Gianni Baget-Bozzo observes: '...the more the bishops speak, the less they are heard as bishops' (Baget-Bozzo 1991: 8). Ecclesiastical solidarity is no longer social and political solidarity. Further signs of secularization include a decline in the publication of religious books as well as a decline in the number who choose the priesthood or other clerical occupations as a career.

Italy is no longer a Catholic country to the extent that it once was. There is no doubt that the Catholic subculture has been tempered. The authoritarian and disciplined elements of the church, which dominated in the immediate postwar period and afforded it an opportunity for social control, have been eroded. Their replacements have not been efficacious, nor are they congruent with the expectations of the populace. Even though religious sentiment has become more important, the church is often perceived as being '...incapable of spiritual motivation [and] ready to enunciate precepts without possessing the legitimacy to guide them' (D'Angelo 1991: 11). The church itself has not realized a consensus as to the role that it should play in political and social matters. Various segments have issued contradictory opinions. Conflict permeates the lay and ecclesiastical units of the Catholic world as well. All of this has been dysfunctional for the socialization process and for the church as a socialization agent.

Ideology

The complexity of the Italian multi-party system has in part resulted from ideological divisions in the society. The Italian political culture provided fertile ground for a broad range of distinctive political parties, each representing a specific ideology. For the greater part of the First Republic, most of the political parties were wed to a distinctive belief system. Parties were conceptualized in spatial terms and placed on a left–right continuum according to their ideological tendency. Analyses of political alliances, political strategies and positions on public policies were spoken of in terms of this left–right orientation.

The gulf between supporters of disparate ideologies has been great. Isolation and insulation of the various groups led to intense partisanship and inordinate hostility among the political parties. These orientations were strengthened by non-overlapping organizational affiliations. As in France, the ideological orientations of Italian citizens have been sharpened and reinforced by class differences. Ideological diversities have related to the political parties' attitudes towards the political order. Thus, political discourse incorporated the terms 'pro-system' and 'anti-system' to refer to the two most prominent ideological traditions, the Catholic and Marxist subcultures, respectively. The animosity between these two forces was greater in Italy than any other nation (Pasquino 1992). These ideological subcultures can also be related to a geographic dichotomy. Traditionally, in Italy reference has been made to the Red and White areas of the country. The so-called Red Belt, which cuts across central Italy, received its name because of the strength and appeal of the Marxist ideology in this area. This superiority was derived from a ferocious anticlericalism, itself a consequence of the church's oppressive role in this zone prior to the unification of the country. The Catholic subculture triumphed in the White areas in the northeastern part of the nation. In this case the church acted as a liberator, supporting the territory in its struggle against foreign rulers.

Multi-faceted change over the last decade has accounted for a startling modification of the left–right continuum as it relates to national politics. Ideological differences have been drastically reduced. The term 'depolarization' is used to describe a decline in the extent of ideological divergence and the concomitant diminution in the hostility among the diverse political forces. Adaptive changes have taken place in all ideological subcultures. Secularization has particularly impinged on political Catholicism, and modernization and changes in Eastern Europe and international relations, as well as the decline in class politics, have taken their toll on Marxism. Even if both subcultures retain some distinctive elements, their differences have been reduced. This reduction in ideological distance has had consequences for the tenor of political debate and conflict, which has mellowed. Although the groups involved in the political process have changed, political leaders still speak in spatial terms, using the labels left, centre, right and so on. However, in the Second Republic there has been a rejection of traditional ideologies.

The ideological cleavage which has marked Italian political culture has been a significant one. The extreme polarization, which characterized the ideological spectrum for the greater part of the First Republic, placed severe restraints on the decision-making process. Non-consensus was prevalent and the language of political discourse was inflated along with group demands. Individual ideologies were important to their adherents. The belief system which each represented served as a point of reference for citizens and members of the political elite alike. Among other things, it defined behaviour in the political arena and determined policy choices and relationships between actors in the decision-making process. Moreover, each ideology functioned as an evaluative mechanism in that each philosophy of life aided in an interpretation of political reality. At the same time as these ideologies interacted, they were a very divisive force, given the depth and intensity of the schisms and the fact that they were reinforced by class and geographic diversities. Their contribution to the extreme fragmentation of the Italian political culture was considerable.

Geography

As described above, in Italy geographic divisions coincide with cultural differences. The northern third of the nation is European in terms of its way of life, the peoples' attitudes and the economy. The further south one travels from the northern borders, the less European Italy seems. The two largest islands, Sicily and Sardinia, are also southern in culture as well as having their own unique characteristics. For centuries, to many observers the southern third of the nation appeared more Mediterranean than European. The middle third of the country, from south of Florence to just south of Rome, has characteristics of both European and Mediterranean cultures.

Other cultural traits divide the North and the South. In the South, one finds that women historically have accepted a traditional role. Loyalty to the primary social unit, the family, has always been great. Elements introduced from the outside or by the establishment are deemed suspicious; often these have been rejected not on merit, but on the basis of their source of origin. In the South, too, security and status are more valued than financial profit. Politics are based on vertical strategies, emphasizing individual relationships as opposed to the case of the North in which horizontal strategies based on collective action prevail. Believing that collective action does not provide adequate individual returns, the political world in the South produces these returns in the form of jobs and favours. In the North, concern is with societal goods. The civic tradition, which is closely identified with the level of socioeconomic development, is weak in the South. It accounts for the more effective response of the North to contemporary challenges and opportunities. Historically, northerners have looked down on their southern counterparts. They have referred to southerners as *terroni* (people of the earth), corrupt, poor, lazy, backward and not to be trusted. According to southerners, the northerners view their part of the nation as a colony. They perceive their colonizers as arrogant and haughty (Leonardi 1995; Negri and Sciolla 1997; Putnam 1993).

In addition to the North–South dichotomy, the existence of sub-national political cultures must be noted. These are of a wide variety, and some are identified with areas that manifest conspicuous ethnic features. Collective historical experiences have been especially important to these local political cultures. The barriers which they present to national harmony are formidable, and their impact on electoral behaviour is weighty. It was thought that modernization would erase or at least weaken traditionalism. However, in spite of profound social and economic change, these local political cultures have shown great staying power. Various regions of Italy were under foreign rule until the *Risorgimento*, and strong attitudes developed during this occupation.

This type of localism is witnessed by the recent rise of the leagues, symbols of regional pride and disgust with the inefficiencies of Rome and what is deemed outrageous financial support to the South. The leagues represent fertile ground for the disaffections and dissatisfactions of certain social sectors. Other examples involve ethnic and linguistic minorities, which articulated their cultural traditions, especially language and ethnicity, with the creation of political parties. Two representative cases include the *Union Vâldotaine* and the *Südtiroler Volkspartei*, identified with the French-speaking population of Aosta and the German-speaking populace of the Tyrol respectively. In various surveys, an overwhelming majority of Italians have given support to existing localisms. There are many signs of acceptance of this parochialism. Institutionally, it was reflected in the creation of the regions, sub-national units of government, which afforded an opportunity to recognize particular identities. It would seem as if parochialism was triumphant. Yet at the same time, in contradictory fashion, Italians feel a European identification, especially with the EU.

An important dimension of political culture involves the citizens' identity with the nation. National identity has been a problem since the days of the *Risorgimento*. Many citizens have lacked a fundamental allegiance to the state; instead, their primary loyalties have been extended to geographic or other subcultures. This places a burden on the political elite, as the support on which it can rely is automatically reduced in numbers. The various facets of this geographic dichotomy have important implications for the political arena and specifically political behaviour.

Attitudes towards the political system

Knowing how citizens view their political order reveals the extent of the legitimacy of the system and serves as an important indicator of political alienation and aspiration. Most Italians do not boast of their political system. Their attitudes demonstrate a lack of civic spirit or *incivismo*. Since the early days of the Republic they have not taken pride in the political system. They have always felt that they exert little influence on government. There is a wide gap between popular expectations as to what government should do and the perception of what it actually accomplishes. As Italy modernized, the people placed more demands on the political system, in many instances creating an overload. Often, decision makers and the political structures were unable to appropriately respond to these demands and popular dissatisfaction was fuelled.

Limits on resources available to the welfare-state, as well as the inefficiency of its bureaucratic structure, generated dissatisfaction within the populace. The Censis research bureau reports an uneasiness and a lack of trust in the welfare-state, local government, the legal system, trade unions and educational arrangements, to name just a few elements. The magnitude of this distrust is greater in Italy than in any other West European nation. *Tangentopoli* further aggravated the situation. It is curious that there is a considerable tradition of legalism and formal laws and structures pervade the society; however, respect for law and abiding by it is not a predominant value in the culture, as it is in Great Britain.

Although Italians view their political system in a negative fashion, their political cognition has been low. Their knowledge of political arrangements is often limited, and judgements might not be based on extensive knowledge and awareness. The fact that alienation has been a fixed facet of Italian political culture is unfortunate, because satisfaction and pride are building blocks which help create diffuse support for a political system. This rain-or-shine commitment is essential to the political elite in a period of crisis. It helps in overcoming difficult situations. Action has been taken to alleviate some of this hostility and alienation towards governmental institutions: a Charter of the Rights of the Citizens that obliges bureaucrats to stick to certain rules and procedures was approved, and the government has solicited citizens' opinions on services. However, it will take much more than these efforts to overcome decades of severe alienation and hostility towards governmental institutions.

In discussing attitudes towards the political system, parties may be singled out for special attention because of the significant role they play in providing the foundation for any governmental arrangement, especially a parliamentary one. In Italy, the political party system, especially in the First Republic, has reflected the various cleavage structures. The geographic dichotomy has impinged on the operation of individual parties. The cultural diversity which pervades the Italian social fabric provides different reasons for individuals' support for and membership in political parties. It has also impacted on the structures of the parties, the nature of participation in their activities and different leadership styles according to place of origin and base of local power (Caciagli 1988).

Perceptions of political parties are an important part of individuals' belief systems. There is a difference between Italians' orientations towards political parties in theory and in practice. Theoretically, Italians have a positive orientation towards political parties. They believe that they provide a vehicle for participation in political life, that they are a prerequisite of democracy and that they are important in terms of defending the interests of the people. Only a small segment of the population believes that political parties are useless. However, in reference to political parties and the real world of politics, this positive view is reversed. A study of attitudes towards political parties in Mediterranean Europe (Italy, Spain, Portugal and Greece) revealed that in Italy, well over 60 per cent of the sample manifested a distrust of parties. It is noteworthy that this study was undertaken before the kickback scandals. An indicator of this lack of respect and regard for parties is a decline of partisanship, electoral turnout and membership in political parties. Italians prefer other channels of participation (Guidorossi and Weber 1988; Richardson 1995). At one time political parties were believed to be the principal, if not the only, vehicles, for participation in the decision-making process, and the best structures for the articulation of interests and values. This is no longer true. Because the image of political parties has been tarnished, Italians are not confident that they can help make government responsive and responsible to the people. Parties are perceived as screens rather than transmission belts. It is the failure of the traditional parties, coupled with a greater saliency of political phenomena in the minds of the citizens, that has kindled the effort to find new avenues of participation (Sani 1992).

These have been found in the formation of new organizations and groups, which, in comparison with the older ones, are less complex and more sectorial in the sense of being more focused either geographically, as in the case of the various leagues, or from a public policy point of view with an emphasis on a specific problem, such as that of the environment (Cazzola 1992a). This is a positive sign. The hostility which has pervaded Italian political culture has been used constructively. Citizens have become involved. An indication of this involvement is the increase in membership in student associations and the increase in voluntarism, especially in the social service area. Citizens are participating more in neighbourhood groups and other grassroots organizations. It is interesting to note that this participation parallels geographic, class and gender dichotomies. For example, the volunteer spirit is more prevalent in the North. It is largely a middle-class phenomenon and males, rather than females, are more likely to act on it (Baccaro 1992). The new political parties of the Second Republic represent a parallel development. These new associations and groups press increasingly for satisfaction of citizens' demands and for the development of institutional arrangements and mechanisms that will protect and legitimize their inputs into the political system. The creation of these new avenues of participation represents a rejection of existing norms and practices. Activists switched from an elite-directed to an elite-challenging strategy. Rather than petitioning political leaders to undertake change, they have assumed the responsibility themselves and taken the decision into their own hands (Nanetti 1988).

Materialism and post-materialism

Italy, like other industrialized nations, is characterized by intergenerational discontinuity. Frequently, when people's basic needs have been met, they become concerned with such things as improving social relationships, belonging, self-expression and seeking a better quality of life. This usually happens in the case of the younger generation. Older colleagues, having grown up during the years of the Depression and the Second World War, periods of financial insecurity and turbulence, have clung to materialistic and acquisitive values, opting for pursuit of a higher standard of living and maintenance of law and order. These two disparate outlooks illustrate a generational gap in the political culture. Some of the younger generation in Italy have cultivated what are known as post-bourgeois or post-materialist priorities, which underscore issues such as ethnicity, peace, environmentalism, feminism and expanded participation. The older people, who dominated the political arena throughout the postwar era and who have not given youth access to the leadership strata, have continued to give top priority to materialist requirements and beliefs, highlighting financial gratification and physical security. This difference in outlook can also be related to the class division. Due to their greater affluence and higher level of education, members of the middle class are more likely to develop the post-materialistic perspective than those included in the ranks of the working class (Inglehart 1989). Over the last few years in Italy, this materialistic–post-materialistic dimension has nurtured what is referred to as a post-modernist culture. It exhibits '…a dissatisfaction with modern politics, its sameness, customary allegiances, its predictability, bureaucracy, discipline, authority and mechanical operation…[and stresses] the emergence of a politics featuring difference, dealignment and realignment, unpredictability, freedom, delegitimization and distrust, power and spontaneity' (Gibbins 1989: 15–6). It is clear that the new middle-class orientation manifests an anti-state attitude. The Berlusconi victory in the 1994 parliamentary elections reflected this postmodernist culture.

Conclusion

In the postwar era, Italian political culture has presented '…a picture of fragmentation, multidimensional change and a psychedelic collage of contemporary attitudes, values and beliefs…' (Gibbins 1989: 17). It thrives on contradictions. It is lamented that the political system does not function, but yet the country progresses with leaps and bounds. Many critical political decisions are avoided in the hope they will work out by themselves. Non-decisions in the political arena stand in the company of considerable technological, industrial and commercial successes. The political culture has been modified, especially in the last two decades. Political cognition has been enhanced, secularization has increased and political intolerance has been tempered. Still the basic orientations identified with the historical subcultures have been transmitted to a degree across generational lines. These elements provide the setting for political life. They

The DC, the nation's long-time governing force, was so hurt by the involvement of several of its most prominent and many of its second-level leaders in the corruption investigations that it changed its name to the *Partito Popolare Italiano* (Italian Popular Party) (PPI) and endeavoured to alter its image. This party offered itself as a new force for renewal in the centre of the political spectrum. Its biggest problem was deciding whether it wanted to be viewed as a centre-right or centre-left party. Its members were deeply divided on this issue and a split ensued. The second largest party of the First Republic, the PCI, also had problems with its image. It changed its name to the *Partito Democratico della Sinistra* (Democratic Party of the Left) (PDS) and rejected old-style communism. In spite of seeming to become something like the social democratic parties of Western Europe, it had difficulty overcoming its historic baggage as a radical party among centre and some moderate left-wing voters. Another problem was the existence of a small group of communists who did not wish to forego ties to traditional communism. This group split away and created *Rifondazione Comunista* (Communist Refoundation Party) (PRC).

Being touched by the corruption scandals, the small parties in the centre and moderate left of the First Republic also felt the wrath of the voters. The third largest party of the First Republic, the PSI, was decimated because of its major role in the scandals. Furthermore, as polarization between left and right became pronounced, the traditional role for the minor parties of the centre in coalitions was weakened. Splits in some parties and problems with alliances made the new party system unstable. The promised stable governments of the first years of the Second Republic became illusory.

Parties in the First Republic

In direct contrast to the Fascist dictatorship, the Constitution of 1948 clearly indicates the desire of the founding fathers to assure freedom of political behaviour. Article 49 states that all citizens have the right to freely form parties to contribute by democratic means to national policy. This statement and others in the Constitution would seem to foreclose on the creation of a new fascist party. However, emphasis on freedom of association permitted the MSI to exist. Given the deep divisions within Italian society, it is not surprising that a multi-party system became a fixture of political life. Throughout the First Republic, such a system was also encouraged by the use of a basic proportional representation electoral arrangement. More than ten parties were represented in the Parliament. Changes in social cleavages, including secularization, lessening of class identification, especially with the expansion of the middle class, and the reduction of ideological politics are long-term factors which have contributed to changes in political party arrangements.

It has been argued that throughout the history of the First Republic Italy had a one-party dominant system. The reasoning behind this description was that the Christian Democrats were powerful beyond their electoral support and dominated all parts of the national government. For most of the First Republic they did not receive over two-fifths of the popular vote, but they controlled 75 per cent of the governmental power. Until 1990, the DC provided all prime ministers but two and dominated every cabinet. Hence, it colonized all sectors of the national government and a considerable part of the sub-national units.

The party system from about 1960 to 1990 has also been described as an imperfect two-party system (Galli 1966). The reason for this appellation was that for a long period two parties, the DC and the PCI, obtained over 60 per cent of the popular vote between them. The remainder went to the numerous minor parties. Of considerable significance is the fact that even when speaking of an imperfect two-party system, there was never any alternation of power in government. The PCI was systematically excluded from governing coalitions. The lack of alternation contrasted with the experience of other major nations of Western Europe. In Britain, in the forty-year period from the birth of the Italian Republic in 1948, the Labour Party and the Conservative Party alternated in power. The Christian Democratic Union and the Social Democratic Party of Germany did the same. In France, in addition to different parties dominating governments, there was a total change of regime with the coming of the Fifth Republic in 1958. In spite of all the governmental instability in Italy, real power did not change hands and this contributed to the governing parties' involvement in corruption.

Another characteristic of Italian parties has been their factionalism (Sartori 1973). Parties all over the world, especially mass parties, are factionalized, but along with Japan and India, the Italian experience with factions has been most pronounced. Many factions, especially those in the DC and PSI, behaved like independent parties. With the numerous parties plus their factions, it seemed as if there were more than thirty parties in Parliament. Often factions received official recognition in party organizations. They were based on leadership personalities, ideologies, interest groups and regional and local elements. There was considerable conflict concerned with influence on policies and the dispersal of patronage among the factions. It is not surprising that competition and intransigence among them contributed to government instability and corruption. Often too, factions made compromise among parties difficult.

Factions are known as *correnti* in Italian, and *correntocrazia* (the rule of currents or factions) is spoken of as a serious political ill along with *partitocrazia*, meaning a network of state, party and economic elites infiltrated by clientelism, corruption and patronage (Kitschelt 1995). In the First Republic, *partitocrazia* caused severe damage to Italian democracy. Party leaders were more interested in promoting and protecting their parties and gaining rewards for them, than working in the national interest. Rigidity and self-protection by the parties contributed significantly to governmental instability and corruption. With a vast public sector, including massive holding companies, the governing parties colonized the bureaucracies. An extensive patronage system made many persons feel they owed their jobs to their parties, which reinforced *partitocrazia*. Also, government contracts with business often led to pay-offs to the parties. There existed a grey area, known as *sottogoverno*, which can be roughly translated as government below the surface. This phrase has been used to describe the semi-legal and illegal practices of the parties. In the 1992, 1994 and 1996 elections, voters were voicing their rejection of *partitocrazia*. In the first years of the Second Republic, some of the parties seemed to continue the self-interest approach to politics.

A paradox of the party system is that it was characterized by a super-politicized polity and a seemingly stable electorate. Its stable nature contrasted sharply with governmental instability. Change in voter support for parties generally came incrementally, and while some new splinter groups appeared, others disappeared. Most of the parties demonstrated staying power. Seven national parties persisted through most of the First Republic, and voter support from one election to another for these parties did not change greatly. There was little volatility in the electorate. With the communists and the neo-fascists excluded from governing circles, and little change occurring in party support, governing coalitions were limited to centre and moderate left parties. Leaders of the governing parties found places in one government after another. Hence, some of the instability was illusory.

Having set forth some of the general characteristics of the party system, the parties of the First Republic will now be examined individually. This will be followed by a description of those parties that became major actors just before the 1994 election. Linkages between the parties of the First Republic and those of the Second will also be considered.

The Christian Democrats

After long years in power, the DC thought of itself as the natural and deserving governing party. It felt its rule had saved Italy from the threat of communism and had provided the foundation for the great economic and social transformations which occurred during the First Republic. However, with the end of the communist threat, the exposure of serious corruption in the party and the severe economic recession which gripped Italy, the DC began to disintegrate. Its demise came unexpectedly and quickly, and meant that the power structure of the First Republic was finished. Among Western democratic parties, in the old system the DC was dominant for longer and in a way no other party had achieved (Giovagnoli 1996). After reviewing its very powerful role in government, one author described it as an iceberg (Tamburrano 1974). The idea portrayed by this description is that what is obviously visible is only a small part of the power of the party. Colonization of all aspects of Italian government, including the police, much of the judiciary and the military, and the parastatal apparatus, made the breadth of DC power and influence remarkable.

The DC was formally born after the Second World War. Alcide De Gasperi, the catalyst in its development, became its leader and the first Prime Minister in the First Republic. De Gasperi did not want the party to become a confessional one, totally integrated with the Catholic Church. Although very close ties between the two developed, De Gasperi's idea of separation was formally maintained to some degree throughout the party's history. The DC was an excellent example of what Otto Kirchheimer (1966) called a 'catch-all party', one which encompasses a very wide range of interests. An interclass party, its appeal traversed wealthy industrialists, rich landowners, middle-class businesspeople, professional people, artisans, workers, peasants and a great number of government employees. The party did more than reach across class lines; it successfully endeavoured to assure that class identity and conflict would not take fluidity out of the political system and rigidify it in such a way that compromise politics would become impossible. It did this through the wide use of patronage and the development of organizations which gave the DC ties to different social strata. There emerged Catholic workers' organizations as well as agricultural, business, professional, social and other groups which paralleled the party. Almost all of these groups were included in ACI, the extensive organization of Catholic laypeople closely associated with the Catholic hierarchy.

It would not have been surprising if the DC had chosen to support a free enterprise system as did its German counterpart, the Christian Democratic Union. Instead, however, it advocated a state capitalist system in which the government and the party had a considerable role. Through giant government holding companies, especially in the 1960s and early 1970s, the DC built a network of support within a vast portion of the economy. While this alienated many in the private sector, favours were offered to them to lessen their antagonism. The massive welfare-state apparatus was also a fertile field for the DC.

One of the characteristics of the DC was an extensive organization. However, it was not an integrated, disciplined one. The extreme factionalism which marked the party led to considerable decentralization of power. The impact of the factions was such that in the case of a few, they were closer to elements in other parties than they were to some other factions in the DC. The territorial factions based in and around large cities and regions, led to the development of powerful political bosses. They had considerable influence because of their ability to deliver votes to the DC and individual candidates. However, this permitted them to act with a great deal of independence. The lack of centralization and discipline did not generally interfere with electoral campaigns. Disparate elements in the party rallied together to fight elections, agreeing on the quest for maintaining government power. This assured that patronage would continue.

The Communist Party

The decade of the 1990s began with Europe's communist parties and communist regimes facing difficult times. The PCI, which had been the strongest communist party in Western Europe, was no exception. Italy's second largest party, it had received up to one-third of the vote of the national electorate. In the 1984 election for the European Parliament it garnered 33.3 per cent of the popular vote, compared to 33 per cent for the DC. It was the first time it had passed the traditional governing party in any election.

However, as the last decade of the twentieth century was ushered in, the electoral prospects of the PCI were severely diminished. As material wealth increased and the standard of living improved, a middle-class mentality rapidly developed. The PCI, which relied heavily on industrial workers, saw this group decline in number and militancy. Also, the Party's attractiveness to youth was in severe jeopardy. The then PCI leader Achille Occhetto urged a radical remaking of the party, which included a change in name and symbol.

The PCI was born in 1921, when its founders split away from the PSI. The latter party had throughout its history had a radical wing composed of anarchists and left-leaning Marxists, many of whom were influenced by Russian social and political thinkers. It was this group which led the way in the split from the Socialists. The newly-formed PCI did not have a long period to solidify and develop, as it was outlawed in 1926 by the Fascist government along with all other parties, except the Fascist Party. During the period of the dictatorship, the PCI developed an effective underground organization. Because of this it played a very important role in the Resistance movement, which gained it considerable respect and support following the fall of Mussolini. After the liberation of Italy, the PCI, led by one of the foremost communist leaders in Western Europe, Palmiro Togliatti, participated in all-party governments, but as the Cold War developed, it soon found itself excluded from governing coalitions.

In Fascist times the party was linked to the Socialists via a Unity of Action Pact aimed at joint opposition to Fascism. In the postwar period both parties were a formidable bloc on the left, but soon the Socialists moved towards the centre and declared their independence. The Communists became isolated. In spite of this, they demonstrated considerable strength in local governments, and when regional governments were established in 1970 they did well in elections for these units, especially in the North. They also continued to be influential through the powerful trade union, the Italian General Confederation of Labour, and other interest groups which were closely allied with them.

In the 1970s and early 1980s the Party's leaders, especially its Secretary, the accomplished Enrico Berlinguer, with the support of some communists in other West European nations, developed a doctrine called Eurocommunism (Boggs and Plotke 1980). It recognized that close links to Moscow on all major issues had become counterproductive. It was publicly stated that not all policies made in the Kremlin might be appropriate for the communist parties of Western Europe. Under the new doctrine, these parties were to appeal to the electorates of their nations on the basis of the needs of their countries, rather than the goals of international communism. Changed positions were aimed at making communist parties less of a threat in the perceptions of the electorates of their nation.

Although not formally related to Eurocommunism, a logical outcome of it was something called the 'historic compromise'. This proposal was aimed at bringing the PCI into the government. This act would have involved a great compromise between the DC and its allies and the PCI, and would have been a momentous change had it come to fruition. The cooperation between the centre-left governing bloc and the Communists would have assured the passage of a great deal of needed legislation and some major institutional reform. Movement towards the historic compromise occurred in the middle of the 1970s when Aldo Moro negotiated with the Communists, while working to get his colleagues in his own party to accept the radical idea. Although the PCI remained outside the government in the period from 1976 to 1979, it did support the DC-led coalition. This was the most productive period from a legislative point of view in the post-Second World War era. Unfortunately, the cooperation between the nation's two largest parties ended following the murder of Moro. The PCI was once again isolated and excluded from governing circles. In the early 1990s, the Party undertook a self-examination focusing on the demographic changes which hurt its industrial worker base, and the problems of communism in Eastern Europe. It became evident that modifications were necessary, and the Party began to look at alternative strategies, which resulted in changing its name to PDS. In some respects, it became a party of the Second Republic before that republic was born.

The minor parties

In the fragmented multi-party system of the First Republic, in addition to the DC and the PCI, which together controlled roughly two-thirds of the vote, there were from five to eight other parties controlling the other one-third. The surprising stability in the party system was demonstrated by the fact that at least five of the minor parties had staying power over a long period of time. Some of these often received less than 3 per cent of the vote. Nevertheless, they were important because some provided the necessary votes in Parliament to assure majority support for coalition governments. In exchange, they held ministries in these governments. Clearly, these minor parties had importance beyond their size and voting strength. They will now be discussed.

The Socialist Party

No party was more adversely affected by the corruption scandals than the PSI, which was devastated. Several leaders, including former Prime Minister Bettino Craxi, were indicted for their role in kickback schemes. The PSI had had an important role in Italian politics dating from its birth in 1893. Until the coming of the Fascist regime, it was the only meaningful parliamentary opposition to the governing Liberals. It represented the increasingly important working class, which felt itself alienated from governments dominated by the middle class. Even in its early history it was a highly factionalized party; from its birth it had a radical wing which existed uneasily alongside more conservative factions. As with other parties, the PSI was outlawed in 1926 by the dictatorship and later distinguished itself in the Resistance.

An ally of the PCI, the PSI came out of the Second World War with great hopes. As the new democratic system was being created, it emerged as one of the big three parties along with the DC and the PCI. However, its influence was soon reduced and it became the lesser of the large parties of the left. The venerable Socialist leader Pietro Nenni declared his party's independence from the Communists in 1956. Socialist leaders saw a bleak future for their party if it remained a junior partner of the Communists. Subsequently, following a few years of difficult negotiations, the party entered a coalition government headed by the DC. The political formula which enabled it to join the government was known as the 'opening to the left' (Tamburrano 1971). Since the coalition involved collaboration between Catholics and Socialists, it was seen as a monumental change in Italian politics.

The new grouping of the DC, the PSI and other minor parties became the dominant formula for all but a few governments for almost thirty years. During this period, most observers agreed that there was no realistic alternative to this formula. The PSI was definitely the largest and most important party among the smaller ones in the party system of the First Republic. From 1963 until its severe decline in the early 1990s, it conditioned the nature of governing coalitions. While never reaching more than 14 per cent of the popular vote, it became the swing party in the political system. The DC could not form a majority government with only the support of the small democratic parties. In the bargaining that led to the centre-left governments, the PSI not only obtained key ministries and important sub-ministry positions, but it also received powerful posts in the parastatal apparatus. Ideology became much less important than patronage. The party provided the second non-DC prime minister in the First Republic, Bettino Craxi, who as party secretary had changed the organization radically (Merkel 1987).

Craxi was an extremely ambitious man. In some respects he modernized the party, but in the process of doing so he solidified his own power and reduced the influence of or marginalized any opposition, especially from people on the left. The older generation in the left-wing faction, many of whom had been active in the Resistance movement, saw their party as an honest moral force working for democratic socialism. Craxi took the party on the road to clientelistic, non-ideological politics. Some saw his anti-communism as an ideological thrust. Even here he exploited the issue primarily for electoral purposes. The quest for increasing power was central in his activities. Craxi hoped his party would develop a role in Italy similar to that of the French Socialist Party. That party, which in no way pursued Craxi's road, provided two presidential terms for François Mitterrand and leadership of several governments. However, the strong Communist Party in Italy and other factors never let this happen.

To his credit, Craxi did advocate institutional and other reforms which seemed very necessary. Even in this area, however, critics saw him making suggestions which would work to his personal benefit. Strengthening the executive power was the purpose of most of his proposals. With socialist and public-spirited principles abandoned, deep loyalty to the PSI was weakened and, to an extent, replaced by loyalty to Craxi. When the evidence of extensive corruption was made public, voters quickly turned on the PSI at the polls. Its electoral support was almost totally wiped out and only a small rump of the party remained.

The Social Democratic Party

The PSI was described as having factions both on its left and right. One of the latter factions left the Socialists in 1948 and created the Italian Social Democratic Party (PSDI). Led by Giuseppe Saragat, who was subsequently elected President of the Republic, members of the PSI who opposed the party's continued collaboration with the Communists founded the new splinter party. As the Cold War intensified, the PSDI was firmly in the Western camp. It even accepted finances from the United States. Generally, it received less than 5 per cent of the vote. In spite of this, by demanding and receiving key ministries, it was included in almost all the governments of the First Republic. Few people thought of it as a truly social democratic party. It got its support from middle-class voters and its activities were marked by clientelistic relations. The party had the misfortune of having some of its leaders, including two party secretaries, imprisoned for corruption, well before *Tangentopoli*. The party was viewed as an integral part of the old political system based on *partitocrazia*.

The Republican Party

While the PSDI did not command great respect throughout Italy, the little Republican Party (PRI) did. Although its vote never exceeded 5.1 per cent, and more often it got less, its influence in government and the legislature was definitely much greater than its vote merited. It was one of those parties which many people when voting think of as their second choice. These voters felt that, while they liked the PRI, they did not wish to waste their votes on a very small party. It was a laic party that believed in a free-market economy conditioned by the welfare-state. In the First Republic, it was described as a moral force. To a significant degree, this reputation developed thanks to its long-time leader Ugo La Malfa and his collaborators. He appeared to be above *partitocrazia*. The Party attracted many intellectuals and prominent persons who added to its reputation.

   The party's good name was tarnished in the early 1990s because it handled some of its finances improperly. Its leader, Giorgio La Malfa, son of Ugo, was tainted by the revelations about party funds. During the transition period from the First to the Second Republic the party was divided over the issue of whether to join a governing coalition following the 1992 elections. To his critics, Giorgio La Malfa seemed to want to avoid responsibility in a critical period by withholding support for a coalition. Like its other small counterparts, the future of the PRI seems bleak in the Second Republic with the polarization of the parties and the change in the electoral system. Also, it has lost most of its idealistic young supporters.

The Liberal Party

The Liberal Party (PLI) is one of Italy's historic parties, which was dominant from the *Risorgimento* to the seizure of power by the Fascists. It is also remembered because of its involvement in *trasformismo*. As a result of the party's role in pre-Fascist Italy, it was generally thought that the PLI would be totally rejected by the electorate following the Second World War. This did not occur because some voters saw it as a meaningful alternative to the Marxist and Christian Democratic parties. It remained small, despite the fact that several distinguished people were Liberals.

Early in the First Republic the PLI had two wings, one of which emphasized its political liberalism and progressive tradition. The other was tied to economic liberalism and had links to the business community and upper-middle-class voters. Over the years the second wing came to dominate the party as its members maintained close relations with *Confindustria*, the influential interest group which represents big business. For the support of the business community the PLI had to compete with the DC, which was perceived as the party with power. Thus, the Liberals' base of electoral support was limited and the party's vote declined over the years. Some of its leaders were implicated in corruption scandals. This fact, plus the support offered to FI by many Liberals, left the Party moribund.

The Radical Party

What must be described as something of a curiosity was the Radical Party. This small party was definitely not traditional. It was better known for its activities in public squares than for its role in the Parliament. It was born when the PLI moved to the right. A small group of progressive Liberals, led by the well-known intellectual leader Ernesto Rossi, split and created the party. In its early years it made very little impact, but this changed when right-wing elements in the Catholic Church and DC decided to challenge a divorce law. The opposition proposed a popular referendum on the issue. The Radicals accepted the challenge and became very prominent in the campaign to maintain the divorce law. The success of the campaign encouraged them to introduce many referenda on numerous subjects, and their party became known as the referenda party.

The Radicals advocated abortion on demand, decriminalized drug use and similar measures, which were considered extreme by most of the nation. In proposing many referenda, they received considerable media attention and conducted what were often unorthodox campaigns where rallies frequently turned into happenings. Their appeal was mostly to middle-class people who had a wide range of interests. Environmentalists, representatives of the handicapped, feminists, drug culture people, pro-abortion elements and persons from other disparate groups became their activists. The party's conferences, led by colourful leader Marco Pannella, have frequently been described as circuses where anyone could speak and counter-cultural representatives dominated (Gusso 1982).

The Radicals definitely had an impact on the public agenda. Their party seemed to be an effective protest outlet in a system that was rigid. With the coming of the Second Republic, Pannella became much more mainstream and moved to the right. The lively elan of the Radicals seemed diffused. Pannella, who was always at the centre of attention within the Radical Party and the media, created a new movement in the Second Republic which took his name, the Pannella List. He supported the Freedom Pole, but not without occasional public disagreement with its right-wing leaders.

Italian Social Movement

The Fascist government of Mussolini lasted from 1922 until 1944. During that period, many people were rewarded by it materially and emotionally. Hence, it is not surprising that a neo-Fascist party, the MSI, would appear in the First Republic. While its voting support was not high, it was visible. It generally received 5–7 per cent of the popular vote. Associated in the public mind with extreme positions and violence, it was attractive to former Fascists, especially second-level leaders who were nostalgic about the past. Others favouring this party were persons who had gained rewards under Fascism and youths, who romanticized the fascist past (Ignazi 1998b). From the beginning the MSI had two wings. One saw the party as a right-oriented group that would work within the political system. The other extremist element was willing to use violence and appeared to be anti-system. Some of its members were implicated in bombings and murders. This wing not only included former Fascists, but several people who were filo-Nazis. The number of members of the moderate wing briefly increased when a monarchist party joined the MSI in 1972 (the monarchists were also having generational problems). An increasing number of alienated young people, especially those having difficulty finding jobs, found the MSI very attractive. The extreme elements saw the party as offering opportunities for direct action in the streets.

Reflecting the political culture, most of the party's strength was located from Rome south. The MSI had difficulty holding outdoor rallies in the North because anti-Fascist groups posed a threat. Mussolini brought many supporters from the South to Rome and gave them jobs in the bureaucracy. Also, the Resistance was not active in the South and the sense of a new democratic beginning found in the North after liberation was not great in the South. Many of the MSI's policies were in some ways linked to Mussolini's Fascism. The party emphasized nationalism and a strong military establishment. Stressing negative characteristics, it was staunchly anti-communist, anti-socialist, anti-liberal and, to a degree, anti-Semitic and anti-immigrant. It stood for law and order – a some-what strange position given its members' involvement in violence – family values and the church. In its calls for institutional reform it emphasized the need for a strong leader and it favoured a presidential system of government. Its role changed at the end of the First Republic.

Other parties

Numerous other parties contested parliamentary elections. Some entered the political scene with a flourish, but soon faded away. Others were regional ethnic parties and they had greater staying power. All of these splinter groups, while having a small number of votes or being regionally localized, further contributed to the fragmentation of the party system of the First Republic.

Parties in the Second Republic

The Second Republic began with a fairly clear division between the left and the right. This polarity is not based on single opposing parties, but rather blocs of parties, including large ones and small splinter elements. Some people believed that polarization would contribute to a period of governmental stability. However, the newly-emerging blocs did not maintain their unity, and stability was undermined. The most notable change of position was the withdrawal of the Northern League from the coalition led by Silvio Berlusconi, resulting in the fall of his government. For the Italian public, the behaviour of the new parties appeared sadly reminiscent of the ills of the First Republic. The Olive Tree coalition government led by Romano Prodi has had greater staying power, although it has experienced several threatening moments.

Another characteristic of the new party system is the legitimization of the major parties formerly on the extremes of the party spectrum. During the First Republic the neo-fascist MSI and the PCI were seen by a good part of the electorate as being radical. This was less the case with the PCI, but nevertheless in the minds of many voters it was perceived as being as much of a threat to democracy as the neo-fascists. The MSI, renamed the National Alliance, became a full-fledged member of the Berlusconi government, receiving a legitimacy it never enjoyed in the First Republic. Berlusconi's public support for Gianfranco Fini, leader of the MSI, in the Roman mayoral elections in 1993 was a critical development for the right. Berlusconi had not yet entered politics, and was known as a prominent businessman. His backing of Fini signalled that the MSI was no longer an extremist right-wing party. Following the victory of the Freedom Pole in the March 1994 election, the appointment of AN ministers clearly supported the assertion that they were identified with a legitimate democratic party.

The Communist Party, having changed its name and its policies, strove to be accepted as a mainstream movement which posed no threat to democracy. With the polarization into left-wing and right-wing blocs, the PDS became the leading party of the left. Politicians on the right continued to argue that it was simply a facade for old-style Communism and was not to be trusted. The PDS accepted PPI leader Romano Prodi as the candidate of the new centre-left forces for the premiership in 1996. This plus the party's moderate rhetoric and programmes convinced many voters that the PDS was mainstream. Also the fact that a left-wing faction split away from it because it was perceived as being too moderate and willing to turn its back on its historical communist background reinforced the view that it was no longer a danger. With the victory of the Olive Tree in 1996, the PDS entered the government and continues to behave in a moderate fashion.

In addition to the above-mentioned factors, which caused the radical alteration of the party system, the change also reflected long-term societal developments. Among the most important of these were the expansion of the middle class and secularization. The middle class, particularly the small entrepreneurs who became the backbone of the modernized Italian economy, had for sometime felt frustrated by the political class in Rome. When the communists no longer seemed to be a significant threat and the corruption scandals appeared, the middle class, especially in the North, felt free to stop supporting the traditional parties and to turn to movements which directly addressed their interests. First, the Northern League was formed. It appealed to regional business and farming interests. Its regional appeal became important both in the party's programmes and in inter-party relations. The middle class also flocked to Berlusconi when he launched FI. He appeared to be a fresh face (Schlesinger 1990) with none of the encumbrances of someone who had served in government, and a person who would defend the interests of the middle class.

Forza Italia

No party symbolized the changed party system more than *Forza Italia* (FI) (Fiori 1995; Mennitti 1997). Never a part of the First Republic, it burst on to the political system in January 1994. No other major party in a western democracy had such rapid success. In the parliamentary elections of March 1994, its first contest, it became the nation's largest party; soon after, its leader, Silvio Berlusconi, became the nation's Prime Minister. From its birth it was different from other parties. It was more of a leadership party than almost any since the time of Mussolini. Also, it was more closely linked to a private sector corporation than any other party had ever been. In a sense, from the outset it was an anti-party operation, even to the point of not using the word party in its title. It clearly emphasized that it would not become a traditional party. The major reason it could become so prominent in a brief time was its effective use of the media; Berlusconi's being, among other things, a media magnate led to the extensive use of television and publications in the party's campaigns. FI has been described as a 'media-mediated personality-party' (Seisselberg 1996). Books written in the United States about presidential campaigns speak of 'the selling of the presidency'; the same phrase could be used to describe Berlusconi's rapid rise to political fame.

FI's leadership dimension is easily recognizable; it is completely the personal instrument of Berlusconi. From its organization to its programmes and electoral campaigns, almost every action is taken under his aegis and in his image. He is an articulate and photogenic person. From his early days on the political scene, he has been described as charismatic. He had the good fortune to be able to overcome past behaviours which, by other political leaders, would have been very costly. He was closely associated with former Prime Minister Bettino Craxi, who was deeply implicated in the corruption scandals. Many charge that Craxi, while in government, helped Berlusconi build his media empire. Also, Berlusconi was involved in what were known as the P2 scandals, which occurred in the early 1980s. P2 was a subversive Masonic group, several of whose leaders were imprisoned. A large part of the public held Berlusconi in high esteem in spite of these connections. Even judicial inquiries into the legality of his holding company, Fininvest, and its officers, including himself, have not to date done irreparable damage to him. Some journalists spoke of him as 'the teflon man', meaning that nothing stuck to him.

Even from an organizational perspective, Berlusconi dominates FI; as he has said, 'I am Forza Italia' (Latella 1994: 5). Its organization features a pyramidal structure reaching from a tight national organization down through an intermediary or regional level to a local one. Berlusconi clearly presides over it, and almost all of its activities revolve about him. There is no second leader in the sense of a potential successor or a substitute. An Italian newspaper captured the situation in an article, the title of which translates as 'The party of only one man' (Testa 1994: 8). It is generally acknowledged that Berlusconi totally dominates the operation of Fininvest, the large-scale industrial and commercial organization he heads. His ownership of three television channels plus a newspaper, magazines and a publishing house make him the most powerful media magnate in the country. His leadership style carried over from Fininvest to FI. There is no doubt that in FI, Berlusconi utilizes effectively his business skills and his company's great ability with public relations.

A unique aspect of the FI organization is the network of clubs which operate at its base. In many respects, these groups act more like clubs which support sports teams than political units. They are like sports fan clubs, with Berlusconi being the star player. A considerable amount of the notoriety that Berlusconi received in the media prior to his entry into politics came from his ownership of the very successful AC Milan soccer team. Even the name *Forza Italia* (Let's Go Italy) has a sports ring. In fact, the clubs were developed prior to Berlusconi's entry into politics, but they were a very effective way to provide an opportunity for broad grass-roots participation. One hundred and forty thousand people are members of the 2,500 clubs (N.A. 1998b). Also, these units mark FI as being very different from the old-style parties. The people who rally to them are mostly middle class and include many youth. A large percentage of club members are new to politics.

The clubs have been a key element in electoral campaigns, and they are considered an imaginative innovation. However, they are not without problems. It became public that during the 1994 electoral campaign the Mafia controlled some of the Sicilian clubs (Bolzoni and Viviano 1995). Furthermore, after the euphoria of the March 1994 electoral victory passed, complaints began to be heard that the clubs were in no way democratic. The autocratic operation of Fininvest seemed to carry over to the clubs as the commercial organization's operators kept the local units under tight control. Some club members complained that they were used during the campaign and then were conveniently forgotten when the election was finished ('Forza

Italia, rivolta dei club', 1994). While there are many of these clubs, they have not been geared to sub-national politics and FI has done poorly in many elections at this level.

For four years there were calls for a party congress to institutionalize the party. It was promised, but not held until April 1998. It was called in response to the discontent which increased following the electoral defeat in 1996 and the poor record of FI in opposition. After arguing for years that his movement was not a traditional party, Berlusconi accepted the fact that it should become a 'party in meat and bones' (N.A.1998b: 6). It was to have a hierarchical organization with the clubs at its base; coordinators for regions, provinces and large cities; other officials at all governmental levels; and regular congresses. Berlusconi, as expected, was chosen president by acclamation.

The congress was theatrically staged in a way Italy had never known. It included a huge march and an outdoor rally. Berlusconi dominated it from beginning to end. He seemed to recognize that some of the novelty of his party had worn off, and the myth of efficient management and free-market ideas was no longer sufficient (Ignazi 1998a). He promised a powerful and inflexible opposition to the government. Changing his mind about the electoral system, he called for the continued use of proportional representation in deference to small parties. As part of an appeal to the Northern League, he emphasized the need for federalism. He continued to criticize the justice system, which is investigating him. He spoke of a fairer judicial system in which the role of prosecutors and judges would be separated. He called for a stronger privatization programme, the elimination of useless public agencies and the reform of the welfare-state. While repeating his support for the European Union, he emphasized that he was opposed to its bureaucracy.

Before and during the congress Berlusconi reached out to Catholic voters, speaking glowingly of De Gasperi and drawing similarities between his party and the DC. The leader of the PPI, part of the Olive Tree coalition, staunchly rejected this idea (Luzi 1998). Concurrently with the congress, Berlusconi made another about-face on a political position. After years of using strong language in condemning the Northern League, he called for a new alliance with it (Lampugnani 1998). The League rejected the idea out of hand and indicated that Berlusconi was simply trying to overcome his problems with the judiciary.

In comparison to other parties funds have been no problem for FI. Money has come directly from Berlusconi, from parts of his holding companies and from industrialists. Several banks have been quick to lend significant sums (Saracena 1995). As with other parties, FI has also received some public funds. The party itself was the work of key individuals and agencies within Fininvest. Berlusconi had a team of trusted and talented executives who did most of the work in creating FI. When he considered entering politics, he recruited key people from his commercial empire plus some from other major business firms. What he created was a marketing team that could sell himself and his party. Fininvest marketing operations did extensive public opinion polling several months before a decision was made to create FI. The results of the polling showed that Italy was ready for a totally new party, especially one that could differentiate itself from the traditional ones.

Emphasizing its pragmatism, FI considers itself non-ideological. With a business mentality prevailing, it is oriented towards problem solving. Thatcherism is often cited in discussions of its policies. It is clear that free market liberalism is a centrepiece of its programme. The reduction of the role of the state in the economy is a major goal. Privatization, which had started before the FI victory at the polls, was accelerated by the Berlusconi government. The party was committed to reducing taxes and government spending. A key element in Berlusconi's 1994 electoral campaign was a promise to create one million new jobs. In a nation where unemployment is high, this promise was favourably received. The fact that Berlusconi was unable to deliver even a portion of the promised jobs brought considerable disappointment, and hurt his government and FI's 1996 electoral campaign. In foreign policy, FI wanted Italy to remain committed to the Atlantic Alliance and the European Union, but on its own terms. The party put greater emphasis on nationalism, and a promise was made that Italy would garner more respect in world affairs. Anti-communism remained a central theme; FI's pronouncements still refer to the PDS as a communist party. In spite of the decline of communism as a major issue, FI seems to believe it is still a subject which is exploitable in electoral terms.

Berlusconi's image as an entrepreneur and media tycoon is not all positive. From the outset of his entry into politics, he has been dogged by charges of conflict of interest. When he became prime minister, he did not divest himself of his commercial empire. He made numerous promises about things such as blind trusts, and created an oversight committee. However, his critics and a good part of the public were not satisfied. Not all business acumen translated easily to the responsibility of governing. The Berlusconi government made numerous mistakes that can be attributed to lack of experience. After its fall, Berlusconi seems impatient and very uncomfortable in the role of leader of the opposition. If bi-polarity is to be a mark of the Second Republic, it should entail a responsible opposition. Discussion of new and well-developed policy initiatives has been sorely lacking.

One area where the position of Berlusconi is clear is his extensive criticism of the prosecutors who have been investigating him and Fininvest. So far he has been indicted and sentenced three times. He has viewed these judicial officers as agents of the left who are unscrupulous in their hounding of him. He sees political enemies everywhere. In spite of some of his major collaborators being indicted or put in prison, including his brother Paolo, he has constantly repeated that he and Fininvest have done nothing wrong. Arguing he has done no damage to anybody, he insists he is being prosecuted because of politics. Given his discrediting of investigating prosecutors, some observers are concerned that the independence of the judiciary, a central aspect of democracy, is being threatened.

National Alliance

If it had not been overshadowed by the spectacular impact made by FI, the success of AN during the early period of the Second Republic would have been hailed as an amazing story. Initially composed primarily of the neo-fascist MSI plus a small group of right-wing conservatives, the Alliance projected itself as a new movement. With a change in name, a change of symbol and most important, a new leader who appears to be a mainline politician, the popular image of the party improved considerably. AN, like FI, is definitely a leadership party. In contrast to Mussolini and early MSI leaders, Gianfranco Fini, the youthful Alliance leader, is not bombastic or given to theatrics. He is a very skilful, suave politician who has worked hard to change the image of the party from extremism to that of a democratic mainline organization. The legitimization process was enhanced considerably when five Alliance members joined the Berlusconi government and the MSI was dissolved.

Engineered by Fini, the formal dissolution of the MSI in January 1995 was not an easy task (Tarchi 1997). It took great diplomatic skills on his part, since large numbers of hardline neo-fascists fully identified with the MSI and Italy's fascist past. Fini argued that, in order to be a party for the twenty-first century, it had to change. He further indicated that fascism died when Mussolini was killed. To the surprise of many, Fini rejected racism and all forms of anti-Semitism. He concluded the congress of the MSI in which the party was dissolved by affirming that the right is no longer synonymous with nostalgia (Messina 1995). National-ism and an anti-left orientation, however, remained central elements for the Alliance. Its strong anti-left stance was seen as serving it well with voters from the centre to the extreme right.

The old guard of the MSI, many of whom had served Mussolini, and the extremist youth led the elements opposed to the dissolution of that party. Among their spokesmen was Pino Rauti, who had not only been an active Fascist but also a pro-Nazi who had served briefly as party secretary. In reference to the MSI, he was quoted as saying, 'Neo-Fascism has never existed. We are Fascists pure and simple' (Taylor 1995: 5). Not only did Fini's opponents disapprove of dissolving the MSI and the creation of a so-called democratic conservative or right-wing National Alliance, but they strongly opposed the rejection of the fascist past. An overwhelming majority of the delegates at the last MSI congress supported Fini, who was not totally displeased when Rauti and his followers created a neo-fascist movement called Italian Social Movement – Tri-Colour Flame (MSFT).

In spite of all the declarations that the AN was a democratic party, many doubts remained in the minds of some political observers. It was asked whether neo-fascism had really been rejected, or were the changes cosmetic and undertaken solely as electoral expediency. It was charged that even where some of the old hardliners supported Fini, they did so only because they saw the possibility of the AN governing. Clearly the behaviour of skinheads, especially their violence against immigrants, and the sale of old fascist tracts, including

Mussolini's speeches, at meetings make many question whether the AN is truly a respectable party (Hallenstein 1994b).

In the early period of the Second Republic, the AN was definitely on the ascendant. The MSI had derived its strength from being a regional party. The AN continues to have its strength in the South, but it has made inroads in the North. At its 1998 congress, in an effort to further nationalize its supporters, Fini expressed sympathy with northern problems and supported a non-specific federalist solution. At this gathering the stance of the party became more modern, more liberal and more European than it had been in the past. It left behind the statism which was so important to it.

Equally important is the fact that Fini surpassed Berlusconi in some public opinion polls ('Sondaggio Fini leader della destra', 1995). This generated speculation that if Berlusconi faltered or had extremely serious legal problems because of Fininvest activities, Fini might emerge as the undisputed leader of the right. Fini's relationship with Berlusconi has not been smooth. The two men have disagreed on major policy issues. Also, when Berlusconi made overtures to Bossi and the Northern League in the spring of 1998, Fini opposed them. The future of Fini and the AN will depend, to a large degree, on his ability to control the extreme elements among his supporters and the right in general. Violence and inflammatory speeches can undermine all his endeavours to present himself and his party as committed to democracy.

The Northern League

The Northern League has its origins in the last years of the First Republic. Although there were antecedents to it, it was officially born in 1984. In the early years it was not well known and it had practically no organization (Woods 1995). Initially it was a loose-knit federation of leagues from different northern regions. Its major breakthrough came in the local elections of 1990. Hence, the party really began in the period of transition between the First and Second Republics. It definitely was seen as a major political force when it became the second largest party in the regions of Lombardy, Veneto and Piedmont. Although overshadowed by FI as part of the Freedom Pole, it became a governing party in the Berlusconi government. It turned out to be a swing party.

Like the two other principal parties in the Pole, the League is definitely a leadership party. It is led by Umberto Bossi, a very colourful, bombastic, crass and sometimes vulgar figure. His strong personality not only characterizes the party but also dominates it. In spite of often erratic behaviour, Bossi generated considerable loyalty among many of the party's members. He is seen as the founding father of the party who continues to keep it in the public eye, in spite of his statements and outbursts, some of which are contradictory. As the party has matured, there have been important schisms and prominent leaders have left its ranks. However, Bossi has not altered his behaviour, although he has changed his politics. Since taking the League out of the Berlusconi coalition, he has had very harsh things to say about his former partners. In spite of the fact that the

League participated in the government and held several important positions, Bossi proved to be erratic in his dealings with its leader. He was not loath to criticize the Berlusconi government and some of its policies. Many contradictions remained unresolved. With lack of experience in the public sector, this government faced a very difficult beginning, and the twists and turns of the League did not help it. Few were surprised when the League left the coalition.

The League claims that the national government helped the South, which from its perspective is a drain on the North. According to the League, the South should become more independent and self-sufficient. It believes the northern region is the only area which contributes significantly to the national economy. When not calling for a separate Republic of Padania, the League has put heavy emphasis on the creation of a federal system, in which the demi-autonomous or independent North would gain considerable or total control over its economic, tax and government systems. Its position concerning distribution of power has not been clear; it constantly varies between federalism and separation. Consistent with the desire of the League to work for Italian citizens in the North is the staunch stand of the party against immigration from Eastern Europe and developing countries. Hostility towards immigrants is based on economic and cultural grounds. They are viewed as another drain on northern wealth. Even though this attitude has been tempered, critics argue that the League is racist and sectarian. Bossi has identified three enemies to be fought: the political left, the Pope and the judiciary.

The party appeals to people who feel the old parties treated the nation and themselves badly (Diamanti 1993). The basic argument of the League is that the government in Rome is corrupt and its accomplishments are few. It offers disgruntled voters the opportunity to register their displeasure with traditional parties and to defend threatened values and culture. The party has had considerable appeal to the middle class, especially among entrepreneurs and managers and lower-level white-collar workers. Youths have also been attracted to it, which puts an emphasis on happening-like situations in big public rallies. Young people seem to react very positively to Bossi's colourful oratory, which is consistent with the party's populist and grassroots emphasis. In spite of being marginally involved in some party corruption scandals, the League has benefited from publicity about the payoffs received by the old parties. It exploited revelations about corruption and argues that its electoral victories against the DC and the PSI cleared the way for prosecutors to move against corrupt government officials and the Mafia.

The League finds itself in direct competition with FI, which courts many of the same middle-class voters. Both parties appeal to former DC members, among which the League has considerable strength. While Bossi has his devoted followers, Berlusconi enjoys a broader constituency. The League is the joker in the political deck. This is especially the case since the party seems to want a recreated centre position by painting its former Freedom Pole allies as extremists of the right. The reason for this argument is because of the natural competition between the League and FI.

The Democratic Party of the Left

When the PCI became known as the PDS and jettisoned the word 'Communist' from its name, it signalled a move towards becoming a social democratic party in the Western European tradition. Before proposing the changes, Occhetto consulted British Labour Party leader Neil Kinnock and former West German Chancellor Willy Brandt ('The New Left' 1989). Because of modifications in the party system, the hoped-for improvement in electoral results did not materialize, and Occhetto resigned as party leader. His hope of creating a moderate-left alliance, such as the one developed by President Mitterrand of France in the early 1980s, was dashed.

Some people charged that in spite of the name change, new policies and dropping the Leninist principle of democratic centralism, the PDS still looked like the old PCI. It remained highly centralized and bureaucratic. The party was hurt by vague charges that it had in the past accepted funds from Moscow. Also, there were public revelations that, on a small scale as it was a non-government party, it had received some pay-offs in the *Tangentopoli* scandals. In spite of the vagueness of the allegations and staunch denials by the PDS, some people linked it with the corrupt parties. Following the Berlusconi victory in the 1994 election, the Central Committee chose Massimo D'Alema as Occhetto's successor. D'Alema, former deputy leader, is an intelligent, articulate and strong personality. He has worked hard to demonstrate the continued moderation of his party. This was particularly important in the period prior to the 1996 election, when his flexibility resulted in the construction of a winning alliance, the Olive Tree.

In a strong action in 1995, the PDS supported the candidacy of former Christian Democrat Romano Prodi for the post of prime minister. This support came well before there was any decision about when an election would be called. The PDS hoped that the new alliance would be seen as a moderate centre-left alternative to a more extreme centre-right grouping led by Berlusconi and Fini. The 1996 election fulfilled this hope. After this contest, the PDS leadership continued to develop its moderate image. In 1997 D'Alema called for the party to become more of a European social democratic party. He angered some trade union leaders with his calls for reform of social services and further changes in the pension system.

In spite of these calls, the PDS was not recognized as a European social democratic force. It had remained in 'no man's land' too long, and had not resolved the communist question. Although Occhetto's courageous move represented a radical departure from the past, it failed to bring the party a new pool of supporters. The outcome of the 1996 election also raised the question as to whether the Olive Tree coalition and its victory were likely to lead to the prospect of a single united party or a permanent alliance of parties.

In an even stronger action than that of 1995, in early 1998 D'Alema convened an assembly in which all relevant forces addressed this question. The *Democratici della Sinistra* (Democrats of the Left), composed of the PDS, Labour, Unitary Communist and Social Christian parties, plus left-wing Republicans, was born. No longer will the constituent parties have individual congresses:

instead, they will meet as one. PDS organs remained in place and were expanded to include the other parties. The new group elected D'Alema as its leader and launched the idea of consultation pacts and programmatic understandings with major interest associations. Representing a new way of thinking and long-term as opposed to immediate interests, its scope is to give Italy a bigger, more European and stronger left. Its agenda includes peace, democracy, human and social rights and the environment. A detailed programme is to be prepared at the first congress, to be held in 1999.

The Communist Refoundation Party

The strength of this party has surprised many people. It seems to be somewhat anachronistic in the contemporary political scene. Initially staunchly committed to its communist past, few believed that there were many people who held this position. Instead, the party and what it stood for struck a respondent chord, particularly among workers, intellectuals and youth who were attracted to its militancy. Known as a party for change (N.A. 1998a), it got a big boost when the Democratic Proletarian Party dissolved and the PRC absorbed most of its members. When the party received 5.6 per cent of the vote in the 1992 election, 6 per cent in 1994 and 8.6 per cent in 1996, it became clear that it is a force with which to be reckoned. Following the 1996 election, the PRC held the balance of power for the government. Although it did not join the coalition, it was a necessary part of its parliamentary majority. Opponents charged that it blackmailed the Prodi government on some issues, such as the thirty-five-hour working week. The party threatened the life of the coalition when it opposed sending Italian peacekeeping forces to Albania and the enlargement of NATO. The government was saved by votes from the opposition.

The PRC had an extreme wing and a moderate one, although this is an oversimplification. The party has had internal problems not only related to ideological position. Party leader Fausto Bertinotti is resolute, effective and somewhat pragmatic. Formal in his ways, he has more than held his own in debates with opposition party leaders. He was never known as a Communist, but rather as a Socialist and trade unionist (Berselli 1997). While indicating there are certain policies on which he will continue to take a hard line, such as unemployment, especially in the South, he seems to have moderated somewhat. He recognizes that if the PRC brings down the Prodi government and causes an election, which the centre-right could win, his party would be blamed. Although he has indicated that he respects Prodi and works well with him, and expects the government to live out the full life of the Parliament, sometimes his actions belie this affirmation. In the early period of the party's life, the extreme wing was led by Armando Cossutta, a long-time leader of the PCI, who was often described as a Stalinist. One of the founding fathers of the PRC, he moderated his ideological position and became less strident than Bertinotti.

The Popular Party

When the DC did very badly in the 1992 general elections, a group of leaders tried to revamp its image. This was a much larger task than anticipated. Some of the old leaders, generally those not implicated in the scandals, did not relish relinquishing their power and influence. There was general agreement that the party should occupy the centre of the political spectrum, but the centre was not clearly defined and there was disagreement about whether the party should lean to the left or to the right. This issue subsequently caused desertions and a split. It was decided that the party needed to change its name and present itself to the electorate as a totally new force.

Thus the PPI was born. From the time of its birth it has had serious problems. Italian voters seem to be skewed towards a bipolar configuration. A considerable portion of the old DC vote went to the Freedom Pole. Having an identity crisis (Bianchi 1994), the PPI must present itself as a reform party, but it can only go so far without undermining its centrist position. The appointment of Prodi as Prime Minister, whom the party supported as one of its own, helped with this crisis.

In 1994, consideration was given by the PPI to collaborating in an electoral alliance with the Progressives on the left of the political spectrum in the face of right-wing adversaries who seemed politically very strong. It was decided not to do this, primarily because the DC had so long rejected any collaboration with the Communists. Leaders of the PPI were apprehensive about losing votes to the right, especially since a right-wing faction broke away and established itself as the Christian Democratic Centre (CCD). The CCD collaborated with the Freedom Pole and had ministers in the Berlusconi government. Members of the government put considerable pressure on the PPI to support them, but the party would not consider collaboration unless the neo-fascist AN was expelled from the governing coalition. With a severe defeat in the 1994 parliamentary elections, the PPI entered a period of significant internal conflict. Whereas the old DC for all of its divisions came together for elections in order to maintain itself in power, this was not the case with the PPI. There was a strong division between left-wing and right-wing factions, which led to another formal split in the party. The once mighty DC, often threatened by schisms, was totally shattered. One group assumed the name the Christian United Democrats (CDU) (U.R. 1995), and the other remained as the PPI.

In contrast to its actions in 1994, in the 1996 elections the party joined the PDS-led Olive Tree coalition. Prodi's bid for the premiership was more than an effort of the progressive elements of the PPI; the feeling of many is that he represents the new politics that the PPI requires. He has staunchly rejected the tarnished leaders of the DC. As an economist of substantial standing, he speaks of a new Italy with a new approach to governance. Although he ran as the candidate of a broad-based coalition, this victory aided progressive forces in the PPI.

The Network

Another group which had a meteoric rise followed by a strong decline is the *Rete* (Network). It calls itself a movement so as to distinguish itself from the traditional parties. It was founded in 1991 in the last period of the First Republic, but it definitely represented the forces which brought about the Second Republic. Its founder was Leoluca Orlando, a former DC Mayor of Palermo in Sicily, who returned to that position as a *Rete* candidate in 1993 and again in 1997. The *Rete* describes itself as a political cultural movement with the goals of defending and developing Italian democracy. Most of the media coverage has focused on its fight against the Mafia. This results from its origins in Palermo. Although its electoral support is primarily regional, it is not a regional organization, but rather a national one. It attracted many prominent persons to its banner, especially after its initial electoral successes. After a serious defeat, especially in Sicily, in the 1994 election it lost several of its notable leaders who believed that the campaign was handled badly. It joined the Olive Tree in 1996 and still performed poorly. The *Rete* is definitely a reform party fighting against the old ways of political life. It aims at an informed citizenry, and includes the environment, justice and institutional reform in its platform. In spite of the attractiveness of its programme, the movement is having difficulty projecting a clear image of its role in the political system. Its future prospects are not bright outside Sicily.

The Greens

Italy has had a poor record concerning environmental issues. In a country with so many problems and unstable governments, it took a long time to raise public consciousness about environmental dangers. The development of Green parties came later than in northern Europe. In the 1970s and 1980s the small Radical Party championed environmental causes as part of its efforts for widespread reform. By the 1980s the major parties began to give some attention to environmental issues. Operating first as interest groups, new environmental movements became more conspicuous. Some of these began contesting sub-national elections with success. There was intense competition among various Green groups. The basic difference centred on focus. There were those who wanted to be devoted solely to environmental issues and those, generally on the left, who viewed environmental issues as part of a general framework. Despite this, a Green list contested the 1985 elections and made its presence felt. After much discussion, a Green Federation was formed in 1990 with the merger of numerous environmental groups. The major parties and movements, especially with the transition to the Second Republic, left little room for the Greens on the political stage.

The Greens fought the 1994 parliamentary election as part of the Progressive Alliance and experienced defeat. As a member of the Olive Tree coalition they did better in 1996, and even secured a cabinet position. They improved in elections to the European Parliament where, although their numbers are small, they have joined other European Green parties in the Green Group of that legislature and have had some influence. It would be incorrect to disregard the importance of the Greens. While their electoral numbers are low, they have affected the public agenda and increased public awareness of environmental issues, especially at the sub-national level. On the other hand, given their internal problems and the increasing bi-polarity in the party system, their hope to become a significant electoral force seems very circumscribed (Rhodes 1995a). Even their past recourse to politics in the public square seems limited. In the movement to the Second Republic, Italians seem much less interested in the politics of public protest by small movements.

Conclusion

The political distance between the parties of the First and Second Republics is considerable. In some respects the party systems are very different. A new polarization has occurred; the centre is no longer dominant. Ideological politics has declined significantly. The subcultures at the foundation of the parties of the First Republic have moderated. There seems to be a different leadership structure in the party system. In spite of all this, there is a nagging sense that, while the worst aspects of *partitocrazia* no longer persist, party behaviour in the Second Republic is not that different from the First. Intensive warfare continues. It may be too soon to judge the party system of the Second Republic. Adjustments and further experience are required before its exact nature becomes obvious.

In the Second Republic, several question marks remain about the party system. They relate to the party interests of three prominent personalities. The first concerns Lamberto Dini. For the 1996 election, he created an electoral list bearing his name and subsequently called Italian Renewal. He has performed well as Foreign Secretary in the Prodi government. However, on several issues he seems uncomfortable with the left-leaning government. Having served also in the Berlusconi government and headed a technocratic government himself, one wonders if the circumstances were right, might he opt to lead a larger new centre party between the Freedom Pole and the Olive Tree alliance?

Also with his eye on a new role in the centre of the political spectrum is Francesco Cossiga, the former President of the Republic and DC Prime Minister. In summer 1998 he formed a political party, the Democratic Union for the Republic (UDR). Although he flirts intermittently with Berlusconi, his party aims to be an alternative to the left and distinct and distant from the right. Cossiga argues that he does not want to replicate the DC. However, it is noteworthy that most of his supporters had strong affiliations with that party and he concluded the meeting, which established the party, with a prayer to Saint Thomas More requesting protection for the new organization. Its actual thrust is not clear, however, and Cossiga's future plans are uncertain.

In many respects, the individual who has the most questions about his intentions is Antonio Di Pietro. After a brief period in the Prodi government, he ran for the Senate under the banner of the Olive Tree. He won handily, but did not join the Olive Tree Parliamentary Group in the Senate. He has made several pronouncements critical of the government. Having created his own movement, he has spoken of constructing his own party. His future intentions are not clear, although the centre and right-wing parties are wooing him. Depending upon what he does, he could have a considerable impact on electoral politics.

One thing that is obvious is that the party system plays by new electoral rules. In the next chapter, elections and electoral systems will be discussed.

4   Elections and electors

Introduction

Elections have several purposes, some for the political system, others for the individual voters. While elections are held in many kinds of political systems, it is generally agreed that they are central to representative democracies. Among other things, they serve as a method for selecting leaders, affecting public policies, offering mandates and imposing limits on government action. Furthermore, elections are central factors in legitimizing a regime in the perception of its citizens. In a similar vein, they socialize the voters in their attitudes towards their parties, institutions and political processes. Elections were a featured part of the First Republic, including its demise; in some respects changes in the electoral rules came to symbolize the death knell of that period. Elections have since been essential to legitimizing the Second Republic and to the creation of its new party system. On the other hand, electoral results have sent mixed messages to the new political class, and this has contributed to government instability.

Italians go to the polls with considerable frequency. Elections are a central part of the operative aspects of the political arrangements as well as the myth system at the foundation of their democracy. Not since 1968 has a Parliament lived its normal life span. Article I of the Constitution establishes that sovereignty rests with the people and they are the source of all power. Elections are among the methods the people use to exercise their sovereignty. In these contests, voters elect representatives for all levels of government, and they participate in direct democracy through initiatives and referenda. Italians vote for the Senate, the Chamber of Deputies, mayors and councils of the regions, provinces, cities, towns and even neighbourhoods, as well as the European Parliament. Frequent votes on referendum issues, some of which have impacts beyond the narrow questions involved, have become a major part of political life. There always seems to be some kind of electoral campaign or discussion about elections.

While the Constitution is clear on many matters, this is not the case regarding elections. There is no question that the founding fathers believed that elections would be a central feature of the new republic, but they did not spell out how they would be operationalized. Designation of an electoral system was left to the Parliament. The fundamental law calls for universal direct suffrage, which meant that women were given the vote for the first time. In addition, Article 48 refers to the vote as being personal, equal, free and secret.

Although declining in recent years, voter turnout has been among the highest of any democracy in the world. In many elections, over 90 per cent of the electorate has voted. The fact that voters have so many parties to choose from encourages participation, but that alone is no explanation of high turnout. Included in Article 48 of the Constitution is the statement that voting is a civic duty. The meaning of civic duty is not totally clear. During most of the First Republic when ideological and experiential differences were considerable, many voters had trouble moving from one political party to another. Instead they returned a blank or spoiled ballot (Mannheimer and Sani 1987). This was especially true for DC and PCI supporters. The number of abstentions and blank and spoiled ballots generally increased over the life of the First Republic, and following the 1979 elections it was observed that the party of 'non voters' became the third largest in the nation after the DC and the PCI (Nuvoli and Spreafico 1990). Since 1993, mandatory voting has been eliminated.

The electoral system: a roadblock to change

The basic electoral system used during the First Republic, with variations between the Chamber of Deputies and the Senate, was proportional representation (PR). It is generally acknowledged that the use of PR contributed significantly to the fragmentation of the party system, but it would be too strong to say that it was the only reason for this. Still, Farneti has written: '...the dominance and diffusion of the proportional representation system as opposed to any less representative electoral system was the institutional expression of historical continuity: namely the persistence of political "subcultures", rooted in well identifiable territories within the country' (Farneti 1985: 47). There are many types of PR. The list system, the one used until 1994 to elect the Chamber of Deputies, the lower house, was a fairly pure form. Its goal was to provide a reasonably clear microcosm of the electorate's wishes. Given the political cultural cleavages, it was believed that a broad array of positions would be represented. The electoral system contributed to the consistency of results from one election to another and over time. In spite of the aim of reflecting the wishes of the electorate as closely as possible, under this system the larger parties were awarded more seats in proportion to their votes than the smaller ones. The really small parties, which on occasion won over five million votes in aggregate, often received no seats because individually they were unable to meet the required threshold.

The list system of PR gives greater emphasis to parties than to individual candidates. The party apparatus was strengthened by the fact that it not only made up the lists but also determined the order in which names would appear. It was possible for voters to indicate preferences among the names on the party lists, but less than half of the electorate generally opted for preference voting. When voters saw ten, twenty or fifty names on a list, they tended to concentrate on making certain their party received their vote. The preference system was definitely confusing to a good portion of the electorate. However, it worked to the advantage of the best-known leaders, who did their best to obtain impressive totals of preference votes. Candidates could have their names included in a party's list in more than one district. Usually the names of prominent leaders would appear at the top of the lists in multiple constituencies. If elected in more than one, they would choose the district for which they wished to sit.

Throughout the history of the First Republic there were numerous proposals to change the electoral system. Nothing came of almost all of these. There was one landmark change for a single election; other reforms had a difficult road, in part in reaction to this experiment. In 1953, with the aim of creating a stable government, DC Minister of the Interior Mario Scelba proposed an election law giving a bonus to any party or coalition of parties which achieved a majority of the popular vote. Given that it was unlikely a single party would achieve a majority, in practice this meant that any coalition of parties which received over 50 per cent of the vote would be allotted 60 per cent of the seats. Proponents had to be defensive about the law because it was similar to one used by Mussolini in 1924. However, the DC, the PSDI, the PRI, the PLI and splinter parties joined in an electoral coalition prior to the 1953 election. The opposition, led by the PCI and the PSI, called the law the 'swindle law' and indicated that it was basically undemocratic. In 1953, the coalition which advocated the law did not achieve the required majority by a very small margin; it received 49.85 per cent of the vote, missing the required 50 per cent by a little over 50,000 votes. The acrimony surrounding the Scelba Law contributed to the problems of realizing other proposals for change of the electoral law, and generally intensified political conflict.

Referenda: the people's voice

Consistent with the new spirit of freedom after the fascist experience, the founding fathers included provisions for direct democracy in the fundamental law. This reinforced their belief in popular sovereignty. The most important elements of direct democracy noted in the fundamental law were two types of referenda. One allows the people to participate in the revision of the Constitution, and the other in abrogating all or parts of a law passed by the Parliament. Referenda involving changes in the Constitution require that within three months of the publication of a constitutional amendment approved by the Parliament, a referendum must be held on the proposal if one-fifth of the members of five Regional Councils request it. Since only minor changes have been made to the Constitution, as of 1998 no such referendum has been held.

More important have been referenda on rejecting all or parts of ordinary laws (Salerno 1992). There are restrictions on the types of laws that can be voted upon. Among those excluded from referenda are treaties, pardons and financial measures. Other laws can be submitted to referenda if five Regional Councils or 500,000 voters so request. To abrogate all or part of a law, a majority of the electorate must vote and a majority of those casting valid ballots must support the change. Referenda have failed because a majority of the electorate did not participate. Obtaining the required number of signatures does not guarantee the issue will reach the ballot. Requests for referenda must be approved by the Constitutional Court, and this body has rejected some proposals as being inappropriate. Also, if parliamentary action changes the status of the legislation in question by repeal or amendment, the issue of the referendum becomes moot. In addition, if Parliament is dissolved the referendum is suspended. Finally, the Constitutional Court has decided that if constitutional implications are involved, a referendum cannot be held.

Although Parliament did enact a law in 1953 giving the Constitutional Court the responsibility of approving the admissibility of referenda, the whole procedure was not established until 1970. Until then the parties in power, especially the DC, were loath to risk giving the left the opportunity to overturn legislation. Many viewed referenda as tools for the left. However, it was conservative forces, with the support of the Catholic Church, which advocated the initial referendum of the First Republic, held in 1974, to abrogate the divorce law. The popular vote decisively went against those wishing to abolish the right of divorce. It was clear that the results of this referendum went far beyond the question of divorce; they provided evidence of the weakening of the religious body in its secular activity.

Right from the first referendum, the implications of this form of direct democracy were seen as having wide-ranging political impact. The span of issues subject to referenda has been very broad, including subjects ranging from public order to financing political parties, to the site of nuclear plants and even abortion and the liberalization of drug laws. These are but a few of the questions put before the electorate. Many people believe it is necessary to place greater limits on the use of referenda. There is concern that too many matters are put before the voters, who are not prepared to handle them. In June 1995 the electorate faced twelve separate questions. Some believe that a few of the issues put to a vote are either frivolous or not important enough to justify referenda. Other people are concerned that the legislature is being undermined by frequent recourse to referenda. Several referenda have had a considerable impact on the public agenda. In general, referenda have contributed to intense political conflict and have lessened the possibility of compromise (Breda 1995a).

Elections in the First Republic

Among the many contradictions of contemporary Italian politics has been the fact that in spite of severe government instability, there has been relative stability among the party outcomes in elections. While there undoubtedly was movement within the electorate from one election to another, such movement was limited. When one party lost votes to another or to abstentions and blank and spoiled ballots, it often picked up replacement votes from another party or parties. Hence, major shifts in party vote totals have been the exception rather than the rule. Incremental change, rather than volatility, has marked electoral results in the First Republic. This situation continued to prevail in 1994 and 1996.

It should be noted that patterns of voting began to emerge as early as the 1946 election for the Constituent Assembly, the body which wrote the Constitution. These patterns were reinforced in the contests of 1948 and 1953, and basically remained without fundamental alteration throughout the life of the First Republic. The fact that there was a single dominant governing party, the DC, and two principal competing parties, the DC and the PCI, limited major electoral shifts. Thus, vote totals changed slowly. When one adds the votes of the third largest party, the PSI, to the totals of the two leading parties, the outcome reached over 75 per cent of the vote, or close to it. Since the vote for the big three was relatively stable, little room for radical change existed for the small parties. Still, these small parties demonstrated remarkable staying power with major shifts up and down in their vote totals occurring on rare occasions. If the German five-per-cent rule had been applied in Italy, several of these parties would have been eliminated from the legislature and possibly would have been dissolved or amalgamated.

Nowhere is consistency more evident than in support for the DC. It began with a very large vote in 1948, 48.5 per cent, but following this it entered a long period of decline mixed with an occasional gain (Caciagli 1990). To illustrate its consistency, one only has to examine the returns for elections held between 1963 and 1979. In this period its support ranged between 38.3 and 39.1 per cent of the vote. In 1983 the DC vote fell to 32.9 per cent, and in the following parliamentary election in 1987 its support rose slightly to 34.3 per cent. What is especially impressive about the consistency of these percentages is the fact that the years encompassing these elections were difficult ones for the nation and the DC. In spite of facing both a wide range of national problems as the governing party and considerable internal strife, the DC consistently maintained its portion of the vote.

The long-term forces of political cultural change were important to the electoral performance of the DC. It became clear that secularization trends hurt the party. Those who considered themselves practising Catholics in 1950 were 70 per cent of the population. This figure fell to 48 per cent in 1968 and to 30 per cent in 1987 (Caciagli 1990). At the same time the intense political activities of church-related groups decreased. Furthermore, women, who had been a bulwark of DC voters, were changing roles in the family, community and the economy. Whereas it has been estimated that in 1948 women provided almost 65 per cent of the DC vote, this figure declined rapidly during the years of the First Republic. Of note is the fact that the party was never especially strong among youth.

From the first election in 1948, the DC did particularly well in parts of the centre and north of the country, but especially in the northeast in the so-called 'white zone'. Likewise in Rome and its environs the DC had built an excellent organization, in part based on government workers who owed their jobs to that party. In addition, the church and church-related organizations helped. As the

DC share of the vote declined in the 1970s and 1980s in these traditional areas of strength, its support in the South improved. It is noteworthy that when the DC vote fell to 32.9 per cent nationally in 1983, it remained at 37.3 per cent in the South. As would be expected of a conservative party, the DC did better in small towns and rural areas than in most cities, with notable exceptions. When the DC vote diminished significantly, especially in sub-national elections, more often than not its losses were to the right and centre of the political spectrum, to the MSI or the Liberals, or to the PSDI. Considerable abstention also hurt the party.

Although the ongoing competition between the DC and the PCI was a critical factor in the politics of the nation, voting behaviour in the case of the PCI was somewhat different than that of the DC. Averaging 24.8 per cent of the vote, the PCI showed steady improvement in all parliamentary elections between 1953 and 1979. Its gains, ranging from 0.1 to 2.6 per cent, were small until 1976, when its support increased considerably. In that year it made a major break-through. Receiving 34.4 per cent of the vote, it improved its standing in the 1972 election by more than 7 per cent.

The PCI seemed poised to finally enter the governing circle. However, the 1976 election turned out to be a high-water mark for the party. In spite of some achievements for the government as a result of PCI–DC collaboration, in many ways the 'historic compromise' was a failure. The PCI lost votes as a result of this and the murder of Aldo Moro. In spite of its condemnation of all types of terrorism, some voters saw the party as somehow related to the politically criminal elements on the left of the political spectrum. In 1979, the PCI share of the vote fell to 30.4 per cent and in the two subsequent elections in the 1980s its support continued to decline, reaching a low of 26.6 per cent in 1987.

The steady growth of the PCI share of the vote until 1979 was a national rather than regional phenomenon. When the party's vote began to decline, it fell in all parts of the country. Still, the distribution of its support demonstrated it was strongest in the industrialized areas of the North as well as certain regions such as Tuscany in the centre of the country. Its third area of strength was in and around Rome and pockets of the South. It has long been accepted in western democracies that, with some major exceptions, party organization is critical to strong electoral results. The PCI was always known for its powerful organization. This type of structure generally can produce the votes of militants and friendly voters. Mannheimer (1990) notes that even with the erosion of the PCI organization, the party's vote increased on occasion. It is the floating voter who decides elections, and given the anti-Communist barriers created by most other parties, the PCI had limits on its potential voter pool. It expended intense efforts to enlarge this pool, but found the task very difficult. It is noteworthy that when it seemed as if the PCI might surpass the DC in the 1976 election, the anti-Communist parties used this threat effectively in their electoral propaganda.

The PCI always received most of its votes from industrial workers. With the reduction in the size of this group, it provided less of a stable source of Communist votes. Also, a less militant workforce lessened the effectiveness of the electoral machine. The party always had major pockets of voters among agricultural workers, and in this constituency its percentage of support remained relatively stable. However, given the drastic decline in the number of farm workers, support from this sector diminished as well. While the size of the middle class expanded rapidly between 1968 and 1987, at first the PCI was not adversely affected to a great extent at the polls; many of the new clerks, managers, teachers and technical workers came from lower-class backgrounds where their families had always voted left. But by the 1980s this tradition had begun to erode. Since the number of female industrial workers was always much less than their male counterparts and women, to a large degree, were more influenced by the church, the PCI always did better among masculine workers. As more women entered the workforce and were less tied to the church, the PCI's potential for attracting female voters increased. The voter profile of the PCI looked more like that of the other parties as the electorate became more homogenized and nationalized. Mannheimer states: '...with the passing of years the PCI conquered an electorate always more similar to that of the other parties' (Mannheimer 1990: 57). One other point needs to be made about communist voters. Until the middle of the 1970s, as opposed to the DC, the PCI always did well among youth. This was one of the great electoral strengths of the party. When the party began to lose the support of these young people, it faced a severe problem. Most of these votes went to splinter parties on the left.

The electoral history of the third largest party, the PSI, must obviously be coupled with that of the PCI. Its hope of becoming the leading party of the left had been dashed. Its electoral results were mixed. It experienced a rapid decline from the first election for the Constituent Assembly, in which it gained 20.7 per cent of the vote. Allied with the PCI in the 1948 and 1953 elections, it quickly became the junior partner in the alliance. Throughout the 1960s it obtained about 14 per cent of the vote. In the 1970s its share fell to just under 10 per cent, and then remained very stable. The 1980s brought new hope when the party increased to 11.4 per cent of the vote in 1983 and 14.3 per cent in 1987. However, the really big advance did not occur, in spite of the severe problems faced by the PCI. The clientelism of Craxi produced a negative reaction among new voters and other small parties.

PSI support from the working class declined throughout the First Republic. As the PCI assumed greater power in the Italian General Confederation of Labour, the PSI was left with its ageing traditional working-class votes and some from the ranks of the Italian Union of Labour. Under Craxi, the profile of Socialist voters became more middle class. The party did especially well among people who owed their jobs or contracts for work in the public sector to the PSI. It had certain traditional strongholds, especially in the North. However, its vote, to a significant degree, was national and the party did as well in small towns and medium-sized cities as in most large cities.

As for the remainder of the small parties, their vote did not fluctuate greatly from one election to another, with occasional exceptions. The major point is that there seemed to be little electoral space left for them when the three leading parties garnered such a large portion of the vote. Hence, electoral competition among the centre-left and far left small parties usually was such that small gains were hoped for or, in some cases, the goal was simply to minimize losses.

As society changed during the First Republic, so did the nature of electoral campaigns. In the early years, campaign methods followed those used before the arrival of the Fascist dictatorship. Campaigns featured frequent large outdoor rallies by the major parties and smaller ones by the others. These rallies remained important, but as television slowly spread throughout the nation, it lessened their impact. A new style of campaigning developed. In spite of the fact that the DC controlled both radio and television throughout a good part of the First Republic, these media developed into significant campaign factors. Special programmes in which the leaders of different parties presented their platforms or answered questions posed by journalists were very popular with the public. The media was important, especially when the DC monopoly of it was broken. It became even more important in the Second Republic.

Public opinion polls did not have a great impact until the middle of the 1970s and the 1980s. Although market research organizations carried on polling, the results were often viewed with scepticism. It was believed that Italians could not be relied on to answer questions truthfully because they did not think they should let anyone know how they voted. This relates to the political cultural value of a lack of trust. Very often the results of exit polls did not correspond to electoral outcomes. Still, the major parties began to do polling and results were used in planning electoral strategy.

Many events and activities are associated with the beginning of the end of the First Republic. Often cited is a referendum held in 1991. Although the issue involved was not of monumental significance, it was soon seen as portent of very important things to come. By 1991, public disgust with the political class was growing, even before *Tangentopoli*. One manifestation of popular discontent was the increasing support for the Northern League, which campaigned as an opponent of the traditional parties. The League began to do very well in several local elections in the North. There was considerable evidence of political ferment in several places around the nation.

On 9 June 1991, the voters went to the polls in a referendum which was aimed at reducing the number of preference votes in elections for the Chamber of Deputies from three or four to one. What is interesting is that the issue of the number of preferences, which did not appear to be of huge importance, captured the imagination of the voters. It would not be too strong to argue that many voters did not fully understand the implications of their votes. What they did seem to grasp was that somehow they were voting against the old party system. Clearly, momentum for significant reform was building. In discussing the referendum of 1991, it has been observed: 'Since the campaign…the theme of institutional reform had entered into mass debate. Before that, throughout the 1980s, only a restricted segment of the political class had discussed institutional reforms' (Corbetta and Parisi 1995: 76).

The 1992 parliamentary election was heralded by the newspapers as an electoral earthquake. It did involve changes which a brief time before would not have been considered possible, and it did turn out to be a serious tremor, which would later be greatly surpassed in the elections of 1994 and 1996. In retrospect, this election can be viewed as a major step in the transition to the Second Republic. The change wrought by the 1992 election was founded on a public condemnation of the party system, which had continuously dominated the political life of the First Republic. Almost the entire political class felt the wrath of the voters. The 1992 election broke the seemingly immutable gridlock of party power, which had existed throughout the First Republic and assured the public that change was possible.

In discussing the 1992 election, Bull and Newell write of a combination of six factors which explain the destabilization of Italian politics in the late 1980s. The items on this list have been touched upon throughout this work, but it is still useful to present them here. The authors note '…the end of the "Communist question", the stagnation of the DC and the PCI, the economic downturn, the rising social tensions, the institutional degeneration and finally the emergence of new movements for change' (Bull and Newell 1993: 204). Only a few of these items need further discussion. The economic problems were not new to Italy. However, after a strong economic recovery in the early and middle part of the 1980s, the nation subsequently felt the economic downturn which was being experienced by most of the industrial world. The enormous government spending and public debt made responding to the recession more difficult than in some countries. As economic conditions worsened, there seemed to be a concomitant increase in social tensions.

Growth in violent crime, especially in the South, was all too evident. The Mafia and other criminal organizations were acting with impunity, and public authorities seemed unable to cope. It began to become apparent that there was some collusion between certain politicians and criminal organizations. Then, a few months before the 1992 election, *Tangentopoli* emerged. While corruption began to dominate the news, the government seemed not only to be unable to deal with the economy and crime, but it did not appear to be doing much about reform in pressing areas, such as education, health, welfare and so on. Also contributing to the ferment were new movements which, more than anything else, were calling for a political change. Foremost among these groups was the Northern League, which was gaining supporters primarily by attacking the political system and portraying itself as a force very different from the traditional political parties. The *Rete* also began to attract attention as a force against the Mafia and existing politics. In addition, movements for referenda which could bring about change, which was seen as being blocked by the old guard leaders, became more prominent.

The traditional parties of the First Republic did not disappear as a result of the 1992 election, but they were severely damaged. All interpretations of the electoral outcome focused on the voters' rejection of them. The turnout for the election was 87.3 per cent, the lowest figure in the history of the First Republic.

Furthermore, when blank and spoiled ballots are added to the number of abstentions, a figure of 17.4 per cent results. This figure is higher than the vote obtained by the PDS.

One would anticipate that the DC as the long-time governing party would especially feel the wrath of the voters. Its vote, at 29.7 per cent, was still considerable, but it did decline 4.6 per cent from its 1987 total. Also, its performance meant that the party's vote had fallen below the 30 per cent mark for the first time. When it is recognized that clientelistic and church-related organizations still provided a solid block of votes for the DC, it was clear that floating voters left the governing party in significant numbers. Nor could the PDS take advantage of the decline of its major opponent; instead, the voters seemed to see it as part of the old system. The result for the PDS was 16.1 per cent, a fall of more than 10 per cent from its 1987 performance. It should be noted that the DC and the PCI, which had combined for 60.9 per cent of the vote in 1987, saw their combined share of the vote drop to 45.8 per cent. Clearly another casualty of the election was the imperfect two-party system. It must be recognized that some of the lost votes of the PDS went to the PRC, which received 5.6 per cent of the vote. Even acknowledging this fact, the decline of the PDS, which had begun in 1979, continued unabated.

In terms of the minor parties, voter shifts were not great. The PSI dropped from 14.3 per cent in 1987 to 13.6 per cent in 1992. The unfolding scandals in which PSI leaders were involved hurt the party. Among the other small parties it was the newer ones, like the Greens and the *Rete*, which, while not getting a lot of votes, did take them from the larger parties. The major victor in 1992 was the Northern League, the outsider party, which went from less than 1 per cent in 1987 to 8.7 per cent in 1992 (Donovan 1992). It became the fourth largest party in the nation, in spite of its regional base. In corruption-marked Milan it became the largest vote-winner.

From the point of view of the government, the electoral earthquake did not clear the picture: in fact, things were less clear than before the election. The four governing parties, which had been expected to produce a government led by Craxi, lost their majority. Some speculation developed that the PDS might finally join the government or give its external support to a governing coalition. The disastrous results for this party made it reject either possibility. The Northern League, which so vociferously condemned the traditional parties, would not consider joining them in a government. Finally, a caretaker government emerged under Giuliano Amato, a Socialist and a professor of constitutional law. The Amato government was supported by the traditional governing parties, the DC, the PSI, the PSDI and the PRI. It was generally perceived as a stopgap measure and not expected to last long, and it did not. Assuming office in June 1992, Amato resigned as Prime Minister on 19 April 1993, following a referendum on a change in the election law for the Senate with which he disagreed.

The Amato government was replaced by a technocratic non-party one led by Carlo Azeglio Ciampi, the former head of the Bank of Italy. For the first time in the First Republic, Italy had a government headed by a person who was not a Member of Parliament. This government was also seen as a temporary affair, something to get the nation through the obvious period of transition. Yet what the transition would lead to was not clear. The Ciampi government had a limited non-political agenda. It was evident that high on the national agenda was a major change in electoral laws. This was to be initiated through still another referendum. The existing electoral law seemed to be identified with the worst things in the First Republic.

As can be imagined, following the 1992 election the winds of change blew more intensely throughout the nation. Part of this was the result of the referenda movement, which gathered momentum. The Committee for the Referendum on Electoral Laws (COREL) was particularly active. With caretaker governments, it was difficult for the Parliament to undertake major reforms. Hence, the people were asked to urge change with their votes. Requests for numerous referenda came quickly. What emerged as the most significant was a call to revise the electoral law for the Senate.

In the past, it had often been difficult to obtain the necessary signatures to get an issue on the ballot. The movement led by COREL encountered no such problems. Almost all parties favoured a reform of the electoral law used for the second chamber. Opponents of the change, such as the PRC, argued that the Parliament elected in 1992 was not sufficiently representative to change electoral arrangements. It was obvious that numerous very diverse questions were confusing for the voters. Furthermore, the wording of the referendum on the issue of the electoral law for the Senate was far from clear. This was an abrogative referendum, which involved cancelling some of the wording of the existing law. The mixed system used to elect the Senate had a heavy emphasis on PR: the change proposed in the referendum would mean that a mixed system would be continued, but the emphasis would be on majoritarianism. It was clear that the voters were voting for reform even without fully understanding the specific issue. The supporters of the reform achieved an overwhelming victory which was a national phenomenon, like the vote on divorce. It was apparent that even voters of the few parties which opposed the change, such as the PRC, the *Rete* and the Greens, voted yes in significant numbers (Corbetta and Parisi 1995).

The problems of electoral reform

Following the victory of the reformers in the 1993 referendum, the demands for change intensified. Parliamentary modification of the electoral laws was more extensive than anticipated. Parliamentarians read the message the people sent in the referendum as more than a call for reform of the Senate's electoral law, and they also changed electoral arrangements for the Chamber of Deputies. Even before the referendum, political parties set forth proposals for electoral reform (Pappalardo 1995). In spite of major differences, almost all of them seemed ready to move beyond pure PR. It became clear that a mixed arrangement was the only thing upon which agreement could be reached. The amount of PR versus that of single-member districts continued to be a matter of dispute. As to be expected, the smaller parties wanted a greater PR component, while the larger ones wanted more single-member district seats. Also, the size of the constituencies for the PR distribution was a controversial issue. Some wanted a national constituency, like Israel, which would help the small parties. It was difficult to find agreement about the relationship between the PR list votes and those for single-member district candidates. Similar to the German practice, the party list vote was to be reduced by the votes the party received in the single-member district contest. This mechanism was called *scorporo*. During the debates, differences emerged between parties concerning the changes, and some parties changed their positions, if not completely then at least in part. For instance, the PDS seemed often to lack consistency in its behaviour. In some areas it seemed very cautious as it endeavoured not to alienate the small parties which might be its partners in a future government.

For almost all the plans, the objective was to get rid of the old guard, the 'barons' who had dominated political life for so long. Another goal was to create a party system which would reduce governmental instability. For the small parties, these goals meant they would have to pay a price because almost all the proposals for a new electoral system would work to their disadvantage. These parties also recognized that they would not be able to stand alone, but would have to join one another or even larger parties in electoral coalitions. Of course, this was consistent with the reformers' desire to reduce the fragmentation of the parties in Parliament. In spite of all the discussions, things continued to appear deadlocked. Prospects for change looked so poor that Prime Minister Ciampi threatened to have his government act by decree if Parliament did not pass new electoral laws. No one liked the notion of independent executive action.

Finally, as pressure for reform built on many fronts, agreement was reached. The change was realized in August 1993. According to the new law, a mixed system, containing some elements of the German arrangement, is used to elect members of the Chamber of Deputies. Seventy-five per cent of the deputies are elected in single-member districts and 25 per cent by PR. The nation is divided into 475 single-member districts in which the candidate receiving a plurality of votes is victorious. One hundred and fifty-five seats are distributed on the basis of PR in twenty-seven constituencies, each of which embraces several single-member districts. In effect, the voters have two votes, one in the district and one for the party list. Voters can split their votes and give the one for the single-member district to one party and the one for the PR list to another. All candidates in the single-member districts have to be aligned with one or more of the lists competing for PR seats. The whole operation requires a complex system of candidate–list affiliation.

Complexity, involving the *scorporo*, also marks the allocation of the seats. The votes to elect victors in single-member districts are subtracted from the party's total in the PR constituency elections. Furthermore, complicated measures are used for the allocation of the PR seats, which is carried out by a National

Electoral Office. A 4 per cent rule is used, which requires that a party garner at least 4 per cent of the valid votes cast throughout the nation in order to share in the distribution of PR seats. No personal preferences are utilized, and the seats are allocated to individuals on the basis of their position on the electoral list. No longer is it possible to run as a candidate in more than one constituency or in both Chamber and Senate races.

The Senate's electoral system is the old one as changed by the deletions resulting from the referendum of 1993. Two hundred and thirty-eight Senators are elected in single-member districts with a plurality of votes required for victory, and 77 are selected by PR on a regional basis. Our discussion will focus on elections for the lower house. Although there have been differences in the electoral results for the two chambers, a detailed analysis of senatorial elections is not necessary for an understanding of basic electoral patterns.

Even as the new electoral laws were passed, there was considerable criticism of them. The great complexity of the new arrangements was thought to create difficulties for the average voter in terms of comprehension. Furthermore, many argued that keeping some PR would assure the representation of some small parties, which would make stable majority government, one of the stated goals of the reformers, difficult. Also, there are nuances in the laws which make electoral engineering by some parties possible. This involves the use of phantom lists, which could change outcomes. Although no illegality is involved, it runs counter to the spirit of the new law (Katz 1995). Dissatisfaction with the new law was widespread, but often for different reasons. There were many predictions that it would be used for one election and then would have to be changed. The new system was employed in the 1994 election and, following this, calls for further reform became frequent. However, due to a lack of agreement on reform, the system was also used in 1996.

The sweeping changes in national election laws reflected a widespread reform attitude, which also touched on sub-national governments and elections. At first there were calls for more devolution of power so that the regions could have greater self-determination in matters pertaining to elections. It was thought by some that the regions should adopt their own electoral laws. This did not occur; instead, Parliament passed general electoral laws which applied to sub-national units. The electoral arrangements resulting from this legislation have been described as the most complicated in postwar history (PDC 1995).

Elections: the beginning of the Second Republic

The 1994 and 1996 parliamentary elections were critical ones. All elections in democracies have special significance, but some are more important than others. Those that signal monumental change in a system are referred to as critical elections (Burnham 1970). In Italy, events since the end of the 1980s seemed to be building up to the 1994 and 1996 elections. The two referenda on electoral laws, the 1992 parliamentary election plus votes in sub-national contests, the change in electoral laws, revelations concerning *Tangentopoli*, the creation of new political movements and the end of the old political order all served as a prelude to the changes wrought by the 1994 and 1996 elections. The 1994 election brought the right to power for the first time in the postwar years; the 1996 election brought the left into the government for the first time since the 1940s.

One thing which marked the 1994 election was the development of party alliances of greater political magnitude than those of the First Republic. Moreover, these alliances were used in different ways. The parties quickly understood that the new electoral laws, with their emphasis on the majoritarian principle even though some PR remained, required them to make alliances to maximize the benefits of their vote. In the same vein, though slightly different, was the recognition that costly competition in single-member districts should be avoided wherever possible. All of this should have been anticipated. One goal for many of the reformers was to reduce the fragmentation of the parties and develop a polarization. It was hoped that two major poles would emerge, and that after the election they would serve as the foundation for a stable government and a responsible opposition.

It was clear that there was considerable political ferment in the transition years between the First and Second Republics. This meant that there was a substantial number of floating voters, many of whom were on the centre-left of the political spectrum. As further revelations about corruption identified with the PSDI, the DC and the PSI became a frequent occurrence, the leaders hoped to appeal to people from these parties who were going into new movements (Rhodes 1995b). Before the entry of Berlusconi into the competition, the PDS anticipated that the opposition would come from the right-wing MSI and the centre-right Northern League. It was known that the latter had considerable appeal as an alternative to the old corrupt party system. The populist approach of these forces on the right was not fully understood by the PDS, and it acted on the basis of a traditional analysis of the left–right spectrum.

As indicated earlier, the PRC had demonstrated strength beyond many people's expectations when it split from the PCI on the occasion of the birth of the PDS. Since the PDS seemed intent on becoming a moderate force deserving voter support to govern, it continued to lose sympathy among militants attracted to the PRC and other far left splinter groups. While the militant position of the PRC caused the PDS difficulties in negotiations between the two parties, it also caused problems for the PDS in its negotiations with other parties and movements to its right. There were still many people in the centre and moderate left of the political spectrum who did not have complete confidence that the PDS had totally cast away its communist past. They saw the PRC as proof that there continued to be a communist threat in Italy. Any alliance between the PDS and the PRC was viewed as clear evidence that the PDS had not completely changed.

Occhetto felt stronger than ever that the PDS would need a broad alliance. The Progressive Alliance, ranging from the far to the moderate left, was formed. Led by the PDS, it included the PRC, the *Rete*, the Greens, two splinter socialist groups, the Reborn Socialists and the remnants of the PSI, the Democratic

of Berlusconi's meetings with the public, as well as press conferences, were carefully controlled. Within this context he proved to be an effective campaigner and a fresh face in politics. By comparison, Occhetto, the leader of the PDS, looked like a traditional party leader who did not seem to represent a complete change from the past.

Following the election, it was asked if it were true that television won the contest (Lerner 1994). There was certainly a TV blitz. With Berlusconi owning three major channels, his staff used innumerable election spots, most of which featured him, symbols of FI and its theme song. The public channels were much more balanced in their presentations, even though they were generally not favourable to the Freedom Pole. One innovation in the campaign was a face-to-face TV debate between Berlusconi and Occhetto. Most viewers interviewed after the programme thought the result was a standoff, or that Berlusconi had a slight edge. Not many opinions about the leaders and their parties were changed. Berlusconi's television performance demonstrated confidence and a mastery of many subjects. However, during the campaign one of the general criticisms of Berlusconi was that he lacked political experience. Although it is difficult to evaluate the total impact of television on elections, in the 1994 election its role was considerable.

Party programmes definitely were less important than leaders, parties and alliances. It was obvious that the Freedom Pole would have difficulty agreeing on a programme. The differences between the MSI-AN and the Northern League were great and often involved contradictory positions. The result was separate and different programmes on a regional basis. All of the partners in the Freedom Pole agreed to strongly emphasize anti-communism and the dangers implicit in a victory for the left. This was a message aimed at the middle class, especially the former supporters of the DC. It was left to Berlusconi to offer a few specific and several general ideas. He promised lower taxes, less government and the creation of a million new jobs. However, the emphasis on image was most important, and he asked the electorate to have confidence in him. It is noteworthy that the Freedom Pole continually stressed that it was different from the old political establishment and that it brought a fresh approach to governance. Following the austerity programmes of the Amato and Ciampi governments, Berlusconi seemed to be an optimist with new hope. Although the Progressives had less difficulty developing a common programme and they were much clearer in their platform, this did not receive a great deal of attention. They stressed a strong European orientation, the reform of social welfare programmes and fiscal responsibility. But it was the Berlusconi forces which dictated the focus of the campaign.

Much has been made of the fact that a new governing class emerged from the election of 1994. The Second Republic had not only many new leaders, but also many people new to politics who were candidates. This was particularly evident in the ranks of FI. Over 60 per cent of the FI candidates came from the business and professional worlds. Neither the League nor FI featured a trade unionist candidate. One outstanding statistic is that just under 21 per cent of the FI candidates had been private sector managers. In addition, over 16 per cent of this party's candidates were medical doctors; in general, Freedom Pole brought a considerable number of physicians into politics. On the other hand, almost one-third of the PDS candidates were either university professors or teachers. Another figure which makes an impression was the 29.3 per cent of the PDS candidates who were professional politicians (Mattina 1995).

Having many candidates with little or no experience in politics meant that few of these people were well known to the public. This definitely impacted on the political campaign, since not having an identity of their own, they were very dependent on their parties and leaders for recognition. Turnout, which reached 86.1 per cent, was slightly down from the election of two years before when the figure was 87.3 per cent. Also, the number of spoiled and blank ballots reached a postwar high. These plus the non-voters totalled 20 per cent (Bull and Newell 1995). Part of the explanation for this phenomenon was the new and complicated electoral system.

The victory of the Freedom Pole was not a massive one. Obtaining 46.65 per cent of the vote, it won a majority of the seats in the Chamber of Deputies (366). While the largest single bloc in the Senate, it did not have an absolute majority in the second chamber. With its 21 per cent of the vote and a vote that was distributed nationally, FI was the largest party in the nation. Since it received many votes from former supporters of the DC, questions began to be asked as to whether it might evolve into a new DC. Four years later, in 1998, Berlusconi cited this as a possibility. The results were different for the two major FI allies. The MSI-AN demonstrated what many thought was surprising strength. It became the third largest party in the country, with a vote of 13.5 per cent. However, its strength was regionally based in the South. On the other hand, the Northern League experienced a slight slippage – from 8.65 to 8.6 per cent – in its share of the vote from the 1992 elections. Due to electoral geography and its alliance with FI, the Northern League's seat total in the Chamber of Deputies doubled, from 55 in 1992 to 106 in 1994.

The Progressive Alliance was a loser, garnering 34.4 per cent of the vote. This compared with 42.8 per cent received by a similar, but not exactly the same, grouping in 1992. It is important to recognize that the PDS actually improved its vote total over that of 1992. It showed a significant gain in the two-year span going from 16.1 per cent to 20.4 per cent. However, most of its allies in the alliance were losers. The hopes, even if meagre, of the centrist Pact for Italy did not materialize. It was definitely squeezed between the two poles. This is demonstrated in part by the fact that with the use of the new electoral system, the payoff to the Pact was less than that of the other two alliances. The Progressives won roughly the same proportion of seats as they had votes. The Freedom Pole did even better, winning a larger portion of seats than its vote would indicate. The Pact ended up with less than half of the seats that a true proportional system would have awarded it (Bull and Newell 1995).

Falling after eight tumultuous months, the Berlusconi government was short-lived. Instead of calling elections as demanded by the Pole, President Scalfaro appointed Lamberto Dini, the finance minister in the Berlusconi government, to head a caretaker government of technocrats. During much of the life of the Dini government, the leaders of the Pole continued to call for elections. Towards the end of 1995, when the Dini Government had accomplished most of its agenda, it appeared elections might be further delayed. Berlusconi changed his mind and agreed with the left that another government of technocrats should be established to change the electoral law and realize other reforms. Believing that early elections would bring considerable success, the AN blocked this proposal. With no alternative, Scalfaro dissolved the Parliament and set 21 April 1996 as the date for elections. This meant Italians would go to the polls for the third time in four years.

Like the 1994 contest, that of 1996 can be described as a critical election. As noted, it brought the left to power for the first time following the Second World War. Also, it demonstrated an alternation of power after the victory of the right in 1994, which many people believed was essential to further democracy. In spite of these important outcomes, the results cannot be considered another electoral earthquake. There was no large shift of votes. Changes in alliances, tactical factors and limited voting switches brought the left to power. Prior to the election, most observers believed a hung Parliament with no majority in the legislature would emerge. It was anticipated that the Freedom Pole would not win; it was thought the Olive Tree had a chance, but an unlikely one.

As in 1994, alliances were central to the 1996 election, given the nature of the electoral system. However, the partnerships were considerably altered in the two intervening years. This was very evident in the case of the Freedom Pole, which lost the support of the Northern League. Another loss which did not appear serious initially was the split in the AN, with the departure of the traditional Fascist group which became the Italian Social Movement – Tri-Colour Flame. It fought the election independently, and took votes from the AN. On the positive side for the Pole was the addition of more former right-wing Christian Democrats, who contested the election under the banner of the CCD–CDU.

While in most respects the centre-left looked similar to the 1994 Progressive Alliance, in practice there were considerable differences. The alliance was now called the Olive Tree. Although the PDS continued to be the dominant force in this arrangement, its prime ministerial candidate was Romano Prodi. He headed a group consisting of former DC supporters who were in the PPI, but remained on the left when it split. Prior to the formal creation of the Olive Tree, Prodi and his followers created grassroots groups called Committees for Prodi. Another new element in the Olive Tree camp was the list headed by former Prime Minister Lamberto Dini. He believed his personal popularity would bring his list success in the PR portion of the election. In addition to the elements mentioned above, the Greens and other small groups joined the Olive Tree.

Another major difference on the left in the 1996 election was the role of the PRC. In 1994 this party was part of the Progressive Alliance. Many observers believe that while it brought votes, especially where the left was already strong, it was not popular with moderate voters throughout the nation, who viewed it as too radical. In the 1996 election, a clever agreement was made between the Olive Tree and the PRC. The latter did not formally join the former; instead, a special arrangement was made whereby the Olive Tree and the PRC agreed not to have their candidates compete against each other in single-member constituencies. This was known as a 'standdown arrangement'. It only involved the election and was a pragmatic measure. It was not supposed to impact on post-election developments.

In 1996, the party platforms seemed to converge more than was the case in 1994. The Olive Tree carefully made no great promises. In a move some observers saw as risky, no tax reduction was promised. General fiscal responsibility and reduction of the public debt were emphasized. Privatization was called for, along with an improvement in social services and institutional reform, especially of the bureaucracy. The PRC muted its demands and seemed to be intent on not embarrassing the Olive Tree. The Pole, and especially Berlusconi, toned down their rhetoric. The lavish promises and most of the extreme language Berlusconi used in 1994 were limited. The anti-communist theme appeared again, but seemed somewhat hollow among marginal voters given that former DC member Prodi was Berlusconi's primary opponent. The Pole emphasized tax relief and simplification of the tax system. Fini accepted more privatization and less state intervention in the economy. Attacks on the *Mani Pulite* prosecutors continued, especially by FI leaders. The League, standing alone, was less clear in its goals. It definitely wanted a better deal for the North, sometimes raising the spectre of separation but more often emphasizing federalism. It continued to be anti-Rome and wanted the South to succeed on its own. Its previous anti-immigrant stance was less prominent.

The 1996 campaign, to a large degree, followed the script of two years earlier. The focus of the Pole's efforts continued to be on Berlusconi and Fini. The novelty of the former on the political scene no longer had the same effect. On the other hand, Prodi's roles in the DC and government did not hurt him. He is a very low-key individual who seemed convincing in his presentations. He travelled around the country in a coach and often was pictured riding a bicycle. This was a clear contrast to the image of Berlusconi, who rode in motorcades and always had a large entourage with him. In a television debate with Berlusconi, a master of this media, Prodi, with little charisma, held his own. He appeared well versed in the problems facing the country. Fini continued to be the number two leader of the Pole, and was viewed as an effective politician who impressed people.

Television still had an important part in the campaign. However, the PRC and the League received less coverage. Instead, both ran intense and effective grassroots campaigns featuring many street rallies. One controversial issue, a fairness doctrine for the media, emerged. This involved a decree called *par condicio*, meaning 'equal opportunity'. Opponents of the Pole felt that in the 1994 election Berlusconi's media holdings provided the Pole an unfair advantage. Since Berlusconi had used his television channels effectively in the 1994 campaign, he avidly opposed *par condicio*. He argued that it was wrong that he could not use his private property as he saw fit. Most observers felt that the decree did not achieve all the promise its supporters thought it would.

The 1996 election did move the party system further towards a division into two broad blocks. However, it remained an imperfect bipolarity. While over 250 parties registered to compete, only a dozen were truly significant. Even this figure must be considered high when the four largest parties, the PDS, FI, AN and the League, received 57 per cent of the vote. If the PRC's 8 per cent share is added to that figure, it almost reaches two-thirds of the vote. Furthermore, in the single-member district part of the election for the Chamber of Deputies, the major alliances dominated, earning over 85 per cent of the vote. When the vote of the League, independent of any alliance, is combined with the non-voters' 17 per cent and the 6 per cent invalid ballots, a figure of almost one-third of the total electorate is reached. This figure is greater if the non-aligned minor parties are included.

In some respects, non-allied parties, the League and MSFT decided the election. Also, the special relationship between the PRC and the Olive Tree was critical. The League, not fighting the election as part of the Freedom Pole as it had done in 1994, was costly to the centre-right. It either won or denied victory to the Pole in somewhere between 50–60 districts in the North. In 1994 the Pole won 161 single-member district seats in the North; in 1996, it won only 61. Even though its vote total was not high, the MSFT took away sufficient votes from the Pole and, more specifically, from AN to cost it up to 36 seats in the South. If the losses to the League and the MSFT had not occurred, the Pole might have won the election or the election could have resulted in the lack of a parliamentary majority (D'Alimonte and Bartolini 1997; Follini 1996).

The electoral system benefited the Freedom Pole in 1994 and the Olive Tree in 1996. The latter's leaders had learned the lesson of 1994. It won 246 seats, to which must be added the PRC's 15 seats in single-member districts. The Progressive Alliance garnered 164 seats in 1994. The Freedom Pole won 169 single-member district seats in 1996. Two years earlier, with the League as part of the alliance, it had won 301 seats in single-member districts. On the left, the PRC went from 6 per cent and eleven seats in the PR part of the election in 1994 to 8.6 per cent and twenty seats in 1996. This gain of 2.5 per cent and nine seats was a solid improvement, and demonstrated both its appeal and staying power. It emerged from the election as a necessary part of the Olive Tree majority in the Chamber of Deputies. However, this support was to remain external to the government, which it did not join. It proved to be an uneasy arrangement. On the other hand, the PDS was something of a loser in the PR part of the election. The percentage of its vote remained stable. It went from 20.4 per cent in 1994 to 21.1 per cent in 1996, but its total number of seats dropped from 38 to 26. The reason for this was the discrimination affiliated with the previously mentioned electoral mechanism, the *scorporo*. The Dini List contributed 8 seats to the Olive Tree on the basis of 4.3 per cent of the vote. The PPI obtained 9.7 per cent of the vote and 6 seats.

In the Freedom Pole, the PR vote for FI remained stable, going from 21 per cent and 30 seats in 1994 to 20.6 per cent and 37 seats two years later. It increased its number of seats due to the *scorporo*. The vote for AN increased to 15.7 per cent in 1996, a 2.2 per cent and five-seat gain. To Fini and his followers, this was disappointing because they expected to do much better. They had hoped to surpass FI. There were positive elements in AN's results. It did much better in the North than previously, and could now claim to be a national party. Also, in Rome, where it had been strong, it garnered 26.98 per cent of the vote. The outcome has to be considered a victory for the League. Given that it was running independently and competing, to a significant degree, with FI for middle-class support in the North, it was not anticipated it would more than hold its own against the two large alliances. However, its total vote increased by 2.3 per cent over that of 1994 and it received 59 seats. Although it showed strength in its performance, it was thought before the election that it might hold the balance of power in the Parliament, if neither of the alliances gained a majority. Since the Prodi government has not needed its votes, its power has diminished somewhat.

Conclusion

If elections were a central feature of the First Republic, the same has been true of the Second. One of the major questions asked in many quarters is whether the Parliament elected in 1996 can last its full term. Most observers believe it could go either way. Also, since the number of parties competing in elections is unlikely to be reduced in the near future, the alliances and their ability to maintain their unity and reach out to minor parties will be decisive for electoral victories. Since there is little agreement about electoral reform, it is likely that imperfect bipolarism will continue.

5 Political behaviour
Interest articulation and aggregation

Overview

An important channel of representation is afforded by interest groups, entities that, on the basis of one or more shared attitudes, make certain claims upon other organizations in society (Truman 1951). These associations, a critical ingredient in any polity, perform many functions, but primarily they serve as a link between the people and the political system. In Italy, as in all industrial societies, there is a plethora of interest groups. The Italian climate is conducive to interest group formation. The substantial cleavages which pervade the nation's social fabric provide a fertile soil for interest group development. The interest articulation pattern mirrors the cleavages of the political culture. Groups tend to reflect the basic population divisions, and as units they tend to be socially homogeneous. In addition to being widely proliferated, their variety is great. Given the nature of the multi-party system, especially in the First Republic, they are often not easily distinguished from political parties.

Within each major area of interest articulation there is further fragmentation on a social, political or religious basis. Few of these groups tend to amalgamate heterogeneous elements. They assume a political connotation, which can impact negatively on the universe of interests because the group process becomes very divided. Consequently, bargaining, negotiation and compromise are difficult. Interests can become quite frustrated, with detrimental consequences for the political system.

Many voluntary associations operate within the political subcultures of the nation. Geographic cleavages are reflected in the interest articulation pattern. Articulation tends to be more intense in northern and central Italy than in the South. The urban–rural conflict is also evident. Voluntary associations are more concentrated in urban as opposed to rural zones. As for membership, given societal patterns, more men than women enter their rank and file.

A factor embodied in the Constitution, which encourages group formation, is the guarantee of political and civil liberties of the private citizen. Very wide freedom of association and expression, which are critical to the creation of interest groups, are provided. As the First Republic matured, the political cognitions and awareness of Italians expanded due to higher educational achievement, socioeconomic modernity, greater diffusion of mass media, advanced communication technologies and a greater saliency of political phenomenon in the people's minds. This change in cultural values has nurtured associationism. Political structure has played a role as well. The devolution of political power has profoundly affected civic engagement (Putnam 1993; Sani 1980). As the responsibilities of government have increased, the number and type of organized interests have mushroomed and the level of group activity has intensified. Italy, as other nations, has witnessed a great proliferation of interest groups, especially in the last few decades. This is a healthy sign. It helps to maintain and expand the basis of democracy. The policy communities have not only become more numerous, but more complex and more competitive.

Resulting from this proliferation of groups are the newer ones, which represent post-materialist concerns, those preoccupations of an affluent society. These relate to the New Politics, which encompass values of the quality of life, individual freedoms and social equality, as opposed to those of the Old Politics, which stress economic growth, public order and national security. The non-economic concerns, reflecting the post-material values, often are linked to a single idea or a single cause, which is highly controversial or scientific and technical, such as peace, environmentalism or feminism. Frequently they are related to social issues with a high moral content. Believing that their concerns have been ignored by the established organizations, those who feel intensely about these post-material matters create their own associations. The prime movers of these interest groups tend to be young, well-educated, occupational and professional people from the middle class, committed to an important idea or set of ideas, and anxious for change. In terms of support, they cut across the established Old Politics cleavage which can be related to a left–right continuum. They take advantage of a large potential for chequebook membership, meaning that by writing a cheque people can make an expressive commitment without assuming onerous responsibilities. These groups have had to labour long and hard to build credibility and legitimacy.

It may be said that Italy has a two-tiered system of interest group representation. The first consists of the so-called established interests, such as business, trade union, professional and religious associations, which enjoy entrée to the various centres of the policy-making arena and participate in established networks. The second tier is composed of the newer groups, which enjoy little or lesser credibility and, having an organization which is not solidified, lack elites authorized to make binding commitments on their behalf. These associations are at a definite disadvantage in the interest articulation game because often they lack access to the appropriate policy makers and thus, their demands '...are expressed outside the perimeter of what can usually be accommodated by a policy style based on inter-elite bargaining' (Kitschelt 1989: 28).

Diverse methodological approaches have been used to examine the relationship between interest groups and the state in terms of the decision-making process. A recent approach is the neo-corporatist, which portrays decision-making arrangements and the role of functional groups in advanced capitalist societies. Neo-corporatism must be distinguished from the corporatist model developed, albeit incompletely, during the Fascist dictatorship in Italy. A generally accepted definition describes neo-corporatism as

> a system of interest representation in which the constituent units are organized into a limited number of singular, compulsory, non-competitive, hierarchically ordered and functionally differentiated categories, recognized or licensed (if not created) by the state and granted a deliberate representational monopoly within their respective categories in exchange for observing certain controls on their selection of leaders and articulation of demands and supports.
>
> (Hernes and Selvik 1981:104–5)

Corporatism is thus a method of formally incorporating certain functional groups, such as capital and labour, into the public decision-making apparatus. It is not easy to decide the extent of corporatism in a nation because of disputes concerning its definition, the functioning of institutions in theory and practice, and the diversity of the policy areas involved (Offe 1981).

Corporatist decision making is a consensual form of government. There is an agreement among the interests on the problems to be tackled, the solutions and the implementation procedures. Conflict is reduced and depoliticized by formally incorporating traditional adversaries, such as capital and labour, into the decision-making process. This is accomplished by establishing tripartite bodies, composed, for example, of business, trade union and governmental representatives. Through negotiation and bargaining, these representatives hammer out policy in a specific area. This structural arrangement is beneficial to all participants. The interest groups involved reap benefits from having been granted public status and privileged access. They enjoy prestige and can exert enormous influence throughout the policy-making process. The state bureaucracy garners a certain amount of control over group behaviour as well as a partner in the implementation of public policy. Theoretically, it can count on rank-and-file compliance with the policy outputs. Moreover, it can take advantage of the groups' resources and expert knowledge. As a result of this type of decision making, the basic functions of legislative institutions and political parties are transformed. The policy decisions taken outside the representative assembly must still receive its approval. But this endorsement may be of the rubber stamp variety because the policies have already been agreed to by the corporatists. At the end of this chapter, we will return to the concept to examine how it relates to Italy.

The Italian interest group universe

Given the number, the complexity and diversity of secondary associations, a problem of classification arises. For purposes of this discussion, these organizations will be presented by category according to a scheme based on the nature of the group, its tactics and the channels it uses to pass its message to the appropriate decision makers. Groups are thus placed in the following categories: anomic, non-associational, associational and institutional (Almond and Powell 1966). It should be recognized that this is a general schema and all groups do not fit neatly into one category. Each of these will be discussed in turn.

Anomic groups

Anomic interest articulation involves spontaneous behaviour, which is manifested in the form of riots, street demonstrations, protest marches, assassinations and the like. The postwar period in Italy, being one of intense conflict, has witnessed a lot of these activities. They are utilized by people who lack access to the decision-making process and are unable to express their demands in another fashion. Such actions are not a new phenomenon in Italian history, which has always been marked by activity in the public square. Examples of anomic manifestations are attacks on the American embassy in Rome and consulates in major Italian cities because of the United States' action in Vietnam, occupation of some Italian universities by students with demand for reform, and the separatist uprisings by ethnic Germans in the northern part of the country.

In many instances, the spontaneity of such groups and such behaviour is merely a pretense because they may be, and often have been, organized and/or aided by other elements, such as extremist groups on the left and right of the political spectrum. Often the leadership effort dissolves, or it may lose control of the operation. Potentially, this type of group action is self-destructive. The immediate effect of this sporadic activity may be powerful – so powerful, that coupled with the nature of the organization, these groups may peter out. Anomic interest behaviour is associated with certain patterns of violence, which are expressions of the fragmented Italian political culture, and are tools that tend to strengthen that fragmentation.

Non-associational groups

Another type of interest articulation is performed by the non-associational group, which is based on kinship, lineage, ethnicity, regionalism, class, religion, linguistic activity, status or other traditional characteristics. Having a relatively loose organization and no permanent leaders, this type of association usually, but not always, articulates its interests in an informal and intermittent fashion through individuals, cliques, influential families and religious authorities.

Often these groups sponsor a conference, the purpose of which might be to examine a specific problem, such as the South. Such gatherings have been organized by a number of intellectuals organized around *Il Mulino*, a monthly periodical. Other non-associational groups are those organized on a linguistic basis, which, in Italy, could be identified with the Italians of the South Tyrol who use German as their principal tongue. Currently they are demanding that road signs be in German. There are also religious groups in this category, along with individual privately owned oligopolies such as Fiat. Given the non-associational groups' intermittent pattern of articulation, their lack of an established method for determining the means of articulation and the fact that there is no continuity in their internal structure, there has been a trend towards a more developed organization, the associational. This has occurred because non-associational groups do not possess the requisite resources to compete successfully in complex interest group politics.

Associational interest groups

As in all industrialized nations, most of the voluntary associations in Italy are contained within the category of associational interest groups, entities specifically structured for the articulation of functional interests on a continuous basis. It is these groups that regulate interest group politics. This discussion will focus on the principal traditional interests – business, labour, agriculture – and the major non-traditional ones – the ecologists, Red Brigades, Freemasonry and the Mafia.

Business

Management, at one time one of the most powerful groups in Italy, is represented by *Confindustria* (the General Confederation of Italian Industry) which united local chambers of commerce and various business groups into a single association. Its membership reflects the dual nature of the Italian economy, which immediately after the war was dominated by large firms but since the 1970s by small and medium-sized ones. Today, small family-run businesses provide the largest component of *Confindustria*'s membership. The association has not released official membership figures since 1982, but these reveal a great contrast. Enterprises with up to ten employees accounted for 58 per cent of the membership, and those with between eleven and fifty employees for 31 per cent. Thus, not too many giants are affiliated with the organization (Lanzalaco 1990). These firms wield a greater share of power than their portion of the membership might indicate. This contrast has been a problem, but within the last decade it has become more pronounced. In spite of an increasing power cluster around the bigger firms, the smaller ones, having increased numerically, demand more authority within the association. In addition to the conflict between large and small enterprises, there is also tension between industrial and financial groups, which is reflected in the decision-making process.

Two different conceptions of the role of *Confindustria* have emerged. On the one hand, it is perceived as an organization in which the large groups should dominate the decision-making pattern and garner the support of the majority of the membership by financing services of importance to it, which would not be affordable otherwise. On the other hand, it is argued that *Confindustria* should be representative of all Italian business interests which, regardless of size, participate equally in the association. The first conception is closer to reality.

An indication of the importance of *Confindustria*'s president is provided by the fact that all policies and political strategies are spoken of in terms of a particular presidency. Reference is made to the Agnelli presidency, the Fossa presidency and so on. Being president of *Confindustria* means that the firm which this officer represents has additional weapons with which to fight competitors. Particular interests may be articulated along with general interests, and dominance over the association is assured because the president controls the selection of the vice-presidents and the working leadership.

In the immediate postwar era, *Confindustria* demanded two essentials. Management was to control the workplace and capitalists were not to be constrained by the state planning advocated by the political left. Other values supported by *Confindustria* were a *laissez-faire*, free market economy, political decisions based on economic and not social or political considerations and a recognition that industrialists, not politicians, should evaluate decisions impacting the economic arena (Ginsborg 1990; LaPalombara 1964). In the early years of the First Republic *Confindustria* was very strong, primarily because of the weakness of labour, its homogeneity and a close relationship with the hegemonic DC. Connections with the DC were further reinforced with the development of a financial linkage. The relationship between the DC and *Confindustria* has been described 'as the relationship between two homogeneous political organizations with separate areas of influence' (Martinelli 1980: 72). The DC was charged with foreign policy matters, building a consensus and maintaining law and order. Economic policy making was the responsibility of *Confindustria*. In return for the privilege of governing the economy, *Confindustria* supported DC candidates at election time. As a kind of insurance policy against potential threats from the PCI and/or PSI which could become real threats with electoral success, business did flirt with and even allocated funds to left-wing political parties and the trade unions affiliated with them.

The decade of the 1960s was a turbulent one for industrial interests. A political crisis and organizational decline were encountered. The relationship between the DC and *Confindustria* was especially difficult. The new societal framework generated diverse factions and alliances in the DC, and *Confindustria* was not flexible in adjusting. Several cleavages developed within the ranks of the association. The labour-intensive sectors were pitted against the capital-intensive ones. Consumer market-oriented firms opposed the industrial market-oriented ones, and technologically advanced enterprises were divided from their technologically backward counterparts. Different factions within the DC related to these disparate cleavages. The extensive fragmentation within its own association, the factionalism within the DC and the networks created between the cleavages in both organizations plus the growth of the state sector of the economy affected *Confindustria*'s ability to operate.

Labour came out of the 1969 Hot Autumn, a period of intense industrial conflict, with increased strength and was more cantankerous than ever. It was quite clear at the dawn of the 1970s that the industrialists' association could not act as a counterweight. Lacking cohesion, each sector had its own perspective.

Disparate alliances and a power struggle ensued. Although small and medium-sized firms numerically dominated the association, the principle of 'he who pays the piper calls the tune' gave control to the larger ones. Italian industry has never regained the homogeneity it possessed in the immediate postwar period. It remains polarized with the private and public oligopolies and the transnational corporations in one camp, and the small and medium-sized firms in the other. In spite of the disparate and often fragile transient alliances within these camps and between them or parts of them, the public enterprises and the private oligopolies have been able to generate favourable governmental responses to their demands to the detriment of the small and medium-sized firms.

When *Confindustria* showed its short-sightedness and rejected the centre-left coalition, it lost much of its contact with the political world and experienced difficulty in continuing to influence the general lines of economic policy. It was at this point in time that *Confindustria* gave more support, financial and otherwise, to the Liberal Party. Redefining its political agenda and undertaking a political turnabout, it eventually abandoned its unswerving loyalty to the DC. In time some members, representing small business, supported the Northern League (Mattina 1993; Salvati 1981). When Silvio Berlusconi turned political leader, he did not enjoy *Confindustria*'s support, as one might expect. He was quick to attack the organization and to separate himself from the business elite. In his eyes, the former's leaders were more progressive than he while the latter represented the traditional establishment.

In the 1970s, when the first attempts at concertation between the government and social partners were undertaken, and throughout the 1980s, *Confindustria* was included in concertation activities. In the 1990s the association has until recently been a willing participant. Important outcomes related to income policies, collective bargaining and pensions. Such participation was in *Confindustria*'s interest because these policies concern national competitiveness. However, on some issues, such as the thirty-five-hour working week which the association opposes, it has hedged calling for new concertation rules. In other instances, interests coincide with those of the Prodi Government, especially those of its economic ministers.

Of note are two organizations independent of *Confindustria*, the *Confederazione Associazione Piccole Imprese* (Confederated Association of Small Businesses) and the *Confartigianato*, the association of craftsmen. Often it is difficult to distinguish between a small industrial firm and a craft business. There is keen competition between these associations. Moreover, other institutions such as banks have become influential. Frequently also, the oligopolies who traditionally were satisfied with representation by *Confindustria* have ignored their organizational affiliation and have acted in an autonomous fashion, articulating their own particular interests to the political parties and the government. It is evident that the cohesion of the capitalist class has not been facilitated and *Confindustria*'s strategy is anything but unified. Although business has its interests articulated primarily by one representational giant and Italian labour is divided and represented by several entities, *Confindustria* is not as powerful as it might seem.

The Italian case demonstrates the waxing and relative waning of the major business interest.

Labour

Being identified with a long and intense syndicalist tradition, it was not surprising that unions were recognized and given extensive treatment in the Republican Constitution. At a congress held in Bari in 1944, the *Confederazione Generale Italiana di Lavoro* (Italian General Confederation of Labour) (CGIL) was established. The association was to be independent of specific political party dominance and it allied the three mass political parties – the PSI, the PCI and the DC – with the smaller Republican and Action Parties. Although the union was supposedly apolitical, it had three secretaries-general, one from each of the principal political parties. Given this situation, its independence from all political parties was questionable. It is not surprising that this unity was short-lived. It was shattered by great ideological cleavages, concomitant political differences and the strains of the Cold War. In October 1948 the Catholics were the first to part company. They formed the *Confederazione Italiana Sindacati Lavoratori* (Italian Confederation of Workers' Unions) (CISL), which was anchored in the camp of the DC. It identifies with the concerns of the regularly employed and better-off industrial workers. Today it is the second largest union in Italy.

A year later, in 1949, the Republicans and Social Democrats withdrew to establish the *Unione Italiana del Lavoro* (Italian Union of Labour) (UIL), which now ranks third in terms of size. Like the CISL, it does not garner large support from the industrial blue-collar workers. It has been known as a bosses' union. These splits left the CGIL allied with the left of the political spectrum. It was primarily communist, but it included socialists and independents. It was and remains the majority confederation. In 1950, another labour union identified with fascist tendencies, the *Confederazione Italiana dei Sindacati Nazionali dei Lavoratori* (Italian Confederation of National Workers' Unions), came into being. It is small in comparison to the aforementioned ones, and of little industrial importance.

In postwar Italy the labour movement is not only fragmented, but each component has been highly politicized. The political orientation resulted from the resistance to fascism towards the end of the war. The effort to rebuild the trade unions was overshadowed by the struggle for national liberation. Thus, unions were born as appendages of the political parties. The political orientations of the three principal confederations – the CGIL, CISL and UIL – are not as significant as they were during the height of the Cold War. There are also independent unions, meaning trade unions independent of the political parties and not affiliated with one of the three confederations. These are particularly widespread among employees in the public sector. In general, however, the labour movement has not been as strong as in other countries because of the fragmentation and the unions' subordination to specific political parties. Trade unions have served as transmission belts between workers and political party organizations. Parties have used them as a mouthpiece and to carry out their major priorities. Due to this close relationship, union membership has been portrayed 'not as a means of defending particular economic interests but as a political act' (Sabel 1981: 236–7).

Much authority was placed in the hands of the political parties, especially in the case of the PCI. This authority has been equated with an unconditional power of attorney. Such centralization via politicization is advantageous in terms of coordinating action and guaranteeing the leaders' security in office. However, it limits an organization's capacity to react to unexpected changes in the political climate. The dependence of the unions on political parties is illustrated by the latter's penetration of the former's governing organs. Interlocking directorates were created. This linkage was strongest in the case of the DC. The unions were dependent on parties because of organizational weaknesses. Political parties provided them with members, finances, legitimacy and other resources not available because of their low membership. Political differences prevented the presentation of a united front in periods of strength and the establishment of a common line of defence in times of weakness (Carrieri 1996; Regalia and Regini 1987). When the kickback scandals tarnished the image of the political parties, all three confederations made a concerted effort to disassociate themselves from political party identification.

In all modern industrialized liberal democracies, the number of trade union-ists relative to the total number of workers is small. In the 1990s this figure decreased still further. In the EU member-states, membership has declined from 50 per cent to 40 per cent of the workforce. Significant decreases were realized in Great Britain (26 per cent) and in France, where membership is at 15 per cent of the workforce. The Italian rate is at one-third of the workforce. Recruiting efforts by unions have been hindered by political differences, and by regional and sectorial differences. The most recent membership figures show that the ranking of the three major confederations has remained constant. Attention must be drawn to the large number of pensioners who make up for the loss of active members in each union. Recent data indicate that the number of pensioners in the CGIL exceeds that of active workers. All three confederations are operating at a loss at their central headquarters. In each case, financial difficulties are attributed to the fact that only minimal resources are funnelled from the periphery to the centre. All these elements indicate hard times ('Italy: now for a party', 1998; Regini and Regalia 1997; Sivo 1994).

Trade unions interact with two different but interdependent systems: the industrial relations network and the political system. In the first, they relate to the workers they represent, employers and the state, and in the second with government and the political parties. Relations with the political system have been deemed more important (Regini 1980), and will be stressed in this discussion.

Throughout the 1950s, the trade unions were isolated from the governmental arena. They were excluded from the social bloc, which was to control economic reconstruction, primarily because of their weakness, their identification with political parties and the government's anti-union attitude and preference for market forces. Changes in the economy led to labour market and political conditions in the 1960s which were more favourable to the unions. In this decade they regained the confidence of the workers and were able to re-establish themselves in the factories. Their priorities changed. Power in the workplace and meeting the demands of the workers became more important than political goals. The unions became less dependent on political parties due to the establishment of a check-off system, creating a new financial resource. The weakening of the ties between unions and political parties was also encouraged by the end of the Cold War, the centre-left coalition experiment, the renewed trust of the workers in the unions and the labour movement's interest in workplace concerns. Independence from political parties was formally recognized in 1969 with the establishment of an incompatibility between union and political party offices. This loosening of political party ties called forth a certain unity of action between the three confederations.

The labour movement was invited by the government to participate in the making of policy as it related to employment and a variety of economic questions. It was integrated into the decision-making process through tripartite meetings in which it participated along with business and governmental representatives. This attempt at integrating unions in policymaking was not meaningful, as the recommendations which emerged from the consultations were not binding on government. In other instances, the involvement of the trade unions was so sporadic that it did not affect policy decisions. Inclusion of the labour movement in policy making on a formal basis was soon abandoned.

Workers emerged from the Hot Autumn strong in numbers and in spirit. The trade unions were to become emergent actors in the political arena, and conflict was their major weapon. Their agenda consisted of three facets: the political, the economic and the cultural. In attempting to realize this agenda, relations with the state and the industrial relations system were transformed. Unions developed a broad programme of social and structural reforms. Having grown numerically and enjoying increased recognition at the workplace, they had even less need for political parties. They carried out many of the functions political parties normally perform, and they entered into direct competition with them. Instead of allowing the parties to transmit their demands to the government, unions delivered their banner of social reform themselves, thus indicating their independence and seriousness of purpose as a vehicle for reform. Although the results of this effort were disappointing, the important fact is that millions of Italians were mobilized. Moreover, the labour movement came to appreciate the importance of political party actors, especially in the Parliament. Although it might not have been successful in obtaining the sweeping reforms it desired, part of the change in the relations between the unions and the state was their involvement in policy implementation.

The labour movement was more successful in the industrial relations system. The focus of its efforts shifted from a concern with defending jobs to one of pressing for improved salaries, benefits and working conditions. Unions were aggressive and could boast of many achievements during the early part of the 1970s, which enhanced their membership. The events of this period had a unifying effect on the major confederations. All three depended on each other for mutual support as they forged ahead. Joint decision making took place. But although the confederations moved closer together, reunification was impossible because of basic differences. In 1973 they reached a compromise. With the signing of a Federation Pact the confederations joined together to create a structure called the CGIL–CISL–UIL. This experiment had become tenuous at best by the end of the decade, and it was eventually dissolved in 1984.

Many of the gains of the unions were dissipated as the result of an economic crisis. In the middle of the 1970s, they relinquished their conflict-negotiation strategy in favour of one of cooperation and participation. As noted previously, unions brought their demands directly to government. They were backed up by mass mobilization in the form of strikes and demonstrations. As in any bargaining relationship, government attempted to resist them. However, it had an incentive to negotiate: the achievement of industrial peace. Thus, the strategy is referred to as conflict-negotiation, and it dominated the period from 1969 to 1975. As a result of an economic crisis and the DC's need for PCI support after the 1976 election, this trend was reversed. The labour movement adopted a new tactic, that of cooperation and participation. Wage restraint policies were advocated as part of a strategy to restore capital accumulation in exchange for control over investments and participation in the development of an economic plan. Labour's advisory role in policy making was extended from implementation to formulation.

There was ample evidence of consistent government–union cooperation and consultation on a wide variety of social and economic issues. The cooperation and participation policy-making strategy reflects the government's preference to minimize conflict and the weak state of the labour movement. The most visible form of cooperation is the direct incorporation of the unions into institutionalized decision-making processes. This was realized in 1983 with the signing of a tripartite agreement between the government, labour and business. As part of the cooperative efforts, policies in specific areas have been fashioned in unison. The exercise has been marked by instability, primarily because of the dearth of organizational instruments available to the union movement as well as the state (Compston 1995; Locke 1990).

A crucial feature of the transition from the First to the Second Republic, concertation, as this trilateral decision-making arrangement is called, has assumed a new importance because of the political crisis, the weakness of each of the participants who need to lean on each other, and the new economic context provided by the Maastricht Treaty of the EU. Such a scheme aids in securing social legitimation and support. Utilizing this pattern of exchange, it has been possible to reach consensus on major issues, whereas previous governments with larger parliamentary majorities remained immobilized (Regini and Regalia 1997; Salvati 1995; Siniscalco 1996). It is not clear if all actors involved view concertation as a permanent arrangement.

A manifestation of the deterioration of the unions' relationship with the membership was sporadic rank and file rebellion in 1987 and the formation of the COBAS, 'new representative bodies operating autonomously from the main confederated and independent unions' (Bordogna 1989: 51). Teachers first formed these units. They assumed their own negotiating rights and came to enjoy the same privileges as the established unions in the educational sector. Other occupations set up their own units as well. These *ad hoc* groups developed at a time when fierce competition between the confederations was resumed. Not only do these groups present problems to the labour movement's leaders, whose authority they continually flout, but they create difficulties for the public with their capacity to disrupt and paralyse public places and services with their strikes and demonstrations. Recently milk producers, unhappy with EU policies, created havoc in major cities and on the highways with animals and tractors.

The problem presented by the COBAS is complex because, although many of the leaders and members are opposed to the confederated and independent unions, they remain as members of them. Their horizons are parochial, and they demonstrate no interest in coordinating their efforts with the more general demands of the category. They are difficult to deal with because it has not been possible to unify these entities in a single sector, much less in different sectors. Moreover, like the established trade union movement, they frequently experience internal splits. They are a distinct thorn in the side of labour, and contribute to its weakness.

Increased enmity between the PCI and the PSI as well as general conflicts in the trade union movement reduced the options of labour at the national level of government. In search of support for its needs and demands, the movement turned to regional governments. It has shown concern for participation in the formulation of regional policies for economic development and unemployment, as well as a greater role for regional organs in framing policies and investment strategies for artisans and small and medium-sized industry. As the industrial structure has become diffused, the trade union movement has had to change its focus and strategy.

The road to be travelled is a difficult one. Its smoothness has been marred by economic crises, high rates of unemployment, difficult encounters with management, the corruption scandal, competition from militant rebel groups and divisions within and between the three principal unions. In the Second Republic there has been a resumption of discussion of union unification. Although meetings among labour leaders produced a plan for a single organization, what happens remains to be seen. Current issues, such as the feasibility of a general strike in reaction to government policy concerning the unemployment problem, divide the movement. It might be that the conditions for a merger are more favourable today than in the past. Changes in the political party system have eliminated traditional reasons for divisions within the labour movement. The corruption scandals have provided the basis for a fresh start, and the Maastricht Treaty has imposed new economic parameters. All of these elements provide new opportunities for trade unions and the rationale to cast aside old stabilities.

Agriculture

The percentage of workers organized in the agricultural sector is greater than in the industrial sector. Like their industrial counterparts, agricultural groups in Italy are fragmented. They are organized on the basis of crop and class, and they have assumed pronounced party and ideological positions. The most influential agricultural interest association is the *Coldiretti* (The National Confederation of Direct Cultivators), a confederation of small independent owners and tenant farmers, which traditionally has been a collateral organization of the DC. It was created in 1944 under the dynamic leadership of Paolo Bonomi, a prominent Christian Democratic politician. Its original focus was on the significant role of the peasant family, the importance of spiritual values and anti-Communism. A more concrete programme emphasized high prices for agricultural products, lower prices for farm equipment and protection for its clientele. Other aims were more technical and educational assistance to farmers, greater investments in the rural infrastructure, increased representation of farmers in structures dealing with land reform, the abolition of inheritance taxes for certain facets of agricultural patrimony and the elimination of taxes on livestock. Moreover, the association advocated a guaranteed agricultural income, development of cooperatives and family-size farms. As is evident, these interests are comprehensive. The same word may be used to describe *Coldiretti*'s highly centralized and active organization, which features a galaxy of ancillary units including a rural youth movement, women's groups, a press and training schools for farmers.

The DC, because of its special relationship with the Ministry of Agriculture, afforded Bonomi's association the opportunity to assume management responsibilities of the units which operate as field agencies for the Ministry of Agriculture. These entities served as part of the power base of the DC and, as a result of its role in their management, the *Coldiretti* acted as an important conduit for policies and services to the agricultural sector. Control of these organizations allowed Bonomi to be the liaison between the small peasant proprietor and northern industry. Furthermore, it afforded him a prominent role in the administration of state funds for rural areas. Combining the resources of these units with the organizational network of the *Coldiretti*, Bonomi was at the helm of a significant empire which dominated rural Italy.

The *Coldiretti* constantly furnished a deep and reliable pool of rural votes to the DC. In return, given the DC's control of certain Cabinet positions, and specifically the Ministry of Agriculture, the *Coldiretti* was instrumental in the selection of an individual to fill that portfolio. In addition to developing an intimate relationship with this ministry, it fostered close relations with the executive in general. Thus, it enjoyed the privilege of exercising leverage over agricultural decision making by courtesy of government itself. As well as directing its members' votes towards the DC, the association gained significant influence within that party, thereby winning seats in the legislature and the European Parliament. Thus it developed several possibilities for articulating its demands through the DC, the executive and the legislature as well as sub-national and European institutions. There is no doubt that throughout the First Republic, the *Coldiretti* remained strong in spite of the massive rural exodus. At its convention in November 1993, these traditional relationships were revolutionized. Feeling that it received shabby treatment from the DC because of the failure to defend it in the face of the corruption scandal and its decreased interest in the agricultural sector, the *Coldiretti* adamantly declared its autonomy from all political parties. The new hope is to escape from the trap of old political relationships, work for unity among disparate agricultural groups and stress trade union-type activities within the context of problems concerning the 'family farm'.

In comparison with the *Coldiretti*, *Confagricoltura* (the General Confederation of Italian Agriculture), the medium and large landowners' association, occupies a less advantageous position, although at one time it was *the* association in this policy area. Recently it experienced difficulties when its president was forced to resign for alleged involvement in kickback scandals. Consequently, local units of the group have shown signs of distrust towards the central organization, which has embarked on an effort to rewrite its constitution. Thus it is difficult to comment extensively on its operation.

Federterra, the National Federation of the Workers of the Land, is the CGIL's rural component. At one time, its members were much better organized than Italy's industrial labourers. It was active in achieving important legislation related to working conditions. Whereas democracy was at a minimum in the ranks of the *Coldiretti*, especially in the Bonomi era, the *Federterra* had many elected institutions within its own structure and in the agricultural sector, and a focus on autonomy in collective decision making. The PCI reaped electoral benefits from its relationship with the sharecroppers, specifically in the rural zones of central Italy. In this part of the nation it was able to counteract *Coldiretti*, but in other areas it experienced difficulty.

As in the case of labour, the agricultural sector experiences difficulties because of deep divisions within farming. Having no umbrella organization, like the Green Front in Germany, it is unable to realize its potential strength. These schisms have led to the emergence of competing groups, the principal one being *Coldiretti*. Some of these groups are geographic in nature, some are based on particular commodities and some result from ideological differences.

The ecologists

An example of an interest representing post-materialist concerns is provided by the ecologists. Originally there were only a few groups taking up this particular cause, but within the last decade the movement has diffused outward from central and northern Europe and environmentalism has achieved greater appeal among Italians. Evidence of this diffusion is provided by the fact that environmental consciousness is strongest in the northern part of the nation and weakest in the South (Alexander 1991). This is congruent with the political culture. With this diffusion came the development of a galaxy of interest associations that cut across all levels of society and the world of work. As these groups developed, their universe underwent a process of moderation rather than radicalization. Due to its multi-layered historical development, organizationally the environmental interest does not have a completely unified structure. It consists of two types of associations, the conventional and the political, which are distinguished by differing strategies for ecology action. The former stress defence and protection, and the latter stress social change (Diani 1990). Moreover, the alliances established by this sector and within it have varied and often have been quite fragile.

The early environmental organizations were of the conventional type. They exerted minimal influence in the late 1950s and early 1960s. Concern for environmental issues was restricted to intellectual and scientific elites and upper-class 'do-gooders' who joined groups advocating the beautification of nature. Typical were *Italia Nostra* (Our Italy) or the *Federazione Pro Natura* (Pro-Nature Federation). These attempted to protect their patrimony against the invasions of economic growth, modern living and the plights of contemporary society. They engaged in traditional strategies, which included volunteer activities related to the beautification of certain areas. Also relying on the status, prestige and social connections of their members, they focused their efforts on the media and public authorities. Their work was primarily educational in nature, and active participation in political debate was not part of this. Activists within these organizations are political moderates and they do not have strong ties with other social movements.

The political ecology group has a very different orientation. Its horizons are broader than those of the conventional camp in that it believes that there can be no environmental preservation without a major transformation of capitalist society. Social change is a prime concern. These associations, born in the mid-1970s, trace their origins to the radical movements of the late 1960s. It is not surprising that many had sympathy for Marxism, radical beliefs and unconventional action. Given this orientation, originally there was little basis for cooperation with the conventional associations. The most prominent organization of the political ecology group is the *Lega per l'Ambiente* (League for the Environment) (Ceri 1988).

The ecology movement continued to blossom throughout the 1970s. It was aided by new forms of class conflict, which created an awareness of issues related to industrial pollution, quality of life and control over the production cycle. Moreover, scholars allied with politically active workers in various endeavours, such as workers' councils in the factories, editorial boards of militant journals and professional associations. These experiments were favourable to the political ecology sector. The National Energy Act of 1977 brought the ecology and anti-nuclear movements together. The Act, projecting the construction of twenty nuclear plants, prompted joint action. The last decade has provided a climate which supported the growth of environmentalism. The role of the traditional class cleavage and ideological disagreements in the political arena was reduced as a result of the diminution of industrial and class strife. There was an enlargement of the middle class in the service sector, which was important to the ecology movement, given the relationship between participation, political interest and knowledge. Post-materialist values became more evident along, with a dissatisfaction with conventional politics and political parties. These values gave priority to new political issues and self-expression. Thus, single economic and social issues were stressed. As they became increasingly important, it seemed natural that environmental concerns should gain prominence. Specific events, like Chernobyl, the nuclear accident in the Ukraine, also facilitated the growth of the ecology movement, as did the population's receptiveness to the issue. Activists engaged in local and national efforts which complemented each other. Moreover, the weakening of ideological and cultural barriers fuelled a more stable and frequent cooperation between both camps of the movement.

Ecologists have utilized various strategies and channels of access to the political system. Although tactics were originally perceived in traditional terms with a stress on lobbying, the influence of the Radical Party and other non-traditional political forces nurtured unconventional political behaviour. There has been a preference for the ideal of fluid, open networks of interaction between political parties and the movement. Victory at the polls has provided this interest in direct representation at the local and national levels of government and in the European Parliament. Relations between environmentalists and organized labour have been tenuous. This can be explained by the fact that often the interests of the two entities do not coalesce, given the trade unions' concern with economic growth and the preservation of jobs. Moreover, each group frequently relies on different tactics. The unconventional behaviour of ecologists, and especially direct action, has divided labour, part of which prefers established institutionalized contacts with governments and political parties.

New opportunities arose within the executive branch with the creation of the Ministry for the Environment in the mid-1980s. Its establishment demonstrates the enhanced significance of environmentalism. The larger ecology groups offer a consultative voice at this level. Environmentalists have been engaged in research and have issued a number of scientific reports with the hope of influencing public policy. They have also used the referendum to challenge the state. In the case of nuclear energy, they were successful. They have voiced their opinions at corporate assemblies as participants, and at stockholders' meetings with their vote. Again they have achieved victory. It is noteworthy that certain industries have become more environmentally conscious.

At a more popular level, ecologists have generated awareness and support via marches, demonstrations and vigils. These manifestations have been of all shapes and sizes. Other tactics have involved urging hog raisers concerned with pollution to paint their pigs green. In addition, investment counsellors sympathetic to the movement have targeted socially responsible investment opportunities for ecologists. The strategies of the environmentalists are wide ranging. Their support has been enhanced and is growing. Although they have achieved several victories, the issue does not enjoy high priority on the public agenda. It was thought that the two camps of the movement, having come together, would be able to accomplish their mission at a faster pace and in a more efficient manner. The centre-right orientation of the Berlusconi government at the dawn of the Second Republic presented a serious obstacle with its lack of sensitivity to environmental problems. Other governments have had to address problems considered to be more urgent.

The Red Brigades

In the 1960s and 1970s, Italy experienced extensive terrorism involving many groups on the right and left of the political spectrum. The principal terrorist organization, the *Brigate Rosse* (Red Brigades) (BR), founded in 1970, received its inspiration from the Hot Autumn. Its origins may be traced to the student movements of this time and to two of the New Left groups, *Potere Operaio* (Workers' Power) and *Lotta Continua* (Continuous Struggle). With the purpose of expanding the conflicts originating in the factories and educational institutions to the total society, these 'autonomous workers' organizations', as they described themselves, were prepared to engage in violent armed struggle and other forms of illegal action. Their aim was to foster civil war between the workers and the employers. This was to be accomplished by destabilizing the political system with the use of violence. Latin American urban guerrilla movements and the Italian Resistance provided models for their operation.

The original members of this non-traditional associational interest group reflected disparate social and ideological backgrounds. Political orientations included Maoism, communism and left-wing political Catholicism. Although some adherents came from the middle class, the largest part was identified with the working class or, if not, a modest social background. There was a similarity between the BR and other political groups on the extreme left of the political spectrum. Until 1974, the organization was limited in size and its activities were geographically restricted to the industrial cities of Milan and Turin. This focus was useful because of the industrial base and large numbers of factories, which offered fruitful recruiting grounds when the organization began to expand. Other sources for recruits were political collectives, universities and small groups on the extreme left of the political spectrum. Later, it recruited in prisons. Being subject to police surveillance and the arrest of many of its members, the BR changed its method of operation from partial to complete clandestinity. Membership was large compared to that of similar operations in West Germany, France or Spain. The organization was self-financing from blackmail and bank robberies. Given its ties with counterparts in West Germany, France and the Middle East, it is believed that funds were forthcoming from these also (Caselli and Della Porta 1991; Kelly 1991).

Initially the BR focused on problems at the workplace. They advocated armed support of the trade union struggle, and intervened in various ways in factory summits. They wanted to demonstrate that armed workers can be successful, and support of the slow-acting PCI could only lead to defeat. Also in their early years they circulated propaganda against the political system. Their violence was aimed at property, with arson being the most widespread form of action. Eventually they turned to the kidnapping of right-wing trade union officials or executives of major firms. In 1974 the BR changed their strategy and launched an attack against the state. Although the aim was to terrorize the ruling elite, the principal target of action was the DC. Arms were used to injure and kill, whereas previously intimidation had been the purpose. Symbols of authority labelled as oppressive were targeted for attack. They included, among others, judicial, police and government officials. The most prominent victim was Aldo Moro. His selection as a victim had the obvious aim of obstructing the policy of collaboration between the DC and the PCI, of which Moro was the principal guarantor.

It is the use of premeditated injury of specific individuals which distinguishes the terrorism of the BR and other left-wing movements from their right-wing counterparts. The latter exercised violence in an indiscriminate way against the general public to demonstrate that the democratic state was weak and unable to combat violence. Thus, the obvious need is for a more authoritarian solution. On the other hand, the approach of the BR was labelled the 'strategy of tensions'. Violence was employed against specific targets with the hope that the state would respond with excessive force, inducing the oppressed classes to revolt (LaPalombara 1987). The BR were not successful in all their acts. Defeats enhanced internal schisms and accounted for a number of defections. Once the internal web of solidarity collapsed, ties with external supporters waned. Arrests and confessions also uncovered the organizational terrain and led to further imprisonment of terrorists and supporters. By 1982 the BR were no longer a force to be reckoned with in the political and social arenas, but they left their mark on both.

Freemasonry – P2

Another example of a non-traditional associational interest group is provided by Freemasonry, a fraternal order which is the largest secret society in the world. Having no central command, the structure is divided among autonomous national authorities called grand lodges. One special lodge in Italy, Propaganda 2, or P2, as it was known, was a subject of controversy. In May 1981, Arnaldo Forlani had to resign as Prime Minister because of a scandal involving this conservative Masonic secret society. It was revealed that almost one thousand of Italy's leading establishment figures belonged to this lodge, which had criminal connections at home and abroad. The secrecy of the lodge provided an excellent terrain for developing political and financial manoeuvres. Membership included a vast array of people: politicians, key administrators, important members of the police and military, journalists, captains of banking and industry, judges and other professionals. These elites were the puppets of Licio Gelli, head of the P2 lodge, an industrialist and a conservative in politics.

Consistent with the politics of the right and centre of the Italian political spectrum, the threat of communism was used as a major political tool by P2. There were suggestions of an authoritarian type of constitutional reform. Describing himself as a puppeteer, Gelli and his 'shadow cabinet' met often to fashion an anti-communist network which was to exert pressure at the highest levels of government. A typical meeting had the following agenda:

> a) the political and economic situation in Italy; b) the threat of the PCI, in alliance with clericalism, directed towards the conquest of power; c) the weakness of the public security forces; d) the lack of a ruling class and the absolute incapacity of the government to bring about the necessary reforms for the civic and social development of the country; e) the spread of immoral behaviour, intemperance and the worst aspects of morality and public spirit; f) our position in case of an assumption of power by a clerical–communist coalition; g) relations with the Italian State.
>
> (Galli 1983: 205)

The real scope of the group was the creation of an organization, which would allow for the control of entire sectors of Italian life and the economy. In the economic arena it was involved with kickbacks linked to deals between corporations and public industries, control of bank credit, the illegal export of currency, the placement of followers in key positions and trafficking related to drugs and arms. South American links were particularly strong, and shipments of arms sold to Arab countries were accompanied with top secret NATO documents. Originally arrested for his activities abroad, Gelli continued his political endeavours. In summer 1998 he escaped from house arrest.

P2 has been implicated with the Mafia (Cipriani 1994). Apparently, Masonic judges, of whom it is believed there are a large number, interfered in many trials which involved those affiliated with the Mafia, arms trafficking and kickbacks. In exchange the defendants stood ready to do away with persons who hinder Masons in their activities. In the words of one repentant Mafia member: 'An organization consisting of attorneys, judges, politicians, police and entrepreneurs…gave us protection, such as acquittals, reduced sentences and domiciliary arrests. In return we killed anybody who annoyed them' (Acciari 1993: 1). A DC Member of Parliament, identified with P2, noted that '…in Italy homicide has become an instrument for the political battle' (Galli 1983: 213). Evidently Gelli arranged the outcomes of several trials in exchange for a promise of votes because he intended to run for public office. As a result of this linkage between Masonry and the Mafia, incompatibility between a judgeship and membership in a Masonic lodge was established. This incompatibility derives from the secrecy surrounding the mission of the organization, the bonds of solidarity among the members and the unquestioning obedience expected of an affiliate once the oath has been taken (Nese 1993). Although P2 was dissolved in 1982 on the grounds of violating a constitutional provision that prohibits secret organizations, investigations have been initiated to probe an alleged relationship between the military and public security forces and the Masons. Many observers were convinced that the long-term goals of Gelli and his cohorts involved overthrowing the state.

The Mafia

Since the mid-1980s, terrorism on the left and right of the political spectrum has waned. The real burden for the Italian state is that of organized crime as perpetrated by the four big Italian criminal organizations: the Sicilian Mafia and its mainland cousins, the *Camorra*, the *N'drangheta* and the *Sacra Corona Unita* (Holy United Crown). These associations display a similar development that parallels social, economic and industrial modernization. The biggest challenge for the state is the Mafia.

As used in the first part of the nineteenth century, the word 'mafia' and its adjectival derivatives meant beauty, boldness and pride. Within a few years, they referred to a league of courageous, vengeful men, and they indicated something that was perfect. When Italy was unified, the label described an association of brigands which in Sicily had direct relations with political life. This collusion between organized crime and political circles has old roots in southern Italy, and the term has never rid itself of this political identification. The geographical application of the word 'mafia' is no longer limited to Sicily, and its significance has broadened as well. It now connotes a particular criminal mentality or mindset, which includes a disregard for the law, the exercise of patronage and favouritism and the possession of a confidence resulting from the protection of the powerful.

The way in which the nation-building process evolves has consequences for the types of groups that emerge in a particular society. The Mafia is an outgrowth of this process. Its birthplace was the island of Sicily. Sicilian history is characterized by great estates, absentee landlords, rebellion, poverty, hostility towards the central authority and, above all, neglect by that authority (Smith 1959). Such an environment generated a good deal of tension and distrust on the part of all concerned. It was the Mafia which served as a guarantor of order and social stability, in a variety of ways. It provided private police functions. When the tenant farmers seized land from the absentee landowners, the Mafia offered protection. It managed the gap between the peasants and the absentee landlords. It controlled access to the land and the availability of water, a scarce resource. Moreover, through an economic network, which it dominated, the Mafia was involved in the marketing of grain, the principal crop of the area. Thus, it linked the countryside to the city. In addition to offering protection to the landed gentry and commoners against non-affiliated criminals, it aided the local population in its contacts with the national government, serving as a conduit for its demands. It acted as a power broker and controlled the channels of communication between the periphery and the centre.

Occupying local positions of power, the Mafia controlled a wide range of financial and patronage resources, which increased its wealth and its hold over the population. Its importance to the central authorities in the form of critical electoral activities and domination of a multitude of local governments was realized; the latter provided the Mafia protection, recognition and legitimation. Moreover, when political deviance at the local level became intolerable, the state, not being capable of exercising the necessary force on its own, called upon the Mafia as its armed agent to quell disorderliness. Mafia power substituted for the state's lack of strength. Due to these critical roles the Mafia acquired a certain amount of autonomy (Catanzaro 1987; Chubb 1989).

The Mafia became a potent force in the political and economic marketplaces, both legal and illegal. In addition, it established ties with parts of the church. Its instruments were and still are the actual use of or the threat of violence and intimidation. However, its delinquency is unique. Criminal means are exercised to achieve status. The Mafia based its power on an age-old rule of silence on the part of others when questioned by legal authorities. This is obtained with the threat of violence, and it affords protection from public prosecution. Political ties between the Mafia and established legitimate institutions have afforded the same security. Utilization of violent methods does not make the Mafia member a criminal in the eyes of the local community. This individual earns respect, legitimacy and social support and is loved and feared. The Mafia is more prone to invoke structured violence as opposed to the erratic violence of its mainland cousins. In the words of a Neapolitan police official: 'In Sicily, they kill at the top level. Here they kill anyone' ('A crime wave hits southern Italy' 1990: 58). Until recently, by convention women and children were not to be targets for Mafia violence.

With the advent of fascism, the Mafia experienced difficult times as the Fascist rulers did not tolerate competition. Its activities were curbed. The state, having a monopoly on force and abolishing elections, no longer needed the services of the Mafia. However, the organization re-emerged in 1943 to provide many of the same services as offered previously. The American Military Government, needing the support of the Sicilian population, used local Mafia leaders as well as American ones to generate that support by appointing them to leadership positions. They served as a liaison between the population and the government. This brokerage role was extended from the political to the economic arena and the Mafia reaped benefits from participation in black market activities.

As the social, political and economic scenes changed in post-Second World War Italy, so did the Mafia. It has shown a great deal of versatility and adaptability. Immediately after the war, it operated primarily in a traditional agrarian environment as in its earlier history. In the 1960s it became an urban creature with the advent of the economic boom, concomitant urbanization, and the extension of the welfare state. Mafia activities continued to penetrate many sectors of the economy. The society developed a grip on public sector contracts, which are thought to be its largest single source of funds today. Other lucrative economic endeavours were and still are related to prostitution and drugs. Extortion and payment of a *pizzo*, the price of protection for a business endeavour, are other ready sources of cash. Those who refuse to pay are eliminated. The Mafia has diversified its activities (Della Porta and Vannucci 1995). Profits from illegal endeavours are laundered or recycled, meaning they are invested in legitimate enterprises.

The success of many of these economic activities is dependent on linkages with a broad array of institutions in the political domain. The term 'politico-Mafia lobby' is used. The Mafia manipulates the political establishment to realize its economic objectives. The political orientation of that establishment is not important. One party or coalition is as good as another as long as it is democratic in nature. The extent of this network of Mafia accomplices in Italian politics is illustrated by the fact that the Minister of the Interior suspended more than fifty municipal councils in southern Italy on the ground that they had been infiltrated by the Mafia. Inept local governments have forged links between organized crime and corrupt politicians. Governmental inefficiency, the Mafia and political corruption feed each other. The Mafia controls provincial and regional councillors, as well as figures at the national level of government. Although the relationship between the Mafia and the DC throughout the First Republic is acknowledged, Mafia turncoats have reported that the relationship was with single candidates and not political parties. Votes were supplied in exchange for favours ranging from court acquittals to construction permits. In many instances, the Mafia is directly represented in government. The Mafia has its tentacles in many worlds, including high finance, international crime, big business and government.

Until well into the 1970s quarrelling Mafia families, people who ignored Mafia orders or leaders of anti-Mafia political parties or groups were targets of Mafia violence. It was only infrequently that members of the establishment were singled out for attack. Even though the society had always imposed its will and resolved its feuds with delinquent means, killing assumed a new intensity. From 1979 to 1992 in Sicily, the Mafia murdered nine judges, eighteen policemen, several politicians, civil servants, journalists and trade unionists, among others that stood in its way. The shooting of the prominent anti-Mafia judges, Giovanni Falcone and Paolo Borsellino, and bombings in Rome, Milan and the famed Uffizzi Gallery in Florence shocked the nation. This new pattern of behaviour was marked by an all-out attack on the state, its institutions and representatives. The society graduated from crime to anti-state terrorism. This terrorism differs from that exercised by organizations like the BR. Theirs is undertaken in order to smash the state, whereas the Mafia wants to capture control of the state. Furthermore, violence amongst Mafia members has increased as well.

As its action became more intense, the tentacles of the Mafia spread to cover a larger geographical territory. The Mafia has a national and international network. It is a complex and flexible organization. Contrary to its public image, it does not represent a single monolithic unit. Although it is fashioned according to a modular plan and is coordinated from the centre, 'it has no single head which, once cut off, might make the organization "acephalous"' (Ferrarotti 1989: 27). The seeming clarity of the formal hierarchical organization does not meet the test of reality. In terms of its social composition, the Mafia was and is largely middle-class in nature. Today it is estimated that between 35,000 and 46,000 people participate in the network with the largest numbers being concentrated in Sicily, the northern industrial triangle (Milan–Genoa–Turin) and Campania. There are membership prerequisites, initiation rituals and security rules that account for the solidarity of the group.

It was the turn to anti-state terrorism that jolted the government into action against the Mafia. Legal innovations were implemented. The police were given special powers to search and question Mafia suspects and to use electronic surveillance. A novel anti-Mafia police force was established, along with a new witness protection programme designed to encourage confessions from Mafia turncoats, new rules for gathering evidence in trials and the appointment of a national anti-Mafia prosecutor. In addition, the government created a special fund to compensate businesses that suffered losses after reporting extortion demands to authorities.

These measures have been effective. Attracted by the prospect of money, reduced prison terms and, in some instances, the possibility of beginning a new life abroad, several hundred Mafia members have turned against the mob to cooperate with police authorities. Significant Mafia assets have been seized. Senior bosses and hundreds of gang members have been arrested. These results are encouraging. The large number of anti-Mafia associations that have emerged throughout the nation provides further optimism. Their rallies and other programmes show that there is a great deal of support for the government's new orientation towards the Mafia.

Much remains to be done. The task is not an easy one (Stille 1995). The organization to be eliminated has shown its persistence and its capacity to adapt to a changing environment and to increase its resources. It is not an external enemy of the government like the BR, but an internal one. It has infiltrated the very institutions which are attempting to eliminate it, and it is determined to establish itself as a state within the state. This is what makes the Mafia, as a criminal organization, unique. The state's task becomes that much more difficult.

Institutional groups

Another type of organization is the institutional interest group, which performs some specific function within the government or society. Its main purpose is not to act as an interest group, but, given its nature, it develops vested interests which it promotes. Institutional interest groups are found within such organizations as churches, legislatures, bureaucracies, the military and other governmental units. Their location within these official structures affords them a power base.

Public corporations

In this category one of the most influential interest associations is the public corporation. The Italian Constitution, like many other contemporary liberal democratic fundamental laws, incorporates an emphasis on social goals and seeks to implement them via socialization. It is the public corporation which organizes business endeavours in the name of the state. Although the state has holdings in many fields, the two most important public corporations are the *Istituto per la Ricostruzione Industriale* (Institute for Industrial Reconstruction) (IRI) and the *Ente Nazionale Idrocarburi* (National Hydrocarbons Agency) (ENI). The majority of governmental activities in the public sector have taken place within these two influential public entities.

IRI came into existence in 1933. It was instituted by the Fascists to rescue the Italian banking system, which controlled a large part of industry and was floundering due to the worldwide depression. IRI was to take charge of all the liabilities of the banks. Its responsibilities expanded as it acquired direct control of a galaxy of businesses that it was only supposed to help via the banks. It literally became a hospital for moribund industries. Given the number of ventures involved, it organized similar concerns into subsidiaries. It was envisioned that when the economy recovered these industries would be returned to the private sector. This did not happen, and within a few years the Italian government commanded a larger portion of industry than any other European state, with the exception of the former Soviet Union (Cassese 1998b).

Assuming responsibility for providing services and intermediate products that could not be easily produced in the private sector, either because of the scale of the projects, the risk involved or the consequences for foreign trade, IRI soon eliminated its original mission of rescuing sick industries. It augmented its operations and became active in many fields, such as communications, transportation and construction. Making a particular effort to expand industries which would produce goods that the nation was importing, it has been connected with the iron, steel and coal industries, as well as with electric utilities. Its tentacles have encompassed substantial, important and varied holdings and have stretched over three operational spheres: services, manufacturing and engineering. It has been known as Europe's largest conglomerate (Guyon 1993).

Another major government corporation, ENI, a postwar phenomenon, was established to unify state-controlled interests in the petroleum industry. It has been primarily concerned with the exploration, production, refining and distribution of natural gas and oil. Also, it has expanded its operation to include other activities related to nuclear energy, plant engineering and construction and ventures in the printing and hotel business. The economic boom of the late 1950s and early 1960s was partly due to the bold policies, methods and activities of both public corporations. In addition to having exerted great economic power, they have left their mark in the political arena. Both entities became a haven of political patronage and the leadership has been appointed on the basis of political party affiliation. A prominent Christian Democrat led ENI until 1979, after which the post became the fiefdom of the PSI. The DC relinquished all rights to the position because politically it needed the support of the PSI. It was understood that the top position in IRI would continue to be held by a

Christian Democrat. Given this situation, ENI has been described as 'a dog on the DC's and PSI's leash' (Turani 1993: 4).

One leader of ENI, the late Enrico Mattei, deserves special mention. He was appointed to reduce ENI in size or liquidate it. Instead, under his energetic leadership in the 1950s and early 1960s, ENI reached the zenith of its power, which was felt throughout the entire governmental structure and in the international arena. Mattei was a stellar left-wing DC politician. In spite of this partisan involvement, he kept ties with all political parties, including the neo-fascist MSI. When asked about the latter affiliation, he asserted: 'I use the Fascists like I'd use a taxi' (Ginsborg 1990: 164). Filling the managerial ranks with ex-partisans who were fearless in business as they were in war, Mattei and his appointees ignored political superiors as well as their subordinates. They acted autonomously and 'corrupted politicians, spied on adversaries, [and] supplied arms to rebels in the Third World in exchange for future petroleum concessions' (Turani 1993: 4) It was said that there were two Italian foreign policies: the official one of the government and that of Enrico Mattei. Mattei often ignored the former and, dealing directly with foreign governments, manufactured his own agreements, which frequently were a source of embarrassment to the regime. In his era, the tension on the DC leash which held ENI was slack.

Mattei's behaviour was particularly aggressive. However, both ENI and IRI have articulated their interests in forceful fashion with various organs of government. They have penetrated the Parliament to obtain support for their demands. At the executive level they have enjoyed considerable autonomy from the traditional bureaucracy, and they were instrumental in the establishment of the centre–left coalition linking the DC and the PSI. Moreover, both financed the DC effort to restructure the party under the leadership of Amintore Fanfani. These public corporations have not been immune to the corruption that has plagued Italian public life.

Both IRI and ENI have been hit by the winds of change. As in France and the United Kingdom, various Italian governments developed programmes for privatization. Divestiture of enterprises was deemed necessary to increase the efficiency of state-owned firms by placing management under the control of competition and financial markets. It was believed that such a policy would make companies more responsive to the needs of consumers and would relieve the public deficit. Both IRI and ENI have been converted into joint-stock companies owned by the Treasury and are undergoing organizational change in an effort to streamline their structures. Divestiture is expected to take several years. Privatization is not an easy task. Divestiture and the rationalization of organizations involve political decisions. A new tug-of-war has emerged, and these public corporations are articulating their interests more intensely than ever.

Interest groups, access channels and corporatism

In order to achieve their goals, interest associations take advantage of certain means and channels of access to the political system depending on the nature of their aims, the existing power relationships within the system and the political culture. The latter is important to interest articulation because it provides a framework for the process. It serves as a point of reference for groups as they interpret and analyse their own situations. Not only does it determine the channels they may utilize, but it impacts on their legitimacy, methods and style.

One of the major actors in the decision-making process with which interest groups interact is the political party system. Various aspects of it affect interest associations. Especially in the First Republic, the Italian multi-party system with its rigid and ideological orientation has had a close relationship with interest groups. In that the organized interests reflect many of the same forces as the political parties, the two entities have a common meeting ground and thus, the party structure serves as an integrating point. Groups and parties that are ideologically similar tend to penetrate one another. Interest groups are not only related to parties as a total entity, but they may also have particular relations with a specific faction or factions. This has happened in the cases of ENI, *Coldiretti* and the CISL. In many instances, the political parties and interest associations exhibited their linkage by interlocking leadership and membership, as illustrated by the relationship between the PCI and the CGIL. Most of the traditional political parties in Italy have had some type of connection with the labour movement and its associations, with perhaps the exception of the Liberal Party whose only interest in labour was that it did not interfere with the position of management. The position of the newest arrivals on the political stage, FI and the Northern League, is similar to that of the Liberals.

In terms of this integration between political parties and interest groups, the question of the power relationships is an interesting one. In some instances, the party rules the interest group, as in the case of the PCI's control of the CGIL; or often a reverse relationship exists, as exemplified by the Catholic Church's one-time influence over the DC. When the political party has the dominant role in this relationship, the interest associations may not always articulate the demands of the rank and file, but instead function as instruments which link the political unit to a segment of the electorate. They mobilize support for the particular party in the form of consensus, votes and the like. Often this lack of autonomy accounts for the development of anomic behaviour and it limits available options and creates immobility within the political system. In such a situation, the party and the interest group are so amalgamated that a vote for the party is a vote for the interest segment.

One of the determinants of the relationship between the organized interest and the political party is finance. In some instances, the interest group serves as a source of funds beyond those supplied by membership fees and other activities. If money is important to the party, the interest group can dictate relations with it. However, when the economic resources of the interest association are weak, such entities merely serve as a drain for party funds and party dominance is reinforced. Such has been the case in trade union situations. Some interest associations, especially those identified with industry and business, use their financial resources to finance governing parties, election campaigns, or even factions or individuals within a party. Financing to individuals has become a common practice as Italian electoral campaigns become more American in nature. Contributions are not limited to a specific area of the political spectrum; instead, because of the nature of Italian coalition governments and concomitant political instability, they are given across the board. Nobody knows what type coalition tomorrow may bring and so for safety's sake, insurance is purchased through these contributions.

The close relationship between political parties and interest associations has consequences for the Italian state. In the words of LaPalombara: 'whereas political parties should serve to filter and to aggregate the demands on the political system, they function instead as instruments of the groups, transmitting to governmental structures demands that are selfish and that do not in any way represent a willingness to compromise. This circumstance...serves seriously to weaken the Italian state' (LaPalombara 1964: 8). Rigid ideologism and particularism, especially throughout the First Republic, have fashioned relations between organized interests and political parties. Attempts at aggregation of interests have been frustrated and efforts at bargaining inhibited. This accounts, in part, for the instability of the Italian political system. It should be noted that the relationship between political parties and organized groups is currently undergoing change. Given the role of *partitocrazia*, interest group leaders always understood the importance of political parties to their cause. However, the recent kickback scandals have discredited the political parties. Whereas previously it was critical for the major organized interests to fashion agreements with political party leaders, the rules of the interest articulation game are changing. These agreements are no longer crucial for the simple reason that political parties have much less to offer.

The nature of the governmental system determines the way in which interest associations operate. Legislatures also serve as a focal point for interest group activities. The legislative arena in Italy has always been important to organized interests because traditionally, with the exception of the Fascist era, the nation has had assembly governments, as in France prior to the Fifth Republic, characterized by coalitions and a dominant legislature. The organization and powers of the Italian Parliament provide much opportunity for interest groups. Given that both legislative chambers have the same power and laws must be passed in identical form by both units, interest associations have more opportunity than their counterparts in other nations to have an impact on public policy. Many organized interests can take advantage of direct representation in the legislative assembly. Legislative committees are fertile grounds for organized interests because of their power in the policy-making process. Under certain conditions they pass bills into law. This practice focuses an interest group's efforts because the assembly as a whole never deals with the bill. The discipline of the political party groups in the legislature is not as great as before. The political parties no longer exercise the same grip over their representatives. Legislators have become more independent, and interest group representatives must pursue single parliamentarians more than they have in the past. Recently, lobbying at the legislative level as well as the relationship between Members of Parliament and interest groups has changed.

In the broadest sense of the term, the executive provides yet another channel of access for interest associations. This arena is especially important, given the contemporary phenomenon of delegated legislation and concomitant rule-making, rule-application and rule-adjudication activities as well as the exigencies of the modern welfare and warfare state. As in other nations, there has been an increased formal penetration of organized interests into the executive. The links between the government and associational groups are well forged. As in the case of the legislature, elite or direct representation has been a primary means of access. Interest group leaders have served in several governments in a ministerial capacity. This identification obviously is of significance to the interest involved. At the executive level, given the nature of coalition governments, interest associations are in a position to benefit from competition between the ministers as well as their political parties. If alternation of power becomes institutionalized in the Second Republic, it will change some of these tendencies.

Further channels for activity are provided for in the processes concerned with the drawing up of Government Bills. These are products of compromise as a result of the bargaining that takes place with extra-governmental and extra-parliamentary units. It has become common practice to consult representatives of social categories on proposals regarding the economic and social life of the country. Important interests, depending on the nature of the issue under consideration, are usually consulted in this manner. Consequently, prior to presentation to the legislature, there is the opportunity to alter government designs for legislation. An important interest, such as a trade union, has great potential power in that it has at least two channels of access in reference to legislation. Government departments and agencies consult it when bills are being formulated, and it can attempt to further alter the legislation in the Parliament.

The kickback scandal has once again raised its head and left its mark on lobbying at the executive level of government. Previously, chief executive officers and other representatives of large corporations would regularly pay a visit to a minister on an informal basis. But now that every contact is open to suspicion and subject to charges of corruption, these representatives prefer only official contacts. Thus, their lobbying activities are basically limited to providing information and data. Whereas before *Tangentopoli*, corporations, including the public ones, were very active in a wide variety of issues, now their attention is concentrated on relations with the Treasury and basic activities or, as they refer to it, 'core business'. This has created a great deal of confusion in the corporate offices that are responsible for institutional relations. They are almost superfluous. Professional freelance lobbyists have experienced hard times as well; their business has reportedly been cut by one-third (Speroni 1993). Recent governments have relied heavily on delegated legislation. This means that for organized interests access to the executive, in general and specific ministries in particular, is crucial. The new environment at the executive level plus foreign competition, privatization and the critical domestic economic situation have opened the door for the banks. Their lobbyists experience less difficulty in penetrating sensitive policy-making points. They are dealing with many colleagues who before assuming their portfolios were active in the banking industry.

Italy has a type of functional representation and something approaching a third chamber with the *Consiglio Nazionale dell'Economia e del Lavoro* (National Council of Economics and Labour). The purpose of this body, which is composed on a vocational as well as expertise basis, is to give advice on legislative matters. The positions are filled by election and by appointment, and the body is empowered to initiate legislation and to carry out studies within its area of responsibility. Most observers feel that the Council, which has been described as operating 'on a level about mid-way between a British Royal Commission and a normal parliamentary standing committee' (Adams 1970: 102), has not fulfilled its promise. There are other advisory committees connected with some ministries on which interest groups are formally represented. These serve as channels of access to the political system.

Given the rule-making, rule-application and rule-adjudication powers of the executive, influence on the part of the interest groups may also be channelled through the state bureaucracy, which, in Italy, is not known for its neutrality. These administrators are not insulated from politics:

> Not only do bureaucrats typically owe their jobs and their promotions (and transfers to limbo!) to political contacts; they themselves are often political party activists. Indeed it takes no time at all to identify…the political party 'notable' with whom many of the most able senior bureaucrats are allied….
>
> (LaPalombara 1987: 209)

It is quite obvious that bureaucrats are receptive to political pressures. Also, industrial representatives are often found in the public service, and a reverse relationship exists in that high-level public servants are included on the directorates of firms in which the state has shares of stock. In many instances, personal contact and common origins similar to the British 'old school tie' concept are relied upon as means of access and a method to bring influence to bear. Often these people interact on a social as well as a business basis.

LaPalombara (1964, 1994) has described relationships in the executive sector with the terms *parentela* and *clientela*. The first involved an identification of the interest group with the former politically dominant DC. Interest segments which enjoyed this special relationship had an entry to the executive arena and thus extra leverage. Such an advantage was not available to associations not connected with the party and they had to concentrate their efforts elsewhere. The *clientela* relationship exists when an interest association is recognized by an administrative agency as 'the representative' of the particular category with which the agency is concerned. Once a group is selected as 'the representative' it becomes the reference point for the business of the agency. Thus, rule making, rule application and rule adjudication reflect the positions of the clientele interest group. The agency established to regulate a certain interest sector is put in the position of serving the interest regulated. This in turn affects executive–legislative relations. *Confindustria* has gained much ground from *clientela* relationships. The *Coldiretti* can boast of both *clientela* and *parentela* linkages. Today these terms are still valid even though changes have occurred in the political party system.

The judiciary is not exempt from interest group activity. Often non-traditional interests, such as the Mafia and P2, have established links with specific members of the judiciary in order to obtain favours. This body is divided into groups distinguished by political orientation, which are useful to their interests.

Sub-national units of government were not considered important points of access for organized interests until the establishment of the regions. Regional governments have actively mobilized interests in support of the implementation of innovative policies and have been prone to strongly interact with economic groups. Many regions have consulted on a regular basis with specific organized interests, such as business, agriculture and labour. These contacts are more systematic in the North than in the South. This collaboration developed because the interest groups accommodated their structure to meet the requirements of the regional state and at the same time they developed a regional perspective on policy issues. In terms of access and availability, interest group leaders have found it easier to network with the regions than with the national government. Perhaps because of this, organized interests have given a great deal of support to regionalism and have defended the regions in their battle with the central government (Nanetti 1988). Given the importance of the EU to regionalism, among other things, interest groups have also been active within the former.

The concept of neo-corporatism was presented earlier in this chapter. Having developed a familiarity with the Italian interest group scene, the notion can be related to it. Throughout this chapter, evidence of corporatist structures has been noted. Organized groups and the state, particularly in the economic area, have worked together. This cooperation has taken many forms. For example, there has been consultation, both formal and informal, on proposed new legislation or public committees have been established on which disparate forces were formally represented. However, in spite of these manifestations, Italy is not a corporatist state. An important ingredient of corporatism is a labour movement strong enough to counteract the weight of business. It has been demonstrated that membership in Italian trade unions accounts for only a small part of the total workforce and that the trade union organization has been fuelled by political divisions. Ideological fragmentation and a low membership account, in part, for the weakness of the trade unions. Corporatism is strongly linked to low strike rates resulting from a compromise between capital and labour organizations. However, strikes are not infrequent in Italy. Early in the Second Republic, the threat of a general strike caused the Berlusconi government to withdraw a proposal for a new pension plan.

Fragmentation is also reflected in other interests that might cooperate with the state in policy making. It generates elite cooperation, which is fragile, informal and irregular. Corporatism assumes a consolidation of interests into a single organization for each sector, and the leaders of each must have the authority to enforce established policies on the rank and file. Given the nature of the political culture, such consolidation is not possible or probable in the Italian case. Corporatism is not congruent with well-entrenched political subcultures that divide a nation. Moreover, union leaders cannot exercise the appropriate internal authority to ensure compliance with policy outputs on the part of the rank and file. The same is true of the business sector and others.

Another barrier to corporatist developments in Italy is the nature of the political party system. Corporatism depends on stability, which certainly does not pervade the relations between the political parties in Italy where contacts among elites have been too tenuous and bitter for corporatism to emerge. Golden (1986) argues corporatism cannot be realized in a setting in which the left of the political spectrum is both divided and largely communist-oriented, as in the First Republic. The importance of the PCI throughout much of this period meant that a large sector of the electorate was in the opposition. In the Second Republic the left is more close-knit, but there are still major differences within it. In corporatist arrangements the role of experts would be maximized and that of political parties minimized. Moreover, corporatist policy making detracts power from representative institutions. In contemporary Italy, both the political parties and the representative governmental institutions are major actors in the decision-making process. Thus, Italy is placed on a low step of a ladder which represents varying degrees of corporatism. If anything, corporatism has been more solidified at the regional level of government where homogeneity is more consistent (Bagnasco 1987; LaPalombara 1987). In Italy. concertational policy making has reinforced old routines and programmes. The various policy-making actors have followed a conditioned path of development that does not allow for major departures. Attempts at innovation are stymied. Institutional and programmatic inertia prevail (Gualmini 1997).

Conclusion

In the postwar period, the Italian interest group universe has experienced great change. An increase in the number of participants has made the policy-making process more representative, thus contributing to the foundation of Italian democracy. The base of interest group participation has been broadened, and this in turn has opened up the political process somewhat, if not completely. Also the influence of many of the traditional interests has been tempered. Italian interest groups, given the instability associated with the government, have had much opportunity to jockey for power in the political arena. The political structure, the power relationships at a given moment and the political culture have had an influence on what channels of access and methods these associations will use to press their objectives and which groups will have the advantage. Organized interests in Italy, as elsewhere, have shown that they are capable of adapting to a shift in the political structure and to use whatever means available.

Political culture has also had an impact on the interest articulation pattern. Its heterogeneity is reflected in the organization of these associations as well as in their objectives. Given their narrow appeal as well as the role of ideology in Italian politics, for a large part of the First Republic their focus was system-oriented and not policy-oriented. They operated within the framework of political subcultures, and this attachment was reflected in dogmatic proposals to change features of the fundamental order. A lack of consensus, reinforced by the fragmented culture, and the role of ideology, caused this situation and made compromise difficult to realize. Fortunately, as the face of Italy has changed, organized interests have become more policy-oriented, especially in the present decade. The significance of organized interests has been enhanced as the image of the political parties became tarnished due to *Tangentopoli* and a decline in their abilities to perform principal electoral and policy-related activities.

6   Parliament

A legislature in search of its role

Introduction

With the rebirth of liberal democracy after the fall of Fascism, it was generally acknowledged that the Italian Parliament, a bicameral institution consisting of an upper house, the Senate, and a lower one, the Chamber of Deputies, would be the focal point of the new political arrangements. It was to represent the sovereignty of the people and perform certain political, legislative, judicial and electoral functions. To fulfil this role, certain obstacles had to be overcome. Like its counterparts in other West European nations, the Italian postwar Parliament had to reckon with an increased rate and depth of socioeconomic change. Moreover, it 'had to identify, test and consolidate [its] role in the newly established constitutional order – especially in regard to parties and government' (Di Palma and Cotta 1986: 42).

Although the functions and role assigned to this assembly were similar to those of other parliamentary democracies, it is limited by certain procedures not found in some similar institutions based on the classic parliamentary model. In the first place, legislation is subject to constitutional review by the Constitutional Court. Moreover, many legislative and administrative powers are devolved to the regional governments and utilization of the referendum may lead to the repeal of some types of legislation enacted by the national and regional legislative bodies. These factors limit the legislative powers of the Parliament. However, as will be seen below, other factors have impinged upon its performance. As a result, the assembly has not consistently been an effective or a central political forum.

The Italian bicameral system is unique in that both houses enjoy the same constitutional status. They are equal in terms of their legislative, political and juridical powers. This 'perfect bicameralism' has consequences for the political system. It means that the government must secure the confidence of both chambers and it is obliged to resign if one house withdraws its support. Second, theoretically members of the government are individually and collectively responsible to both the Chamber of Deputies and the Senate. Third, both houses exercise the legislative function. Last, a political directive issued by one house instructing the government to act in a certain manner is only valid when consensus is achieved in the other legislative chamber.

In spite of this constitutional parity between the two houses, there are some differences. These focus on their structure, composition and electoral base. In the first place, they may be differentiated on the bases of size and age. The Chamber of Deputies consists of 630 members and the Senate of 315. Members of the latter are older in that candidates must be 40 years of age, whereas those contesting a seat in the Chamber only have to be 25. The electoral base of the two institutions differs as well. Participation in senatorial elections requires that the elector be 25 years of age, whereas one must only be 18 to vote for members of the Chamber of Deputies. It was assumed that different electorates and age qualifications for candidacy would produce diverse legislative chambers. Thus, they would complement each other as far as membership was concerned. Originally there was a difference in the electoral terms of the two houses, but this was not maintained. A constitutional reform in 1963 provided that the Chamber of Deputies and Senate be elected at the same time for a period of five years.

The Senate is not totally an elective body because it includes a small category of non-elected members, known as Life Senators. All former Presidents of the Republic are automatically senators for life. Also, the head of state may appoint as Life Senators five citizens who have distinguished themselves, and thus the country, in a social, scientific, artistic or literary capacity. It was believed that such persons would enhance the deliberations of the Senate by offering another perspective and by not being subject to electoral and political pressures. Most of these appointments have gone to former prominent political leaders as a reward for long service. Given the nature of these few differences between the two chambers, it may be concluded that they are minimal. Thus, one house is almost a replica of the other. However, through usage the lower chamber seems somewhat predominant.

The parliamentary career

The characteristics of parliamentarians aid in explaining legislative behaviour and the nature of the parliamentary institution. For the most part, the composition of legislative bodies around the world mirrors the dominant social patterns of their respective nation. The Italian Parliament is no exception. Italian legislators tend to have more education than the rest of the general population. Moreover, their occupations are identified more with the professions and white-collar employment than is true for the society as a whole. Also, their income is higher than the average and the parliamentary profession is primarily a male one.

Although postwar Italian parliaments have been characterized by a preponderance of representatives from the middle and lower-middle classes, throughout this period one witnesses a change in the occupational profile of the legislators. For many years the Parliament was dominated by the legal profession and then by teachers and journalists. There was a period of relative stability in terms of this occupational profile. However, by the dawn of the 1980s the appearance of the legislature changed. There was a decrease in the parliamentary presence of the higher social strata and an increase in the representation of the managerial and white-collar occupations as well as academics and politicians by profession. As these occupations rose to the fore, the legal field experienced a decline. Over time the number of business people, farmers and manual workers has been minimal. It used to be that the occupation of legislators varied according to political party affiliation; however, as in other nations, the Italian Parliament is now predominantly middle-class in composition. Moreover, an examination of legislators and their career patterns in the First Republic reveals similarities between the principal political parties. Responsibilities related to political socialization and parliamentary selection were assumed by the political parties. Party affiliation was important in terms of professional identities and roles (Di Palma and Cotta 1986; Guadagnini 1983, 1984).

In the first two parliaments of the Second Republic, those elected in 1994 and 1996, not only was there a noticeable change in the backgrounds of the legislators, but there were also variances by political party (Istituto Nazionale dell'Informazione 1996; Verzichelli 1995, 1997). Part of this change can be attributed to the new electoral system which fostered pre-electoral alliances of various types. There was a decrease in the number of parliamentarians whose occupation was professional politician. Also, business and professional interests became much more prominent. Emphasizing the productive categories of the middle and upper-middle class, the Northern League and FI were identified with these interests. FI's parliamentary contingent, with its industrial and managerial base, featured business people, managers and a broad range of professionals, especially physicians, engineers, consultants and judges, in addition to theatrical personalities, journalists and other opinion setters. Most of the Northern League's representatives are small business people, artisans, consultants and freelance professionals. In sharp contrast are the parties of the left and the right – the PDS and the AN – which, as successors to parties of the First Republic, witnessed little change in terms of their representation. In spite of the overall decline of professional politicians in the parliamentary ranks, these people figure prominently in both of these party delegations. Lawyers are also important to the AN. The various professions, academicians and public administrators account for over 80 per cent of the PDS delegation. Parliamentarians in the Second Republic are younger than those in the First. Also differences in educational levels are less marked than in the past. Education achievements are high for most parties (Istituto Nazionale dell'Informazione 1996).

There has also been a change related to the number of female representatives. In part, due to cultural attitudes towards the role of women, the female contingent in the Italian Parliament has been very small. Over time, however, the number of women parliamentarians and also their role within the legislative institution have increased. The Parliament elected in 1987 was labelled 'the most feminine assembly in forty years of Republican history' (Damato 1987b: 1). The 1992 elections handed women a setback in the Chamber of Deputies, where they registered 8 per cent of the total membership. In the upper house their representation increased by 2 percentage points to 9 per cent. The decrease in female representation in the Chamber was attributed to a new electoral law which allowed only a single preference vote. Moreover, with the exception of the PDS, the political parties tended to slight female candidates by not assigning them 'safe' electoral districts (Orefice 1992). In the 1994 elections the feminine presence in the Senate remained stable and in the Chamber it recovered, rising to 14 per cent. In this election a requirement, which has since been abolished, required that the names on the ballot for the proportional vote alternate on the basis of gender. Such a practice, it was hoped, would ensure more female representation. Female candidates in single-member districts were less successful than those running on a party list. The nature of the electoral system put them at a disadvantage. The lower house elected in 1996 is 11 per cent female and the Senate is 8 per cent. There is definitely a gender gap in both cases. Variations between parties are evident. The PDS and the PRC have a significant feminine component, whereas the AN, reflecting its ideological roots, does not.

As in any large organization, in the Italian Parliament one must look beyond the formal rules in an attempt to understand behaviour. An examination of the parliamentary career reveals the importance of unwritten rules. It is clear that in the First Republic, seniority and the assumption of leadership positions in a party's parliamentary organization were crucial to appointments in higher legislative organs. Also, significant and high-level parliamentary experience was a requisite for entry into a governmental position. On the other hand, leadership posts in the Parliament very often have been given to people who have filled prestigious governmental and political party posts. Furthermore, legislative experience has been important to the chief of state in that Presidents of the Republic have been prominent parliamentary leaders. The significance of a parliamentary career spreads beyond the executive organization. Increasingly, it has impacted the electoral or appointive function of the Parliament. It has been found that appointments requiring parliamentary confirmation have more and more frequently been based on legislative experience. A parliamentary career serves as a stepping stone to many other offices (Baldassare 1985). In the First Republic, most legislators launched their parliamentary career with some previous political experience. However, many Members of Parliament elected in 1994 and 1996 had little or no political experience (Recchi 1996).

As in other nations, an effort is made to ensure the independence of legislators in carrying out their parliamentary responsibilities. Thus, they receive a salary which is established by law. Italian Members of Parliament are among the best paid in all of Europe. In addition, to help defray their living expenses in Rome, legislators are paid a per diem when Parliament is in session. They enjoy franking privileges as well as free train and air travel within Italy, among other amenities. Further protection for the parliamentary members lies in parliamentary immunity, that is, the right not to be indicted for opinions or votes expressed in the exercise of legislative responsibilities. Moreover, parliamentarians enjoyed penal immunity as well. Thus, no judicial action could be taken against them without the permission of the chamber in which they sat. The purpose of penal immunity was to ensure that the liberty of representatives would not be limited at the discretion of the executive power. In several instances, authorization to undertake judicial action was denied and sometimes not even deliberated for purely political reasons (Musso 1986). Between 1987 and 1992 there were 337 requests for authorization to proceed against individual Members of Parliament, and only 43 were granted (Gilbert 1995; Solazzo 1992). The most noted case involved former Prime Minister Craxi who was protected by this mechanism on the so-called 'day of shame', when Parliament did not grant the authorities authorization to proceed. In part due to the national outrage which resulted from this decision, the Constitution was amended in 1993 and penal immunity was altered. No longer is parliamentary permission required to subject a legislator to judicial action; this is only obligatory when a parliamentarian's personal liberties are limited, for example, in the case of house arrest prior to trial.

Again with the scope of maintaining the independence of the representative and avoiding conflict of interest, matters of ineligibility and incompatibility are addressed by the Constitution which states that specifics are to be determined by law. Certain sub-national officials, such as mayors or prefects, are ineligible to contest a parliamentary seat as long as they hold their public office. In terms of incompatibility, Members of Parliament may not hold trade union or university teaching positions. They may not be nominated for positions in the public or private sectors by the government or organs administered by the state, nor may they serve as administrators or consultants for any entity that manages services for the public sector. However, very often legislators assume such posts after they leave their parliamentary seats. In addition, the fundamental law provides that legislators 'exercise their functions without restraint of mandate' (Article 67). For all practical purposes, this stipulation is null and void. The political parties, particularly their parliamentary organizations, as well as other elements and informal practices limit the freedom of the legislators. Thus, although there are mechanisms to ensure the autonomy of parliamentarians, not all of them have been effective.

Governing organs and parliamentary groups

According to the Constitution, each chamber convenes the first working day of February and October. Each may hold extraordinary sessions that may be called by its presiding officer, the chief of state or by one-third of its members. When one house sits in extraordinary session, the other is automatically convened. In addition, in cases established by the Constitution the two chambers sit in joint session. Primarily this occurs when Parliament exercises its electoral and judicial functions.

The first task of the legislators when a new Parliament is convened is to elect a governing organ for each house, consisting of a president, four vice-presidents, three questors and a number of secretaries which allows for the representation of each Parliamentary Group, the basic unit of the political party organization in the legislature. As a whole, this body exercises budgetary, administrative and personnel functions. The president of each chamber has multi-faceted responsibilities. Representing their respective chambers in their entirety, these officers do not formally identify with the parliamentary organization of any political party, nor do they participate in parliamentary debates or votes. Both presidents have ample powers related to the operation of the legislative process, the internal administration of their respective houses and the functioning of the governing organ. It is noteworthy that five of these presiding officers became President of the Republic. The incumbent occupies a key place in the intricate political network. Prior to dissolving the legislative chambers and in the course of consultations, which follow a governmental crisis, by convention, the chief of state is obliged to consult these legislative officers.

The presidency, as well as other legislative structures, reflects the multi-party system. In addition to specifying the process for electing the governing body, the parliamentary rules note that all the parliamentary groups are to be represented in it. Until 1976, practice deviated from this rule. The positions were distributed among the political parties in the governing coalition on the basis of inter-party agreement. Thus, throughout most of the First Republic the PCI was excluded from representation. However, in 1976 a PCI leader was elected President of the Chamber of Deputies. The PCI was given this leadership position as part of the price for its abstention on the vote of confidence in the one-party Christian Democratic Government led by Giulio Andreotti. At that time it was believed that this measure would serve as a prelude to the PCI's entry into the parliamentary majority (Pizzorusso 1981). Also, it is significant that even though the PCI eventually returned to the opposition, it retained this post. Although positions in the presidency are no longer limited to political parties in the governing coalition, they are still distributed on the basis of inter-party agreement. Very often, accord among the political parties on this issue is a prelude to agreement on the composition of the government.

The heart of parliamentary life is the Parliamentary Group, a legislative and political party organ. Bringing together parliamentarians from the same political party, this unit serves as a liaison between Parliament and the political parties. In order to be able to form a Parliamentary Group, a political party must elect a minimum of twenty representatives in the case of the Chamber of Deputies, and ten Senators in the case of the upper house. Sometimes smaller political parties, meeting specific requirements, are allowed to form their own group. Often, parties that fail to satisfy the minimum numerical requirement join together to form a hybrid parliamentary party, known as a mixed group. One can imagine that it is difficult to achieve consensus in a group of this nature, which combines diverse and often antagonistic political orientations. In all cases, each Parliamentary Group chooses its own officers.

The Parliament elected in June 1987 was referred to as a 'record parliament' (Damato 1987a: 1) because both chambers contained more parliamentary groups than in the past. The same trend was evident after the 1992 parliamentary elections. Thirteen groups were formed in the Chamber of Deputies and ten in the Senate. Although the new electoral system used in 1994 was supposed to reduce the number of parties represented in the Parliament, it did not. The number of parliamentary groups was reduced, even though the number of parties represented (twenty) was not. The reduction in parliamentary groups (to nine) in the Chamber of Deputies occurred because the laws relating to their formation were rigidly applied. The Senate, having more liberal regulations, increased its number of groups by one. In the legislature elected in 1996, each chamber added a Parliamentary Group. In spite of good intentions, fragmentation of the party system has remained a mark of the Second Republic as it was in the First. Consolidation of a new party system has failed (D'Alimonte and Bartolini 1995; Manzella 1996; Verzichelli 1996). This has consequences for the organization of the Parliament.

These party organizations are important to the functioning of the Parliament. This importance is recognized in the parliamentary rules as well as in the Constitution. Primarily because of these structures, reference is made to *partitocrazia*. The groups invoke party discipline within the legislative framework by obliging their affiliates to respect political directives, in spite of the constitutional provision concerned with the exercise of legislative responsibilities and restraint of mandate. An analysis of the constitutions of the various political parties of the First Republic (the Radical Party excepted) as well as the parliamentary standing orders reveals a strong linkage between the legislators, the parliamentary groups and the political parties. It has been asserted: 'Now the groups exist with an imperative mandate from the party headquarters… the parliamentary groups…are merely "plenipotentiaries" without powers …commanded by external forces' (Spadaro 1985: 48–9). Although parliamentarians agree to accept political party discipline before being seated, it does not always hold. Also, the parliamentary groups are responsible for designating components of other units of each chamber, such as the commissions, and they have a role in setting the parliamentary agenda. Empirical research shows that in the First Republic parliamentary group discipline was more respected by Communist legislators than by Christian Democratic ones. Moreover, the former were much more dependent on political party resources for the performance of their parliamentary duties in general (Leonardi *et al.* 1978).

Differences between parliamentary groups also relate to continuity. In the First Republic, the rate of turnover in composition varied from one Parliamentary Group to another. DC and PSI turnover was especially low (Cotta 1990). In the 1992 parliamentary elections, in both cases, turnover was under 30 per cent. This contrasts sharply with the situation within the PCI parliamentary groups and more recently within those of the Greens. In the 1992 parliamentary elections in the newly divided communist movements, the PRC and the PDS, turnover was 65 and 50 per cent respectively, and in the case of the Greens it was 80 per cent ('Montecitorio' 1992). The assembly elected at the dawn of the Second Republic in 1994 is known as the 'Parliament of new faces'. This label is justified in that in the lower house, 452 of 630 members (73 per cent) were new. Turnover continues to be a mark of the parliamentary groups after the 1996 elections (Verzichelli 1995, 1997).

In the First Republic, difference in turnover resulted partially from diverse party views concerning the importance of a parliamentary seat and from the different roles of the political parties within the total political structure. The low turnover in the DC Parliamentary Group may be explained by the fact that a seat in Parliament represented the zenith of a political career and a privilege. Also, the DC put a great deal of emphasis on solidifying its organizational structure. Continuity in the Parliamentary Group afforded the opportunity to establish and consolidate multi-faceted links with diverse sectors of society. Networking as well as the strengthening of party organization was important to the DC's power. Similar trends are evident in the case of the PSI (Guadagnini 1984).

On the other hand, the PCI viewed a parliamentary seat as only one of many high-level positions. For a portion of the prominent party leaders, there was longevity in a parliamentary career. Experiencing severe organizational problems, not only did the PCI have to overcome its organizational crisis, but it had to undertake efforts to broaden its base and solidify its rank and file as well as its leadership. It generally did not allow its representatives to occupy a parliamentary seat for too long. The Party implemented a fixed strategy of elite circulation by strict supervision over the construction of electoral lists. Thus, rotation from one political position to another was prevalent. Sometimes this involved a change from a position in Rome to one in local government. For the PCI, this was a way to keep in contact with local government and to cement and capitalize on its ties at this level. Trade union or other party activities were also possible assignments for former Communist parliamentarians. One advantage of this rotation system is that it familiarized decision makers with the problems, demands and viewpoints of many societal constituencies.

An important factor related to the legislative function is control of the parliamentary agenda, which in the Italian case has been within the purview of the individual chambers. Frequently, in situations where the assembly controls its own agenda, its law-making function is great. Originally the president of each chamber was responsible for scheduling the agenda. Practically, this meant centralization of decision making and control by a single political party, the DC. This pattern was interrupted in 1971. Parliamentary business was no longer arranged by the leader of each house, but collectively by the Conference of the Presidents of the Parliamentary Groups and a representative of the government. Unanimous agreement was sought on the subject matter as well as the length of time to be devoted to each issue. Given the relationship between the political parties, this was rarely achieved and the chambers proceeded on a day-to-day basis with no long-term planning. The majoritarian principle was reintroduced and the parliamentary calendar was based on governmental initiative. Italian parliamentary procedure differs from that of other nations, particularly Great Britain and France, because government business has not enjoyed precedence. With the 1990 changes in the parliamentary rules, the government can take advantage of a preferential route for certain priority measures, such as financial ones. This is an important step towards the

The Italian practice of parliamentary commissions sitting in legislative session is unique. The commissions have the possibility of conducting the entire proceedings on a bill, including the final vote. Thus, the parliamentary commissions possess, with some limitations, the same powers as the legislative assembly. A commission functioning in legislative session possesses a maximum of autonomy, which contrasts with the limitations imposed on the same body acting in another capacity. This practice is limited by the Constitution. In the first place, the commissions must be composed in such a manner as to reflect the various proportions of the parliamentary groups. Second, at any time before the final vote takes place a bill must be submitted to the chamber for debate and a final vote, if such is requested by (1) the government, (2) 10 per cent of the house involved or (3) one-fifth of the members of the commission. In the same manner, a bill which has passed through all phases in commission must be submitted to the parent assembly for its final approval, if this is similarly requested. Rarely have these prerogatives been invoked. Last, it is provided that this decentralized legislative procedure may not be adopted for bills dealing with constitutional and electoral matters, for those delegating the legislative power, for the approval of budgets and for the ratification of treaties. To this list the Chamber of Deputies has added bills concerning taxes, and the Senate has added the conversion of decree laws. Concomitant with the principle of executive management in a parliamentary system, the standing parliamentary rules require that the government be represented when a commission considers a bill in legislative session. In order to ensure the representation of all points of view and to reflect the opinion of the entire chamber involved, every parliamentarian, even those who are not members of the particular commission acting in a legislative capacity, has the right to participate in the deliberations, but not to vote.

This so-called decentralized legislative process represents the rule and not the exception. In the First Republic, most legislation – approximately two-thirds – was enacted via this procedure (Attanasio 1994). The rate is higher in the two Parliaments elected in the Second Republic: 95 per cent and 71 per cent respectively (Giuliani 1997). Legislative output is definitely controlled by the parliamentary commissions. The decentralized legislative process has generated a great deal of discussion. Critics have dwelt on the negation of the fundamental principles of representative democratic theory, the deprivation of a parliamentarian's legislative powers, the weakening of the relationship between the legislative body and its electorate, the limited publicity given to the proceedings as well as their closed nature, and the facilitation of 'laws of favour, of privilege, of special interests, of personal advantage' (Garruto 1965: 755). The general thrust of the negative sentiments has been captured in the words of Ugo La Malfa.

> The Constitution has provided for a system of legislative commissions....But in Italy every commission is a small Parliament in itself. The articulation of Parliament is non-existent; there are no certain general principles and thus

legislation…approved in commissions disregards any general vision of problems. Instead we have small parliaments which nobody controls.

(La Malfa 1971: 111)

On the positive side, one can cite the restrictions on the practice and the fact that it reduces the impact of the erosion of parliamentary power, a major mark of recent decades. Moreover, in terms of handling an increased number of bills and the specialized technical consideration that is available with this decentralized legislative process, the Italian Parliament is better equipped to perform its legislative function than many other deliberative institutions. Perhaps most important is that it is easier to achieve compromise and agreement between divergent political forces in the confines of a parliamentary commission than in the limelight of public opinion in the chamber (Morisi 1992).

The Italian Parliament also features select commissions of inquiry, which are temporary and often bicameral in nature. The Constitution provides each chamber with the authority to establish commissions for the purpose of investigating matters concerned with the public interest. These bodies enjoy the same powers and the same limitations as judicial authorities. Thus, they have a great deal of leeway as far as subject matter and powers are concerned. A decision to establish such a commission must receive the support of the parliamentary majority, which also provides a lion's share of the commission's membership. It is noteworthy that the government, if party solidarity prevailed, could ward off requests for inquiries. Consequently, some doubt about the role of these commissions has been raised (Pizzorusso 1981). In other political systems they are directly related to the control function, serving instead as an instrument through which the legislature is able to exert control over the executive and the opposition over the majority. Given the manner in which these organs are operationalized, the control function is definitely diluted. Select commissions have dealt with a wide variety of issues. Subject matter ranges from the general to the specific. Although their subject matter is timely, often the findings of these commissions are released to the public with extreme tardiness. As a result, some of their value is lost. Major problems encountered by these entities focus on their proportional composition and the interpretation of their fact-finding authority.

More directly related to the control function are the watchdog commissions. These are permanent and joint structures consisting of an equal number of representatives from each chamber and sometimes outsiders. Examples are the Joint Commission on Impeachment, the Joint Commission on Regional Affairs and the Joint Commission on Scrutiny over the National Radio and Television Authority. In addition to the three types of commissions discussed above, each chamber is allowed to establish special structures to deal with problems beyond the scope of the regular commissions. For example, the lower chamber has established a commission to deal with EU affairs. Legislative structures analogous to the commissions are the *giunte* (councils). These organs are distinguished because their members are selected by the presiding officer of each chamber, and they are organized around particular problems. Most important in this category is the Rules Council, which deals with proposals to change the standing orders, matters related to interpretation of them and conflicts concerning commission jurisdiction. The Senate has a *giunta* for EU matters. In both chambers councils handle electoral matters and parliamentary immunity.

The core of the Italian parliamentary committee system is represented by the specialized permanent commissions. There is no doubt that they have a critical decisional role, which has been emphasized at the expense of their other functions. The operation of any legislature as well as its commissions is conditioned by the nature of the party system as well as the parties' internal organization. Party politics and leadership patterns have taken their toll on the overall operation of Italian parliamentary commissions. Political parties have been stronger than the commissions' transformative and institutional resources. In the words of Di Palma, 'the commissions, for all their decisional powers, are short on the institutional means, the special mores, and the capacity for socialization typical of committee-centred legislatures' (Di Palma 1976: 158). Although written over two decades ago, this observation is still valid. In short, political parties have served as an obstacle to the commissions' complete institutionalization.

The legislative process

Each country develops a unique legislative process based on its culture, traditions and general political organization. Italy is no exception. Its law-making function may be divided into several distinct phases. The first deals with initiative or the introduction of bills. Reacting to Fascism, in the post-Second World War era an attempt was made to implement participatory democracy. As part of this effort, the number of actors in this first stage of the legislative process was increased. Bills may be introduced by the government, individual members of both chambers, the electorate, providing certain requirements are met, the National Council of Economics and Labour, an advisory organ to the government and the Parliament based on functional representation, and regional councils.

Of all these sources, the second is the most active. In the post-Second World War era, most bills have originated from individual parliamentarians. In part, these Private Member Bills account for the heavy workload of the Italian legislature, which does not restrict the opportunities for these proposals as is the case in many other nations. The proportion of legislative proposals coming from this source is much higher in the Second Republic than in the First (Dickmann 1995; Giuliani 1997). Often these bills lack the support of the Parliamentary Group involved, and frequently they fail to mesh with the political programme of the majority. Thus, many are destined to failure (Cuocolo 1990). Also Government Bills have experienced the same fate because there have been various formal and informal ways for the assembly to sabotage them. Empirical research has demonstrated that the quantity and the type of proposals the government submits to the Parliament are influenced by the number of political parties included in the governing coalition. Even though polarization has diminished, fragmentation continues to take its toll on the policy-making process. Governments have not been able to provide its thrust. The percentage of governmental legislative initiatives approved by the legislature has decreased considerably. Moreover, only a small number are discussed (De Micheli 1997; Kreppel 1997).

The Italian Constitution provides for popular initiative, which can be exercised if a proposal enjoys the support of a minimum of 50,000 voters. It also provides for the right of petition to the chambers for purposes of requesting specific legislative action to remedy a problem or exposing common needs. It is these provisions which afford the populace instruments to express their own ideas. Although these instruments are important in terms of developing participatory democracy, they have not been frequently utilized (Honorati 1995). Regional Councils, sub-national legislative assemblies, may also introduce bills, as may the National Council of Economics and Labour. Both types of entity are limited in that they may only introduce legislation pertinent to their interests, that is, regional issues and social and economic matters, respectively. These organs have utilized the power of initiative parsimoniously. As a result, as far as the introduction of bills is concerned, sources other than the government and individual parliamentarians have had a minimal impact on the legislative system.

Once introduced, as noted above, the presiding officer of the chamber involved decides to what commission or commissions a bill will be assigned and in what capacity these organs will sit. Regardless of which commission assumes primary responsibility for a bill, if it involves the raising or expenditure of funds, the Budget, Treasury and Planning Commission is automatically invited to prepare an advisory opinion on its financial aspects as well as its impact on the national economic programme. The second phase of the legislative process, the examination or discussion phase, commences once a bill has been committed to a legislative commission. This stage has been addressed above in connection with the discussion of parliamentary commissions. A legislative proposal is reported to the entire assembly by a spokesperson for the commission, who is selected from and by its membership. In order to protect the rights and interests of the minority, dissidents may also select a member to present their views. In addition, the government may present its opinion as well to the chamber. Discussion in the chamber focuses on the general aspects of the project as well as the individual provisions. The assembly votes on each article and then on the entire proposal. For a bill to be approved it must receive the support of a simple majority or a majority of all those present.

Both open and secret voting are used. The secret vote was adopted in order to protect the autonomy and dignity of the legislators against the powers of the various political party organs. Independence of thought and liberty of conscience were to be afforded to the parliamentarian. It has been noted throughout this work that Italian political parties may be labelled 'strong'. They might have been even stronger, if this secret vote had not been introduced. In part, what has prevented the party system from becoming completely institutionalized was the lack of complete control over the parliamentary troops (Spadaro 1985). A major thorn in the side of the political parties has been the secret vote. It decreased their command. Moreover, the secret vote arrangement provided camouflage to the *franchi tiratori* (snipers) in the various political parties who fail to vote according to party line and, thus, freely revolt against party leadership as well as the government. In addition, the linkage between the elected and the electors has been seriously weakened in comparison to the relationship in other nations, and accountability has been non-existent. Executive–legislative relations are affected as well. In essence, the government of the day has been placed at the mercy of the legislature, specifically at that of the occult agreements and unstable collusion between parliamentarians. This voting arrangement contributed to the weakness of the Cabinet, which has fewer resources to secure its tenure than its counter-parts in other nations.

At one point, the Government of Bettino Craxi in its life of about 1,150 days had been placed in a minority position as a result of the secret vote 163 times, which meant almost once a week ('Italy: Roman power' 1988). Situations, such as this one, do not enhance opportunities for effective government. In no other parliamentary system has the secret vote been utilized as extensively as in the Italian one. This generated a great deal of controversy, which culminated in placing severe limitations on the practice. The final vote on bills is to be open and the secret ballot may be adopted only for selected issues. Such a reform carried connotations for governmental stability.

Once a bill secures the approval of one legislative chamber, it is automatically transmitted to the other. In order to become law, it must be passed in identical form by both houses of Parliament. The legislative process in both chambers is basically the same with only minor exceptions. However, in dealing with a proposal, both chambers do not have to utilize the same legislative procedure. For example, if the Chamber of Deputies uses the decentralized legislative process in its treatment of a bill, this does not mean that the same must occur in the Senate. There are no institutionalized mechanisms to work out disagree-ments between the two chambers. The proposal merely shuttles back and forth until agreement is achieved or until the term of the legislature expires, creating a guillotine for all bills. The process always has been a long and tedious one. Thus, a major innovation in the newest parliamentary rules is the establishment of time limits for the legislative process.

The last phase of the legislative process consists of promulgation and publica-tion of the law. All laws are promulgated by the President of the Republic within a month of their approval. They are then made public and go into effect, unless otherwise stipulated, fifteen days after their publication in an official document, known as the *Gazzetta ufficiale* (Official Gazette). The President may, if so desired, return a bill to the Parliament for further consideration accompanied by a message outlining the reasons for such action. If the measure once again receives parliamentary approval, promulgation must be forthcoming. Usually when a President does not automatically promulgate a bill, its chances for becoming law are reduced significantly.

Decree laws and referenda: a parliamentary perspective

Parliament's legislative authority is tempered by the government's power to issue decree laws. As set forth in the Constitution the issuance of these measures was intended for the purpose of meeting emergency situations. The legislature must convert a decree into law within sixty days or it loses its validity. In the early years of the post-Second World War era the decree was not utilized, but with the dawn of the 1970s it became a favourite weapon of governments seeking advantage over the legislature to avoid the cumbersome parliamentary procedure. Recourse to decree laws has constantly increased; they have doubled in number over the last five legislatures. Their subject matter has been quite varied and often conflicting in nature. Almost one-third of the legislative output has been based on decree laws, and approximately two-thirds of all public expenditures have been passed as a result of them. It is quite clear that the decree law has been used for purposes other than those originally intended, and it has accounted for a change in executive–legislative relations as envisioned by the Constitution (Furlong 1990; Giuliani 1997).

Frequently the Cabinet will resort to a decree law in an attempt to force the hand of Parliament and the political majority. Usually it has been weaker governments that have most relied on decree laws. It must be realized that using a decree law does not necessarily make a weak government strong. Parliament is put under a great deal of pressure as a result of this measure, and it has been charged that some of its prerogatives have been usurped. The assembly has been put in the position of not being able to fully debate issues that must be decided quickly. Moreover, it has lost some control over the legislative agenda. Given the government's weak hold over the assembly and voting arrangements, the Parliament has utilized its power of amendment in revenge. Well over 90 per cent of the decree laws approved by the legislature have been significantly modified, and their rate of conversion has decreased to around 16 per cent (Bozzi 1985; Giuliani 1997). 'Thus the decree law, instead of constituting a typical display of the government's political orientation, ends up fragmented and lost in an uncontrollable flux of vague and incoherent legal pronouncements' (Ciaurro and Posteraro 1980: 22–3). The situation has become quite complex in that very often decree laws have been presented to the Parliament in conjunction with a vote of confidence. It is quite clear that they are one thing on paper and another in practice. Moreover, they illustrate the government's inability to control its own majority, the failure of party discipline and the heterogeneous and transversal attitudes of the legislators.

Parliament's authority over the law-making process is further restricted by the possibility of a referendum which, as noted earlier, may be used to totally or partially repeal a law voted by the legislature. Although referenda abrogate existing laws, they do not guarantee replacement laws to embody the popular will. The referendum was originally introduced as a tool of participatory democracy. However, it has come to assume functions diverse from those originally intended. In the First Republic it became a weapon for use in competition between governing political parties, especially between the DC and the PSI, as well as between parties on the left of the political spectrum, specifically the PSI and the PCI (Morlino 1986). Moreover, the Radical Party made a national reputation on its activities related to referenda. The referendum is one of the many weapons in the arsenals of the political party leaders who have been accused of promoting referenda to enhance their individual popularity.

The control function

It is generally recognized that in the contemporary era there has been a shift in the distribution of power between the executive and legislative branches of government, to the advantage of the former. This trend has put more emphasis on legislative oversight. Acknowledging that the executive has acquired greater importance, given the complex nature of the welfare-state and the general development of delegated legislation, parliaments are concerned with scrutiny or oversight. As one prominent scholar has noted:

> The problem to be solved is that of making parliament a more effective channel through which a stream of democratic influences may be brought to bear on the administrative process, in order to stem the growth of that arbitrariness which is the occupational disease of bureaucracy.
>
> (Hanson 1964: 295)

In addition to others mentioned in the discussion of commissions, elements traditionally related to the control function are: (1) the power of the purse, (2) questions, (3) interpellation and (4) motions.

Historically, parliaments have exercised power as a result of their control of the purse strings. The Italian budgetary system is dominated by the concept of strict parliamentary control. The Constitution requires that Parliament examine and approve the budget as prepared by the government. In reality, the legislature's power of control is somewhat limited. Given the idiosyncrasies of the Italian budgetary process, the significant powers of financial control have been with other entities, such as the *Ragioneria Generale* (General Accounting Office), a division of the Ministry of the Treasury, and the *Corte dei Conti* (Court of Accounts) which carries out a post-audit on the budget, rather than the legislature (Della Sala 1988; Honorati 1995).

Important instruments in the operation of many parliamentary systems are questions, interpellation and motions. The Italian Parliament makes use of all these mechanisms of control. Parliamentarians may present to the presiding officer of the chamber in which they sit a question with a request that the response be either written or oral. Most responses are written. Basically the questioner is seeking information from the government or an individual minister as to whether an alleged fact or piece of information is true, if the government is aware of some need or news, and so on. Each day that the Parliament sits, at least the first forty minutes of the session are devoted to questions. This time is known as the question period. The parliamentary rules of order contain time requirements for responses. Interpellation is somewhat similar, but yet more detailed and specific in nature. It consists of a written request for information concerning the motives or the intentions of the government as they relate to specific policy areas. The parliamentary rules provide that a legislator who has posed an interpellation and who remains dissatisfied with the response may initiate a discussion on the reply offered by the government. Thus, interpellation may lead to the introduction of a motion. Although it may be initiated independently, a motion generates political discussion on a particular issue in which all members of the house are entitled to participate. Moreover, the discussion concludes with a vote by which the legislative body indicates to the government the course of action that should be pursued in a particular area. The severest type of motion is that of no confidence in the government. It is the debate and vote which distinguish the motion from the question and interpellation.

Conclusion

The Italian legislative system initially did not meet the expectations of the founding fathers. For the first decades after the Second World War, the Italian Parliament was not a meaningful central political agency, nor did it provide a stable fulcrum for the political structure. Moreover, the institution fell short in terms of its contribution to national integration. One reason for the Parliament's poor report card is that it did not become institutionalized (Di Palma 1987). Its role, its structure and the political climate in which it operates have not always been congruent. For a lengthy period, the Italian Parliament consisted of members attempting to reconcile the irreconcilable: the political climate within which the legislature operates, its structure and its functions.

Although formally the Parliament was expected to be a proactive body, in reality this has not always been the case. Rather the institution has been a reactive entity, used as an instrument to give parliamentary legitimacy and approval to issues raised and decided in another context. At first, the Parliament primarily passed legislation authorizing the allocation of public goods and services, which upheld the interests of the DC. The legislative institution was not an initiator or an innovative force. Significant decisions in many areas, particularly economics and foreign policy, were raised in Parliament only after they had been substantially decided elsewhere. Moreover, it is clear that legislative activity has been fragmented and dispersed. Decisions have been made in corridors of power external to the legislature, usually by the extra-parliamentary political parties, and, more specifically, by the secretaries of these entities or by certain potent interest groups. Norberto Bobbio, a Life Senator and a foremost student of Italian politics, has poignantly remarked:

> The sphere over which the supreme representative institution, parliament, has any real control is daily becoming limited…The most important economic decisions are made by forces which are not only to a considerable extent private, but increasingly international rather than national.
>
> (Bobbio 1987: 82)

In addition, the use of decree laws and referenda has served to further distance Parliament from the heart of decision making. Moreover, the legislative institution was not equipped to defend itself from this external onslaught. The fact that the Parliament was captured by external actors in general, and by the political parties in particular, cannot be overemphasized.

This is not meant to imply that the Parliament is not a working body or that it is devoid of output. It has been astutely noted that 'It [Parliament] decides too much and it decides nothing' (Baslini and Vegas 1984: 23). This judgement may be related to the quantity and quality of the legislation produced. The Italian Parliament is distinguished by its high legislative output. Each year it approves on average three times as many laws as its British counterpart (Lombardo 1984). In the legislature which sat from 1992 to 1994, 651 of 3,738 bills were approved. In the five-year period from 1987 to 1992 the Parliament approved 1,041 of 8,200 legislative bills and in the previous Parliament (1983–7) it approved 1,159 of 6,258 bills (Dickmann 1995). An examination of the nature of these laws, however, reveals the narrow and parochial character of many. They are statutes, which fail to embody global norms and which satisfy micro-interests. Italy is known for its disproportionate number of laws in comparison with other legal instruments, such as regulations, circulars, guidelines, and so on. Other European nations rely more on regulations. Legalism has been identified as an important characteristic of the Italian political culture, and the number of laws reflects this trait.

The parliamentary rules drafted in 1971 served as the starting point for the institutionalization of the legislature. This effort was aided by a social environment coloured by the student revolt of 1968, the Hot Autumn which mobilized a significant part of the working class and the birth and empowerment of other forces. Political cultural changes were also important to this endeavour. More specifically, the Catholic subculture was integrated into the democratic system of values and the PCI into the policy-making process. These factors favoured a new role for the legislative institution. Parliament became an important centre for decision making, the fulcrum of which shifted from the DC to institutionally-based settings. It not only became a new type of decision maker, but it became responsible for monitoring the implementation of significant social and economic reforms (Nanetti 1988). After decades of extensive allocation of power to the executive branch and the dominant DC, the Italian Parliament assumed a role closer to that envisioned by the founding fathers. In spite of the foregoing, with the arrival of the Craxi Government and those which followed it, the continued development of the role of the Parliament was severely limited.

Most recent discussions of parliamentary reform have focused on ways to curtail the legislative power and enhance that of the executive branch. The parliamentary regulations, which went into effect in April 1990, reflect this new attitude. The government has been granted a new status in the Parliament with limitations on the secret vote, strict regulation of the parliamentary agenda, restrictions on obstructionism and priority for some governmental measures. These elements have consequences for the government's relationship with the chambers. The pendulum has swung in the other direction. It is too early to determine if this new relationship will become fully institutionalized in the Second Republic.

A new type of government was created in 1992 after the former governing parties had been badly besmirched by scandals. A government headed by Carlo Azeglio Ciampi and composed mostly of technocrats emerged. It was a transition to the Second Republic and it proved effective in facing issues, such as a change in the electoral law and a budget, which addressed the huge public deficit. This government was seen as a temporary expedient that would last until the results of a new election, subsequently held in March 1994, could provide the basis for a new governing majority. The following December, after the fall of the Berlusconi Government which emerged from this election, it was deemed necessary to rely again on this new model of governance, and a technocratic government was formed by Lamberto Dini. In both cases there was no possibility of creating a regular party government that could command a majority in the Parliament. In the First Republic, in periods when there were similar problems, the DC provided an interim caretaker single-party minority government until a majority coalition could be formed.

The Ciampi and Dini Governments received majority votes in the Parliament on the basis of limited agendas. When the Ciampi Government completed its mission, it resigned. The specific terms of the programme of the Dini Government were less precise, and there was considerable debate as to when it was complete and when new elections should be held. Both of these technocratic governments attracted excellent people and accomplished a great deal. They took on difficult problems, such as reform of the bureaucracy and the pension system. Party governments had difficulties addressing problems such as these. Obviously, not having been elected, the technocratic government can last for only a limited duration and must be considered a stopgap vehicle. The fact that the Dini technocratic government was necessary early in the Second Republic troubled many people, who had hoped that governments based on stable majorities would develop in the new era.

The coalition which emerged after the 1994 election definitely represented a centre-right formula. The right was not entirely moderate in nature, thanks to AN's neo-fascist past. The League and FI, however, were moderately to the right in terms of policy orientation and in their strong anti-left attitudes. The centre-right coalition had been dominated by a single personality, Silvio Berlusconi, in a way no individual had controlled a coalition since the first few years of the First Republic. This was also viewed as a break with the past. The coalition's early demise and the return to the technocratic formula of government raised questions as to whether anything truly fundamental had changed in Italian politics.

The centre-left, reform-oriented government of Romano Prodi, which should not be confused with the centre-left formula of the First Republic, followed that led by Dini. It includes former Communists, which troubled people in the centre and on the right. Since the former Communists were generally moderates, most of the nation did not seem troubled by them. The coalition has had its share of polemics, which has impacted negatively on its unity. On occasion, it has been necessary to convene special gatherings of the participants to cement agreements on specific matters. Contentious issues, in addition to the Southern Question and unemployment, include public funds to religious schools, general education reform, the creation of a parliamentary commission to examine *Tangentopoli*, and the commitment of the PRC to the government. The latter is not willing to guarantee its support for the full term of the legislature. It has selected to offer programmatic support in the form of 'critical confidence' to be evaluated periodically as new issues arise.

The legal bases of the government and its formation

Part of the problem with the executive is that the Constitution does not spell out the functions of the government and for a long while it operated on a diffused system of laws which were passed at different times in the nation's history. Some of these legal instruments dated back to the period of the monarchy (1860–1946) and others were passed during Fascism. Usage and custom rooted in over 150 years of experience were also of significance. To help clarify some of the difficulties and inadequacies related to the operation of the executive power an important reform law, Law Number 400, was passed in 1988 (Labriola 1989). The following discussion makes extensive use of this law.

Formal reference to the government includes the President of the Council of Ministers or the Prime Minister and the individual ministers who head departments and, with the Prime Minister, collectively form the Council of Ministers. The ministers without portfolio, under-secretaries and other high officials are not constitutionally part of the government, even though they are frequently referred to as such. Ministers without portfolio do not head departments, but they are treated like the ministers who have ministries (Giuglia 1988). Examples of ministers without portfolio are the Minister for Relations with the Parliament and the Minister for the Public Function. The number of ministries is not fixed and, in part, depends on the priorities of any given government. Also of importance is the number of positions which must be distributed in order to satisfy the various partners in the coalition. Most of the ministries, such as foreign affairs, internal affairs, justice, defence and so on are constant features. In recent years a Minister for the Environment was added. The Berlusconi Government, formed in May 1994, included a Minister for the Family which, it was thought, would appeal to committed Catholics and conservatives in general (Hallenstein 1994a). The Prime Minister may assume one or more ministries. This often occurs after a resignation or a cabinet reshuffle.

The formation of a government following the election of a new Parliament or the fall of a government can be a very complex matter. The Constitution gives very limited guidance for this procedure. It refers to the nomination of the Prime Minister by the President of the Republic and to the fact that on the proposal of the Prime Minister, the President nominates the ministers. Until the Berlusconi victory there was no personal mandate of a leader as occurs in Great Britain. In the First Republic, voters did not know who would emerge as Prime Minister. They only knew it would be one of the leaders of the parties which would circumstances which require urgent action. It is not clear how and under what circumstances urgency is determined. The Constitutional Court can review such decrees, but its practice has been to accept the wishes of the government. Law Number 400 addresses the issue of decree laws. Article 15 states:

(a)   no further delegation of legislative power should occur;
(b)   the decrees cannot deal with material which calls for the regular legislative procedure;
(c)   the Government cannot set forth through decrees that which the Parliament refused to convert into regular law;
(d)   the Government cannot re-propose anything the Constitutional Court has rejected.

The government can also adopt regulations, which take the form of administrative acts. These must conform to law, and if they conflict with a law then they are superseded by it. Also, interministerial committees and even single ministers can issue regulations, but they are inferior to those of the whole Council of Ministers (Pizzorusso 1997).

The President of the Republic: more than a traditional head of state

It is not exactly precise to speak of the President of the Republic as part of the executive power. The President, who is head of state, is supposed to be above any and all of the day-to-day operations of the government and politics. He represents the unity of the nation and is the guardian of the Constitution. The presidency is monocratic, involving only one person, while the government and Parliament are collegial, comprised of a group of persons. Hence there should be no interplay of politics in the office. However, given the nature of Italian politics and the experience which each of the people who have been President brought to the position, it is not surprising that on numerous occasions the heads of state have been involved in what were thought to be governmental areas of responsibility. All of the occupants of the presidency have had long experience in political life before assuming the presidential role. While the Constitution is explicit in setting forth the powers and responsibilities of the President, the men who have held the office have given considerable definition to it. Compared to the powers of the head of state, those of the government and the Parliament are much less clearly stated. The Constitution definitely limits the role of the President, but this has not made the position unimportant. Primarily because of the rapid turnover of governments and crises of various kinds, Presidents have exerted a significant influence on Italian political life.

  The moments in history and the orientations and personalities of the Presidents have determined, for better and in some cases for worse, the activities of the heads of state. All of the men who have held the office, with the exception of one, for the most part endeavoured to act within the limited constitutional mandates of the position. While occasionally straying beyond the traditional expectations related to the role of head of state, their behaviour in office was close to the conceptions of the founding fathers of the Republic. One man, Francesco Cossiga, who held the office from 1985 1992, seemed to believe that the President had to have a very active role in the discussions concerning several of the major problems that the nation faced. His activities were condemned in many quarters. However, even Cossiga often acted in areas where the President was ascribed some role.

The President of the Republic is elected by an electoral college consisting of all members of the legislature and representatives of the regional governments. There are three delegates from each region (except for small Aosta, which has one) elected by Regional Councils in such a way as to ensure minority representation, although this is not always provided. The number of regional delegates is small in proportion to the parliamentary electors, but it still offers an image of a broad national base for the President, instead of a reflection of the narrow interests within the assembly.

The electoral college votes by secret ballot. This has meant that party discipline cannot be maintained and, hence, until the balloting is completed the outcome is rarely clear. No single party alone can elect a President and an image of a broad national majority has been projected. Strangely enough, the subsequently outspoken and divisive Francesco Cossiga was elected on the first ballot. In this case, parties of the government, fearing a protracted election would damage the stability of the governing coalition, agreed on his candidacy and members of these parties followed their leaders' agreement in overwhelming numbers. On the other hand, it took twenty-three ballots and sixteen days to elect Giovanni Leone in 1971 and twenty-one ballots and thirteen days for Giuseppe Saragat to be selected in 1964. The election of Oscar Luigi Scalfaro in May of 1992 was conditioned by two major external factors. One was *Tangentopoli* which, hurting the traditional parties, caused them not to put forward their best-known candidates. Second, during the thirteen days of the election Judge Giovanni Falcone was murdered by the Mafia. This gave a sense of urgency to the electors. All but the extreme left and the extreme right, plus the small PRI, rallied around Scalfaro, seemingly to reassure the nation.

Any citizen who possesses political and civil rights and hence can vote in national elections, and who is fifty years old, can be a candidate for the presidency. The age requirement is one of several formal and informal limitations which have placed an emphasis on older people dominating the political class, and accounts for the fact that up-and-coming leaders in their thirties and forties have found it difficult to break into governing circles. The term of office is seven years. The goal of the long term is to offer a stable institution with a tenure longer than any single Parliament. Therefore, the President should never be the product of an occasional majority. The chief of state is eligible for re-election without limits. However, no President has been elected for a second term, even though some desired to continue in the office.

Fourteen years for a single individual seems too long for the Italians, who are understandably concerned about a concentration of power in the hands of one person.

The President of the Senate substitutes for the President if he is unable to fulfil his duties. Short-term illnesses or brief absences from the country have caused no difficulty. However, long-term incapacity is a grey area. In August 1964, President Segni had the first of two strokes. He clearly was not able to fulfil the duties of the presidency. Still, he did not resign until December 1964. Some commentators have suggested that the DC, of which he was a member, prevailed upon Segni to delay his resignation, which it believed would undermine the fragile governing coalition directed by that party. The important fact is that no specific criteria exist for judging the capacity of a President to carry out the responsibilities of chief of state.

On paper the President seems to have extensive functions, but careful consideration demonstrates the limits of the office. First and foremost is the traditional role of head of state which some holders of the office have argued is the foundation for many serious responsibilities. In the early years of the Republic, one prominent author stated:

> the President is the Head of State and represents national unity (Art. 87) traversing the plurality of organs and functions of the system: it is an organ which personifies the majesty, the continuity, the force of the State beyond and above the changeable wishes of the majorities, of coalitions, of parties and factions.
>
> (Marchi 1950: 105)

These words would apply to heads of state in many parliamentary systems. However, because of some of the unique experiences of the Italian nation several phrases take on special meaning. As has been emphasized, the Italian peninsula has been deeply divided for centuries and severe divisions have marked the modern nation since its birth. Accentuating this have been some calls for a separate northern state by the Northern League. Like many others, President Scalfaro saw even more moderate proposals for a division of Italy as a danger, and he forcefully rejected the idea. Hence, presidential representation of national unity is very important.

Closely related to the issue of national unity is the constitutional custodial responsibility for the protection and maintenance of the fundamental law. Again, specific actions cannot be easily identified, but the influence of the office is thought to be critical in this area. The President has the constitutional power to speak out, and can be expected to do so. Problems arise when one attempts to precisely define when the Constitution is threatened. What is considered of constitutional merit by some is viewed as strictly a government policy issue by others. Obviously, Presidents should avoid becoming publicly involved in the government policy area. One of the more interesting presidential efforts occurred following the electoral victory of Silvio Berlusconi. President Scalfaro, stating that it was his responsibility to guarantee the Constitution, wrote to the new Prime Minister as follows:

> Mr. President:
>
> I want – even to clarify mistaken interpretations that can cause misunderstandings – to recall your responsibility concerning some problems, which eventually not having a clear solution could damage the Republic both internally and externally.
>
> 1) Those to whom you will assign responsibility for foreign policy must assure full fidelity to [existing international] alliances, European unity and peace.
>
> 2) He who will be responsible for the Ministry of Internal Affairs – a Ministry which has a prominent role in preserving the unity of Italy and respect for Republican legality – must not assume political positions which contrast with the tenets of liberty and legality, nor with the principle of Italy 'one and indivisible', which are the foundation for and the spirit of our Constitution.
>
> 3) The government which you are about to form must also respect the principle of social solidarity which is manifested above all in the protection of employment with particular regard to the possibility of guaranteeing work to youth.
>
> I felt and feel this responsibility as guarantor of the Constitution. I am confident that you will give every personal guarantee for these concerns that touch the life of the democratic state.
>
> With warm greetings.
>
> (Il Quirinale scrive 1994: 3)

This was the first time a President had written such a strong public letter to a new Prime Minister.

The formal powers the Constitution gives to the President can loosely be grouped into elements in the executive, legislative and judicial sectors. Most of these powers are carried out in the name of the President, but in reality are the work of the government. In the executive area the head of state, as is the case in other nations, has some responsibilities in the international sphere. According to the Constitution, the President represents the state in its international relations. Heads of state generally embody the sovereign power of their nation, at least in titular form, in dealing with other nations. In this role this official accredits and receives foreign diplomats and ratifies treaties when authorized to do so by the Parliament. The President formally declares a state of war, but only after the legislature and the government indicate it is appropriate to do so.

In representing the nation, Presidents have travelled abroad extensively. Scalfaro, one of the most-travelled Presidents, seems to believe travel puts a spotlight on Italy and elevates its prestige. On several occasions, while outside the nation, chiefs of state seemed to have crossed the fine line between representing Italy and becoming involved in foreign policy. This has also occurred in public statements made at home about foreign issues. For instance, President Pertini spoke out several times condemning international terrorism and dictatorial regimes. On occasion, the Ministers of Foreign Affairs have been angered and embarrassed by the words and actions of Presidents.

In the military arena, the President is the Commander-in-Chief of the armed forces. However, this role in military affairs goes beyond the traditional one associated with heads of state. The responsibility of presiding over the Supreme Council of Defence is an additional source of presidential power. While no public charge has been made about Presidents abusing this power, two Presidents, Gronchi and Segni, seemed to have too close ties to military intelligence. In addition, President Cossiga gave the impression that he was currying the support of the military in some of his wide-ranging activities. In a nation where government instability and frequent crises have been the rule, there has been some apprehension about the intervention of the military in politics. Hence, any questionable action by a President in this area is seen as a threat to democracy. One scholar, Arturo Carlo Jemolo, has warned that the President of the Republic:

> cannot have contacts with military organs which are not purely formal in nature and he must go through the Minister of Defense. Furthermore, the General assigned to the President as a military advisor continues to be subordinate to the Minister of Defense and he must inform him of every-thing that develops between the President and himself. This extends even to politics if it relates to things about which the responsible minister should be informed.
>
> (Quoted in Occhiocupo 1973: 22)

The foremost prerogative of the President is the power to appoint the Presi-dent of the Council of Ministers or the Prime Minister. While this has been discussed earlier in conjunction with the making of a government, a few additional comments are necessary. Of course, when governments are being constructed the President is supposed to be strictly apolitical. However, there have been several violations of this principle. It is generally acknowledged that some Presidents have asked Prime Ministers to nominate certain people for specific ministries. There have also been charges that Presidents have insisted that certain people be excluded from Cabinets. Soon after Silvio Berlusconi formed his government, Gianfranco Miglio, at that time of the Northern League and an advocate of federalism, claimed that President Scalfaro insisted that he not be given a ministerial position. In addition, it has not been unheard of for Presidents to try and influence the political direction of governments. During governmental crises the President is at the centre of attention.

Presidents not only have a role in the construction of governments. They also have the responsibility to accept the resignation of the Prime Minister and his

Cabinet. Some Presidents have refused the resignation of governments in the hope that a crisis could be avoided. On occasion this has gone against the wishes of certain parties in a coalition. Other powers of the President include the authorization of Government Bills for presentation to Parliament. Some commentators and political leaders have argued that the President has the responsibility to withhold authorization, if it is believed that a bill is counter to the Constitution. Presidents have been requested by opposition parties to withhold such authorization, but this has never occurred; and if it did, this would probably cause a constitutional crisis.

The President also promulgates decrees, some of which are put forward in his name. However, it is actually the government which initiates almost all of these decrees, and the presidential authorization is merely a formality. A minister must countersign all of these acts and others. Some of the decrees are of a legislative nature, and some have an administrative impact. Law 13/1991 sought to reduce the number of decrees issued by the President of the Republic. However, certain kinds, such as those nominating high civilian and military officials, those involving early dissolution of city and provincial councils and acts directing and consolidating regional government activities, among others, continue to be used.

In the legislative arena, as noted, the President authorizes the presentation of Government Bills, fixes the date for the first meeting of a new Parliament and can assume the initiative to convoke extraordinary sessions of the Parliament. The power of the President to dissolve one or both of the chambers of the legislature is very important. This power is less clear than many of the others possessed by this office. The Constitution does not state for what reasons and under what circumstances the President should dissolve Parliament. When Parliament approaches the end of its normal duration, five years, dissolution is pro forma and the government normally asks the President for dissolution on a specific date. However, the last seven Parliaments were dissolved before they ran their normal course.

While it is clear that there are certain circumstances under which the President must dissolve Parliament, there are times when some discretion in the matter is required (Breda 1995b). Dissolution may be delayed in the hope that the crisis can be overcome, and calling new elections serves only as a last resort. The head of state cannot dissolve the Parliament during the last six months of a presidential term. The reason for this is to limit the President from trying to bring into existence a Parliament which might favour his re-election. Obviously, the six-month period with no possible dissolution could cause serious problems. If a government falls and no majority can be found to form a new one, a protracted crisis would result.

The President has a suspensive veto over laws passed by Parliament and thus the power to not promulgate a law, but to send it back to the legislature for reconsideration. When this happens, the request for reconsideration must be accompanied by a message containing the reasons for the presidential action. If Parliament passes the law a second time, the President must promulgate it. This power has been used sparingly in the first fifty years of the Republic. The messages sent to Parliament are considered formal in nature and must be countersigned by a minister. Presidents are not limited to sending messages only with bills they return to Parliament. Many such messages have been delivered on a variety of topics (Grisalia 1986). Of course, the people of Italy are the real target of many of them. The use of messages to the nation has been extensive. During the very heated electoral campaign of 1994, President Scalfaro appealed to the judges handling the corruption trials and the press and television to calm the intensity of the electoral scene. More recently, on the occasion of Berlusconi's indictment, he underscored citizen respect for the law. Also in the legislative arena, the President has the power to appoint five life members to the Senate.

As might be expected, the role of the President in the judicial arena is less extensive than that related to the executive and legislative sectors. Still, it is not without significance. On his own, the President appoints a third of the judges to the Constitutional Court; hence, presidential impact on this institution is considerable. In addition, the head of state appoints other magistrates on the recommendation of the President of the Council of Ministers and the Minister of Justice. Furthermore, the presiding officer of the High Council of the Judiciary, a supervisory body, is the President of the Republic. Since this is a collegial body, it is thought that the President's role should not be extensive. It has generally been agreed that while the President presides, the Vice-President of the Council should be the effective leader of the organization. However, Presidents have used the Council as a forum to speak out on judicial matters. Some commentators believe that the independence of the judiciary demands that the President take no position on judicial proceedings or related subjects. The whole issue of the President's behaviour in this role became very controversial during the presidency of Francesco Cossiga. This controversy was as severe as any involving Presidents throughout the history of the Republic. Cossiga was highly critical of the Council and made public pronouncements on the matter. Even many of the people who agreed with his criticism felt it was not the role of the President of the Republic to become embroiled in what became a political controversy.

As with other heads of state, the President possesses the power to declare amnesties and grant pardons. For the most part, this is done on the recommendation of the government. However, Presidents retain a certain initiative, which on occasion has resulted in controversy. For instance, when a Communist Resistance leader was pardoned in 1966 after being convicted of six murders during the war, President Saragat was intensely criticized by the centre and right-wing press and parties (Indrio 1971). Scalfaro endured criticism when he refused to pardon Adriano Sofri for his role in terrorist activities after he had demonstrated over two decades of good citizenship.

The President undertakes other activities that do not fit in the categories cited above. These include awarding honours, which are generally given on the recommendation of the government. The President also makes formal visits throughout Italy to places, such as new schools, hospitals or industries or sites involved in commemorating an anniversary of an important event. Presidents have also visited areas hard hit by earthquakes or other tragedies. In the last category are trips to sites of acts of terrorism or funerals of victims of violence. As the representative of the nation, the President also holds audiences with many diverse groups and individuals.

To a certain extent, a considerable part of the role of the President can be explained by the issue of the formal responsibility of the President. Article 90 of the Constitution states: 'The President is not responsible for acts undertaken in exercising his functions except for high treason and crimes against the Constitution.' The question of criminal behaviour seems quite clear. The issue was raised in the last months of the presidency of Giovanni Leone when rumours circulated about a financial scandal in which he was supposed to have been involved. He resigned before any legal action was taken.

A lack of clarity is raised about the responsibility of the President in conducting the normal business of the office. Article 89 of the Constitution establishes that no act of the President is valid unless it is countersigned by the Prime Minister or an appropriate Minister. These figures then assume responsibility for it. Since the President is supposed to be apolitical, he cannot take on political responsibility. This approach has its origin in the period of the monarchy when the king could not be held responsible for any act of the government or, in other words, 'The king could do no wrong.' Some constitutional scholars (Barile 1991) argue that today the purpose of the countersignature control is to make sure that when the act is a presidential one, it is constitutional, and on the other hand when the act is that of the government, it is the President's signature which assures its constitutionality. Seemingly, in most cases it means that the President is being kept informed of what the government is doing before it acts. More generally, it can be said to mean that consultation is taking place between the government and the President and that the head of state has the opportunity to request a revision before an act is made public.

The question of countersignature becomes truly murky when it involves the resignation of a government and the appointment of a new one. It is generally agreed that it would be inappropriate for the outgoing Prime Minister or ministers to countersign their resignation and the nomination of the new government. Some commentators argue that the offer to form a government is an oral act by the President and does not need a countersignature. Others believe the new prime ministerial nominee is demonstrating acceptance of the office by countersigning the decrees of the resignation of the outgoing government as well as the acceptance of office.

The foregoing has demonstrated that the presidency, which is supposed to be above politics, has frequently found itself involved in controversial situations. It is noteworthy that throughout the early years of the Second Republic, President Scalfaro has been at the centre of both action and controversy. On the basis of defending the unity of the country and the Constitution, he has spoken out against certain governmental acts, behaviour and statements of political leaders, and certain groups, such as the farmers represented by COBAS, as well as selected action by investigating judges. On the other hand, he has defended these same judges. In addition, he took a firm hand in nominating two technocratic governments and making certain no election would be held until he thought the time was appropriate. The entire period of his presidency has been very delicate and a vacuum of power definitely existed at various times. He felt responsible for filling this vacuum, since no one else was available. Clearly a position which was supposed to be above politics has been thrust into the centre of the political arena. Given the nature of Italian political life, it is not surprising that Presidents have acted in ways that were beyond the scope of most heads of state in parliamentary systems of government.

Conclusion

In this chapter, the emphasis has been on the instability of government and the apparent resulting ingovernability. Blame to a significant degree has been placed on the party system and *partitocrazia*. The hope that the election of the Berlusconi Government would mean an end to political gridlock did not come to fruition. The resort to governments of technocrats and the necessary increase in the activities of the President of the Republic intensified calls for reform of the executive power. During the Prodi Government, which has been long-lasting by Italian standards, a major attempt at institutional reform was undertaken. The bicameral group responsible for this effort gave considerable emphasis to the executive. Earlier attempts at reform also focused on transforming the power of the executive. After achieving considerable agreement on a semi-presidential system, the most recent effort unravelled as party politics overtook the desire for change.

8　The public administration

Functions and traits

Of all the political institutions in Italy the one in the most urgent need of reform is the public administration. Citizens experience less than desirable treatment from bureaucrats, and from a structural and personnel point of view, administrative arrangements manifest several weaknesses. Never having been integrated into the economic, social and political fabric of the nation, they have lagged behind other sectors in terms of sophistication and modernity. Bureaucratic power has been strong, extensive, clandestine and pervasive. Members of the bureaucracy look for and are suspect of any effort to reduce their spheres of influence. Inefficiency and cost are other problems. Reform is especially difficult, given the highly fragmented administrative apparatus and the diversity of its vested interests. The Minister of the Public Function is without portfolio, and success of reform efforts thus depends on the importance assigned to them by the chief of government (Della Cananea 1997).

The public administration performs a variety of functions for the polity. It assists political institutions in exercising with certainty and predictability their governing tasks. It provides the activities that are essential to the attainment of public goals and the implementation of specific public policies. It serves as a mediator for and defender of interests articulated by various social groups. Also of importance is the production of benefits, goods and services for the collectivity. There are responsibilities directed at organizing offices, recruiting staff, finding the necessary finances for the operation of administrative arrangements and institutionalizing relevant procedures. Each of these functions taken individually does not provide a problem, but from a total perspective problems exist. The major one is not the number of tasks to be performed, but the complexity and variety of these activities. Much functional differentiation is required. Behaviour and organization appropriate to a specific function are not necessarily appropriate to another or to others. Often the organization and its operative facets are not congruent with the assigned functions.

Characterized by a high degree of pluralism and incoherence, Italian administrative structures have grown in rapid and haphazard fashion. They include a galaxy of ministries and their field services, sub-national officials, *aziende autonome* (autonomous enterprises), state agencies responsible for administering state monopolies, public corporations, and the *enti pubblici* (public agencies), special agencies primarily identified with the social service network. This bureaucratic maze was never integrated in a rational manner. Each element remained unique unto itself and, consequently, the bureaucratic landscape features a plethora of parallel bureaucracies, theoretically under state supervision, and an irrational allocation of resources. Given the multiple functions of the public administration and its myriad of units, it is no wonder that its budget has accounted for almost 50 per cent of the gross national product and that employees in public administration overwhelmingly outnumber those in other sectors.

All social organizations take on a mix of traits produced by the culture in which they operate, the goals to which they aspire and their legal framework. The Constitution establishes certain principles related to public administration. It notes that popular sovereignty serves as the only source of legitimacy for public power. It is required that the public administration be subordinate to the law and there be citizen participation in the administrative process. Democracy, institutional pluralism and devolution of power relate to administrative arrangements as well. Pluralism and decentralization are reflected in the administrative structure with territorial and structural distribution of power. Administrative functions are further divided between the state and the autonomous enterprises, public corporations and public agencies.

Even though the ministries have political and administrative functions, the public administration is a structure distinct from that of the government. Administrative arrangements are organized according to the provisions of the law and civil servants are exclusively at the service of the nation. They enjoy a margin of independence in applying the law and implementing directives and regulations. The separate identity of the state apparatus is established by the fact that it is self-governing, theoretically in such a way as to exclude any potential intervention by external forces (Pizzorusso 1984).

Two fundamental properties of the administrative apparatus are centralization and hierarchy. Important decisions are taken at the top of the structure, and intermediate and lower strata are responsible for implementation, planning and technical operations. There is a chain of command. This centralization contrasts with the fragmented and pluralistic state. Given the division of labour within the administrative structure, there are small bureaucracies, each associated with a specific responsibility. Frequently there is competition and conflict among these various units. Professionals who work at specific tasks in which they become experts staff the public administration. Specialization, repetition, mechanistic behaviour, obedience and conformity to the rules all impact on administrative behaviour. Impersonality, stability and continuity are also identified with administrative arrangements (Rescigno 1990). These nurture antagonism between the bureaucracy and the citizen.

A feature of the bureaucratic structure is its lack of organs to coordinate specific projects (Freddi 1992). From formulation to implementation, an administrative act must pass through several phases of the administrative process. Each requires attention from operational offices 'which need approval from one authority, advice from another, consultations from a third, guidelines fixed by yet another, and so on' (Cassese 1993: 320–1). Power in the system is distributed in such a way as to maximize the number of actors and the veto right of each one. As the administrative process unfolds, each organ involved performs its function in a parochial fashion so as to protect its territoriality and without consideration for other participants. With no coordinating organ, projects often get buried or lost. The administrative machine moves at the pace of a snail. Italian service structures are less efficient than those of other European nations, and their cost is greater.

There are very rigid controls in each facet of the administrative process, which contrast sharply with the lack of control after its completion. This contradictory situation occurs because 'efficiency and results seem not to carry any weight. Attention is focused on procedure itself rather than outcome. The implementation of political measures is often poor, and generating barely any sanction' (Cassese 1993: 321). The state loses a great deal of time in implementing useless formal controls rather than surveying what it should. A former Minister of the Public Function asked: 'Why should I, a minister, have to countersign the employment of a school bus driver in a town which I cannot even find on the map, while expenses and thousands of billions of lire thrown out the window cannot be calculated?' (Lepri 1992: 28).

Professional secrets are identified with all professions. Some information obtained as a result of one's work because of its nature cannot be released. Penal sanctions exist if the requirements of the professional secret are violated. The notion of the secret has other facets as well, which are of social and political importance to Italian administrative arrangements. Very often bureaucrats refuse to divulge information because secrecy works to their own political advantage. Information serves as a potent weapon as one jockeys for personal position. Also, secrecy insulates one from criticism. There are political ramifications to the release of information over and above the concept of the professional secret. Often the private interests of the public functionary prevail over those of the administrative system.

The Constitution sets goals for the public powers. Efficiency and impartiality of administration are established. Closely related is the principle that private citizens will have recourse against the acts of the public administration. Administrative lag has been attributed to the constitutional position of the public administration. Being subject to the law and government ministers, and given the large number of laws and their inflexible and detailed nature, bureaucrats are forced to act within very narrow limits. Many believe their major purpose is to enforce the law. This attitude has been a principal cause of the malaise which pervades the public administration (D'Auria 1995). Efficiency and impartiality have not been achieved. Anonymity and impartiality, hallmarks of the British civil service, have not been incorporated into the Italian administrative tradition. When wanting to frustrate a policy, Italian civil servants are known for their exercise of blatant obstruction and non-cooperation.

An organization deaf to its clientele

As in France and England, the central and peripheral structure of the state is based on ministries, which are organized mainly by sector and directed by a minister who is a member of the government. The ministry is responsible for executing, enforcing and formulating public policy concerning matters under its immediate jurisdiction. Law determines the number, competence and organization of the ministries. It prescribes ministerial objectives and details with what instruments these goals are to be sought. Ministerial operation is regulated with many laws, some of which are of a very minute nature. This firmly establishes the principle of legality and assigns the legislature extensive powers over administration. Stringent regulation was to protect the citizen against the arbitrary power of the bureaucracy:

> In reality…it led to the unparalleled confusion of an estimated 100,000 laws and directives governing administrators' activity, and to a hierarchical civil service where the lower grades were unwilling to take initiatives or move outside the straitjacket of the regulations.
>
> (Ginsborg 1990: 146)

Although the various ministries cover a wide variety of subjects, they can be classified in five different groups based on their function (Pastori 1991). The first category consists of those with responsibilities focusing on the management and defence of the national and international juridical order, such as the Ministries of Internal Affairs, Foreign Affairs and Justice. In terms of age, this group is the oldest and its members coordinate activities of ministers in other sectors. With the establishment of the regions and readjustments in the interests of other ministries, this role has been tempered. Second, there are the financial units whose primary concern relates to the acquisition of and employment of fiscal resources for the functioning of the state and other public authorities. As opposed to the case of the first group, the coordinating responsibilities of these ministries have increased significantly. This is understandable in view of the growth of the welfare-state. Third, a part of the ministerial structure, including the Ministries of Agricultural, Food and Forest Resources, and Industry, Commerce, and Artisanship, focuses on specific economic undertakings. The functions of the fourth group relate to planning and the utilization of territory, infrastructures and services. It includes the Ministries of the Environment, Public Works, Transportation and Navigation, and Post and Telecommunications. Last, there are ministries with a general social service focus, such as Public Instruction, Labour and Social Security, and Health. The ministerial units included in the last three categories demonstrate the fact that responsibilities pertaining to a specific sector often are of interest to several entities, leading to a duplication of policies, overlapping of functions and jurisdictional uncertainties.

The number of ministries has served as a source of debate. In the post-Second World War era, ministerial bureaucracies have increased in number as well as size. In part, this accounts for the overlapping of responsibilities. Calls for a reduction in the number of ministries have been heard from many quarters. Ministries have been eliminated, but new ones have been created. The Prodi Government, in an attempt to streamline the ministerial bureaucracy and to redistribute the workload, has projected changes in ministerial organization. To date, these have been implemented on a piece-by-piece basis, commencing with foreign affairs and cultural resources.

Ministries are exceptionally complex organizations, given the number of persons they employ, the nature of the workload and the types of offices they feature. Each one may be thought of as a pyramid consisting of various layers with the minister, who oversees the employees and the organization of the offices, at the peak. At this official's side is the cabinet, usually consisting of legislative, research and press offices, as well as a secretariat. The first level of the pyramid below that of the Minister consists of the decision-making element, the *direzioni generali* (Directorates General), offices responsible for a specific branch of the ministry. For example, in the Ministry of Public Instruction, there is a Directorate General for primary education, one for secondary education, technical training and so on. Each Directorate General is proliferated into divisions which, in turn, are divided into sections. Depending on the ministry involved, there might be further devolution or some variation of the above. This compartmentalization is extensive, and it is a source of concern. By segmenting single policy areas, it creates organizational problems. The ministerial cabinets, positioned between the minister and the top-level bureaucracy, whose principal purpose was to serve as a link with the directorates, have acquired broader powers than envisioned. Instead of acting as a filter and political liaison between the minister and the directorates, they, rather than the latter, determine the general thrust of policies (Barile 1991).

In addition to their central organization with its seat in Rome, about half of the ministries have a peripheral dimension with field offices in the single regions, provinces and even in more local areas. This peripheral organization is often very complex in that some ministries feature a multi-tier geographical structure and different sectorial branches. Peripheral units vary in terms of their role. In some cases they have decision-making powers, albeit under the control of the centre, whereas in others, all decisions are made in Rome. Each ministry also includes advisory organs. Mention may be made of the *Consigli Superiori* (High Councils) consisting of experts in a specific area. They were created to ensure that technical competence and professional expertise would be brought to bear on administrative decision making. Other advisory units, the administrative councils and disciplinary bodies, have pure administrative functions. Ministries take advantage of advisory organizations external to their structure, such as the Council of State and the National Council of Economics and Labour. In some cases consultation is obligatory and either binding or not binding and in others, it is voluntary. In the last few decades, especially with the development of regionalization, many ministries have established other collegiate organs, the *Consigli Nazionali* (National Councils), composed of ministerial and regional representatives. Having as their scope the enhancement of coordination and collaboration between the state and the regions, they focus on technical elaboration and implementation of programmes. In addition there are other national councils which represent only single administrative categories, such as the universities, and science and technology.

The President of the Council of Ministers is required to guarantee the unity and consistency of political and administrative policies by promoting and coordinating the activity of the ministers. This unified front has been lacking. Single ministries are not necessarily responsive to the collegial will of the government. They are much more sensitive to the will of a network consisting of their unit, the corresponding parliamentary commission and interest groups in the sector. Unity of administrative programmes presupposes parameters which the government is incapable of providing. Circulars from the Presidency of the Council of Ministers deal with problems in such abstract and vague terms that they fail to unify. They are viewed with impunity. Nor do administrators respond in unified fashion to governmental political programmes. Political parties and specific party factions have penetrated bureaucratic structures and influence administrative behaviour (Calandra 1986). The administration is definitely politicized and often serves special interests. Administrative programmes and style develop within the confines of specific ministries and bureaucracies identified with particular units.

For purposes of managing activities related to the production of goods and services, the public administration includes autonomous enterprises which stand between ministries and public agencies. Even though they are affiliated with the ministries, the autonomous enterprises have their own governing board, a separate budget and different accounting and contractual procedures. The structure responsible for the road system, which is linked to the Ministry of Public Works, is an example. The minister who heads the specific ministry involved serves as president of the enterprise which is modelled on ministerial organization. It features administrative councils composed in such a way as to include high level civil servants from the responsible ministry and others having an interest in the subject matter. The power centre in the autonomous agencies varies. In some instances, the minister, the chairperson of the board, has the advantage in terms of decision making and in others, the major actor is the director-general who is responsible to the minister. In spite of their name, these organizations lack real autonomy and the model is often bypassed in favour of another structure, the public agency.

This type of organization has been useful in instances where needs did not mesh with the demands of a uniform administrative system. The public agency, even though it acts in the interest of the public and is subject to the direction of a ministry, is not directly headed by a minister nor is it a part of the ministry. It is a legal entity separate from the formal state apparatus. Embracing a wide array of diverse activities and numbering over 41,000, public agencies differ in terms of functions and origins. Some, such as the national institute in charge of social security and pensions, deliver services, whereas others, such as the national electric power board, are business organizations. They also differ in terms of the types of law that regulate them and the amount of control to which they are subject. Being separate from the state apparatus, they do not have to meet civil service recruitment regulations, and thus they provide a vast pool for political patronage.

The civil service career

A principal factor which determines the operation of any administrative structure is the character of its staff. In Italy, the personnel situation varies from one component of the public administration to the other. For example, in the case of public agencies, employees are governed by as many different regulations as there are bodies. For purposes of simplicity, this discussion will focus on the state civil service system, which is unique because it does not feature a civil service commission. Each ministry manages its own personnel needs.

According to the Constitution, entrance to the civil service is based on the merit system and on competitive examinations 'unless otherwise laid down by law', meaning there can be exceptions. Some of these exceptions refer to the highest echelons of the bureaucracy and to the lower levels, where a certain percentage of available posts are reserved for the disabled. The examinations are to ascertain a certain level of general knowledge or cultural literacy, rather than a penchant for professional specialization. Expecting successful candidates to spend all their working life in the civil service, it is assumed that professional training will take place within its ranks. Acquired experiences and skills are then transmitted to the next generation of employees. This type of recruitment institutionalized a resistance to change especially evident among top-level bureaucrats (Freddi 1992). In practice, to a considerable degree, admission to the civil service is based on co-option. The public administration governs the entire recruitment process. Even though formalities are involved, the basic conclusion does not change.

Ordinary recruitment mechanisms are frequently circumvented. Individuals are employed on an adjunct basis, and after a period of time an exemption granting them a regular position with tenure is legislated. How many people receive civil service positions in this manner is uncertain. It is estimated that from 1973 to 1990 approximately 350,000 persons were recruited without having to undergo competitive examinations. In the same seventeen-year period, 250,000 people were recruited into the ranks of the civil service with an examination. In the last years, 70 per cent of state employees were hired without taking the competitive examination (Puledda 1993). Sources also report that as many as 500,000 people are working in a temporary capacity. No ministry is capable of stating exactly how many stipends it pays each month and to what type of employee. Silence is often preferred. The issue is embarrassing for politicians and trade unionists because a large part of their membership consists of these temporary employees. Not only have these people helped to fill labour needs, but in the First Republic, the DC and PSI enjoyed a resource of electoral support (Cassese 1993; Meletti 1992). Politics and administration are intertwined. The constitutional mandate represents the exception, not the rule.

The civil service structure is not attuned to individual specialization, but is based on a generalist approach. Training, the assignment of tasks and promotion are tailored in such a way as to create bureaucrats ideally capable of performing satisfactorily in various areas. Career civil servants are divided into two large groups. The first consists of eight functional grades based on the importance and complexity of the activities to be carried out. There is a smaller group of directors, the managers responsible for the operation of the Directorates General and Sections. An excessive number of appointments from outside the civil service at this level has impacted negatively. This group of managers has had limited influence on the public administration. Planning for them fell short of the mark, with the number of posts exceeding the needs of the bureaucracy. Also, planned educational endeavours to assure appropriate organizational skills were not realized in timely fashion and economic rewards were not adequate (Pastori 1991).

Another problem area concerns relations between this managerial class and politicians at the helm of the ministries. The two constituencies represent diverse age groups, career paths, training and geographical origin. Administrators tend to be older than the ministers, and twice as many of them are southern in origin. The administrative caste usually has a career limited to one ministry. Such does not pertain to a minister. The continuity–turnover dichotomy is also relevant, with the first facet representing the administrators and the second representing the ministers. Moreover, the minister often has little time for or interest in the needs and requests of administrators. Mutual suspicion, resentment and separation characterize relations between these two groups.

There is a lack of integration between the two worlds at the top of the administrative pyramid. Top-level administrators are blocked because they lack access to the decision-making process and are only used in the implementation phase. The ministerial cabinets as well as the ministers are politicized and extraneous to the administrative apparatus. Administrators resent any political interference in their realm and they defend themselves with a shield of legalism, which delays or completely obstructs policy implementation. In reaction, the political class utilizes the appointment power to bypass administrators. These two sectors coexist in a very unstable equilibrium, which has negative connotations for the policy-making process. To date, bureaucratic reform has not paid sufficient attention to relations between the top-level administrative and political wings of the bureaucracy.

The career structure of the civil service is a vertical one. There have been very few cases of horizontal mobility. This career pattern can be explained by the rigidity of the bureaucratic structures. Also, it was believed that transfers from one ministry to another could deflate the morale of internal ministry employees, who would witness the promotion of personnel from other ministries over their heads. Moreover, the trade unions, having a veto over transfers, have been able to obstruct them.

At the end of the 1960s, perhaps in response to the ideological environment at the time, the government as well as the major trade unions reacted to the disparity of treatment, both juridical and economic, among the various types of public sector workers and of employment. An attempt was made to harmonize the situation and make it more equitable. This effort resulted in a general reform in 1983 which provided that salaries and working conditions in various sectors would be determined by collective bargaining between trade unions and the government. Such a measure reduced the power of Parliament over the civil service. It was hoped that it would be possible to regularize procedures and the subjects for negotiation and to invoke objective criteria, things which were to appeal to the trade unions, as well as to allow the government to control public spending by stipulating that contracts must be compatible with the budget. The reform created more problems than it solved (Sechi 1992). The wording of the legislation created disparities and uncertainties in its implementation. One author, labelling it a 'cross-eyed reform' (D'Orta 1990), seems to be saying that it had lost its original straightforward thrust.

Italian civil servants are not well paid. Although the initial salary might be appropriate, the differential between the various grades of the civil service is quite small. At a certain point there is a general wage levelling. Many functionaries work the bare minimum and hold second jobs, often in the so-called 'black economy'. Often a civil service career is selected not for the remuneration offered, but for the security. Italian public administrators are notorious for their work habits. Their schedule has been the famous eight o'clock in the morning to two o'clock in the afternoon, Monday through Saturday with the possibility of two afternoons of overtime per week. This type of schedule is convenient for those civil servants that pursue second jobs. Given the propensity for coffee breaks, a high level of absenteeism and other reasons for being away from the desk, the Italian functionary works no more than three hours per day (Cassese 1988). This work pattern has repercussions that relate to productivity, efficiency and the public's accessibility to services. Of all Europeans, Italians have the least accessibility to public offices, museums and so on.

The severity of this problem is underscored in light of the practice of other EU member-states. Believing that Italians must become Europeans, an effort was made to bring public services more in line with those of the EU. Work schedules are being adjusted to service needs. Offices are open longer and unions have lost power to the managers. The possibility of being fired or laid off is new for the non-performer, and many of the traditional privileges which distinguished Italian civil servants from their counterparts in the private sector are being abolished. Time off for trade union purposes, extraordinary leaves and so on have been cut. Sick leave has been reduced. The employee's salary is reduced by one-third for the first day of sick leave, to deter people from using such leave for a long weekend. These actions, taken in the interests of efficiency, productivity and competition, indicate the desire to move from a bureaucratic and clientelistic culture in the work world to a managerial one. It is doubtful whether changes will come automatically from a decree. The firmly entrenched bureaucratic mentality must be changed as well.

Italian civil servants are excessive in number, poorly distributed and dissatisfied. The North–South dichotomy applies to the public administration. There has been a tendency for it to take on a social function in the underdeveloped South by offering extensive employment opportunities. Given the relative weakness of the southern economy, a civil service career is very attractive. Rather than employing people on the basis of work to be done, decisions have been made to increase vote-getting potential and alleviate southern unemployment crises. The South has twice as many ministerial employees as the North. The supply of personnel is definitely in a ratio opposite to workload (Puledda 1993). An effort is being made to selectively recruit on the basis of regional origins with a stipulation that after being appointed an employee must remain in a geographical location for a certain amount of time.

This maldistribution not only has a geographical dimension, but may also be looked at in relation to particular ministries. Several have an excess of personnel. In many of the ministries, there are hundreds of employees who literally have no work to do and many of the High Councils have not met in years. Efforts have been made to rationalize this situation. Only 15 per cent of those who retire are to be replaced. Five per cent of this group will come from within the bureaucracy, and the other 10 per cent can be selected from internal or external sources. This is another instance in which unions have lost power. No longer are they able to block internal transfers, and the employee who refuses one has the alternative of being laid off or retired. High-level administrators will work on a contractual basis with evaluation at the end of each legislature. Stipends will be based on merit and responsibilities. In addition, many of the High Councils have been abolished along with other committee structures deemed superfluous. As one might imagine, there has been resistance to these efforts towards efficiency and cost-cutting (Cassese 1998a). This is a difficult moment in which to undertake a reduction of the public bureaucracy. General unemployment is high, especially in the South. If its economy were in a stronger state, even though it is not easy to insert employees in a productive environment with a completely diverse dynamic, it would be possible to consider a flow of personnel from the public to the private sector.

Italian public administrators do not have a positive attitude towards their work. Not only are they unhappy with their jobs, but they are severely critical of their organization and the public administration itself. They lack motivation, which perhaps is related to low remuneration and a lack of real rewards for innovation and productivity. Relations between the citizens and members of the civil service are less than desirable. Among the citizenry there is a lack of confidence in and widespread dissatisfaction with the public administration. More than 60 per cent of the population has evaluated it negatively (Cassese 1998b). It seems as if civil servants take out their discontent on their clients. They are known to act in a discretionary, arrogant and autocratic manner.

To ask for a service from a public office has literally meant to put oneself into the hands of a functionary who was not obligated to furnish any explanations or guarantee any scheduled response. Very often, the carrying out of a request has depended on whom the citizen knows and what influence can be brought to bear on the civil servant(s) involved. The Catholic subculture has been related to this idea of mediation. In Catholicism, for the faithful, the saints serve as mediators with God: 'in the public administration…the patron who mediates between the client and the all-powerful appears. Sometimes the patron is the all-powerful himself' (Ginsborg 1994: 75). The traditional notion of service to the public is warped, and a sense of duty is lacking. Laws which should protect the public's rights *vis-à-vis* the administration frequently are overlooked.

Although Italians are unhappy with administrative output, they have not rebelled against the public service. The public administration is endured, but not supported (Cassese 1988). This contradiction within the administrative framework contributes to the malaise of the Italian state, and problems of specific governments. Efforts have been made to enhance the public administration's relations with the citizenry. A 1990 law has established norms for the administrative process. Criteria related to single administrative acts are set forth, along with general principles and norms concerning administrative procedures. Administrative activities must not only seek the ends determined by law, but particular attention must be paid to cost, effectiveness and publicity. These requirements apply to national and sub-national governments. Codes of behaviour carrying penal sanctions, if not respected, have been established along with the citizen's right to information and to examine and photocopy documents.

An attempt has been made to disseminate information related to public services and to provide channels for the population's reaction to them. A toll-free number was introduced to ascertain the nature of citizens' experiences with the public administration so that they could be used to better services. People responded to this opportunity. Another innovation was the silence–approval mechanism, meaning that if a public office fails to give an answer in a period of from thirty to sixty days depending on the situation, the response is automatically understood as a positive one. Responsibility and transparency of administration provided the major thrusts for change. Almost all of the ministries have implemented the new principles, but at sub-national units of government the situation is less than satisfactory.

Candidates for entry into the bureaucracy are relatively young. Basic educational prerequisites exist, but none pertain to practical training or work experience. It is not usual for people to become civil servants at mid-career. In terms of education, a large number of civil servants have a legal background and a smaller group is trained in economics. Law is such a popular field with bureaucrats that it seems to be the one factor that unifies a large and diverse lot. It has been observed that an understanding of the law and legal language is essential to the personal position of a public servant, given its role in and the legalism of the Italian administrative culture. This knowledge, as the saying goes, allows the functionary to enforce the law for enemies and interpret it for friends.

The training received by civil servants is not completely adequate for the demands of a modern administrative structure, be it public or private.

Although Italy has borrowed much from the French administrative tradition, it has neither the famous *grandes écoles*, one of which is the prestigious *Ecole Nationale d'Administration*, or the *grands corps*. The former are the selective educational institutions which train higher civil servants whose best graduates enter the latter, the small specialized and highly cohesive elite networks of top administrators. The difference between the two countries can be explained by reference to the Italian state and society. Traditionally the power of the state, reflecting its social and constitutional roots, has been weak. Also, a demand for equality and the concomitant social antipathy towards the privileges and prestige identified with a select administrative corps, in spite of its utility, deterred its creation. This low level of statism in Italy contrasts sharply with the legalism mentioned throughout this chapter and thus provides the basis for another contradiction in the Italian administrative structure: high legalism–low statism (Cassese 1993).

The geographic origin of civil servants has been important to the operation of the public administration. Although southerners are a dominant factor in the civil service, this has not always been the case. Immediately after unification, northerners, specifically those from Piedmont, ruled the administrative world. The scene began to change at the beginning of this century, and by the third decade the extent of the transformation was so considerable that it established the trend for the present scene. Currently, 70 per cent of public servants are southern in origin and of the highest ranking, the percentage rises to 90 (Cassese 1988, 1993). The consequences of this imbalance are considerable. Values identified with the South permeate the civil service. Given the long-time prevalence of the peasant outlook in the South because of its state of economic development, there has been a lack of an industrial type of productive mentality in the civil service. Coming from a part of the nation which has long been a victim of multi-faceted inequities and not having career alternatives as their northern counterparts, southern civil servants, manifesting a desire for justice and equality, have demanded certain guarantees relating to their status and career prospects.

They have also developed a very possessive attitude towards their positions, which they expect to keep for the rest of their working life. This attitude and the pre-industrial culture with which southerners were traditionally affiliated generated the 'flight from the state' which, in the administrative arena, accounted for the creation of the public agencies described above. Southerners in the civil service have definitely manifested different behaviour than their counterparts from the North. Although legal background and the law unite them, territorial origins separate them. Cassese (1993) attributes the poor quality of the public sector to this geographical factor. Personnel are united and divided, providing another contradiction: a centralized but divided administration.

Gender and age are less severe divisive factors. Only a small number of civil servants reach the higher echelons of the bureaucracy, and of these only a minuscule percentage are under forty. Gender also negatively conditions the career, but to a lesser extent. Other observations may be made to illustrate the centralized administration–divided administration dichotomy. There is a difference in the characteristics of national and regional public administrators. Those at the national level are older, more educated and work in an environment more attuned to their knowledge and education. Their unexcused absences are minor in number as compared to their regional counterparts. They have more role models and more occasions to utilize superior skills. Their sensitivity to discipline and controls is greater than that of those who work in the region, as is their dissatisfaction with their pay and financial incentives. Regional bureaucrats travel the career path at a faster pace, and their discontent focuses on the belief that professionally they are not utilized in an appropriate fashion. They are more apt to complain about the organizational and professional deficiencies of their offices (Bettini 1990). Acknowledging all of these variables and the behaviour they generate, one can appreciate the centrality of personnel recruitment to the healthy state of an administrative structure.

Ineffective controls on the public administration

In theory, some of the negative aspects of the bureaucracy should have been overcome by controls, which exist, but their impact is not what it should have been. In a public statement, a former Minister of the Public Function asked: 'How is it possible that in 1990, 100 million formal controls on administrative acts were carried out, without succeeding in blocking half of a kickback payment?' (Puledda 1993: 43). There are several actors involved in the control of the public administration.

A major role is played by Parliament. It must be remembered that ministers are responsible to Parliament for their policies and actions, and that legislative bodies assign major importance to their scrutiny and oversight powers. In addition to featuring Select Commissions of Inquiry, established for the purpose of investigating issues impinging on the public interest, and Joint Permanent Commissions, assigned specific 'watchdog' functions, parliamentary control over administrative matters may be exercised through its law-making authority, power of the purse, questions, interpellations and motions. In addition, the State Audit Board is responsible for supervising ministerial expenditures. Acting in this capacity, it reviews all administrative decisions involving the expenditure of public funds, which means practically all of them, prior to their implementation, and it reports to Parliament annually. The Constitution provides for recourse against decisions taken by the public administration. Administrative law is an important component of Italian legal arrangements, and administrative justice is meted out by several tribunals, including the Court of Accounts, and the Council of State. Other courts participate in control of the public administration because civil servants are held accountable for four types of responsibility: administrative, penal, civil and financial.

9 The politics of justice

Introduction

Democratic states pride themselves on the independence of the judiciary, and their citizens fully expect fair and equal treatment. Increased pressures have been placed on judicial systems in liberal democracies as a result of the growth of the welfare-state and state intervention in the economy. More extensive regulation of economic, social and political relationships has meant an increase in conflict concerning the rights of individuals and the community at large. Dealing with the authoritative distribution of values in a new environment, the judiciary's role has become more pronounced and more political in nature. In the revolution that has occurred in Italian political life, the judiciary has played a critical and expanding role. While the judicial culture has ancient roots, its prominence in judicial proceedings has never been greater.

A nation's legal tradition, and its fabric and processes of justice, provide the setting for a major portion of its political life. The Western political tradition has generated two disparate foundations for Western European legal arrangements: one grounded in civil law and the other based on the common law. Unlike the Anglo-American tradition, Italian legal structures are rooted in civil law, which is written law or code law. Legal principles are incorporated in an authoritative code of general rules. The tendency of civil law is to create unified legal arrangements by working out with utmost precision the conclusions to be drawn from the basic principles on which they rest. The task of the judge is to apply these conclusions in specific instances. The civil law decision sets forth the applicable provision from the code or from a relevant statute, and the judgement is anchored on that provision. It is the letter of the code that is significant.

Legal careers: attorneys, judges and prosecutors

The quality and training of professionals of the law reveal a great deal about a particular legal system. They influence the role, structure and style of the judicial system as well as the climate in which it operates and the quality of justice. An enduring division in the Italian judicial world is the distinction between the careers of judge and lawyer. Being two distinct entities, those desiring a legal career must decide between the bar and the bench. Although the legal profession has been open to women since 1883, they number less and earn less than their male colleagues. A breakdown of the profession by gender and site of practice shows that most females practise in northern Italy, with the central part of the nation and the South following. This pattern is congruent with trends in the political culture related to gender (Contri 1991).

Judgeships are the most critical legal positions in any society. One of the unique characteristics of the Italian magistracy is its recruitment system. Judicial appointments are linked with a civil servant-like career. The corps of judges forms a hierarchically structured career service in which there is no lateral entry. Those entering this service do so directly upon leaving law school, and they are selected on the basis of their performance on an examination. This means the professional socialization of judges takes place within the magistracy. Once admitted to the bench, a person enjoys a good salary, security and an excellent pension. Moreover, one cannot be transferred without personal consent nor removed from office without legal cause. These benefits have been especially attractive to the southern Italian who traditionally has had more limited career opportunities. Similar to the case of public administrators, a great number of judges come from small communes in the South.

Some of these benefits, particularly the one related to transfers, have caused difficulties in carrying out justice. Statistics indicate that although crime has increased throughout the nation, a significant portion of this criminality is concentrated in the South. The supply of judicial personnel in this part of the nation is not adequate to the need. The number of cases in certain areas is often three times above the national average. Judges became targets for the violence of the Red Brigades and the Mafia. Many are reluctant to practise in the South. To keep judicial offices open, it has often been necessary to send newly appointed judges, popularly known as *giudici ragazzini* (kid judges). It has been especially difficult to fill positions with people possessing the appropriate expertise and experience.

Judges in Italy are appointed, promoted and supervised in the main by their colleagues. This has been the case since the downfall of the Fascist regime, which constantly interfered with the judiciary. As a negative reaction to Fascism, the judiciary acquired a great deal of autonomy. It enjoys more autonomy than any of its counterparts in constitutional democracies (Di Federico 1989). Internal supervision was deemed essential to achieving a modicum of independence from government and politics. Through its governing organ the judiciary controls recruitment, career ladders and discipline. In most civil law nations promotion in a judicial career is usually based on some combination of examination, seniority and merit. At one time these criteria applied to Italy, even though a great deal of discretion was exercised by those at the top of the hierarchy and political influence was brought to bear. The usual evaluative criteria for promotion were abolished. Once awarded the title of judge, the neophyte's competency is no longer evaluated. Promotions are automatic because they are based, to a large extent, on seniority. The Italian judicial career represents a haven of lifetime security.

The fact that a judge does not have to submit periodically to various forms of control has consequences for the overall exercise of the profession. The internal independence of the judiciary has been established. There is an increasing lack of personal and technical professionalism among Italian judges who often devote more attention to extra-judicial activities in the administrative or parliamentary sectors than to their judicial responsibilities. Judges know they will be promoted with limited or no effort. This affects the efficiency of the system and the public image of judicial officials in a negative way. The professional qualifications of magistrates are no longer guaranteed. Critics of the present practice have argued that 'a judge is not a priest who once ordained never has to submit to controls, engage in continuing education and appraisals of one's merit' (Graldi 1986: 7). One positive consequence of the prevailing system is that it has afforded an opportunity for the injection of some new blood into the upper echelons of the magistracy, which, by definition, have supported the status quo. Advancement in the judicial career ladder means increased financial rewards. Judicial independence was reinforced when the method for the determination of judges' salaries was changed. Originally following the process of other liberal democratic nations, remuneration was established by the legislature and was linked to the pay scale of other public administrators. The Italian magistracy was successful in obtaining large salary increases and the right to determine its own salary scales. Independence knows few limits.

The doors of the magistracy were opened to women in 1963, and those of military tribunals in 1989. There are even fewer female judges than attorneys. However, more women have hopes of sitting on the bench, and among the younger judges they are in the majority. It is possible that in a short period of time women judges will equal their male counterparts in terms of numbers, and perhaps even surpass them, as has happened in France (Gasperoni 1997; Luccioli 1991). Most women judges are northern in origin. As opposed to other nations, given the standard for career advancement in Italy, female judges theoretically are not subject to discrimination on the basis of gender. However, they have not reached the highest legal positions in significant numbers, nor are they a force in the governing bodies of professional associations or other judicial control organs, in spite of their candidacy for leadership positions. Even though for the first time a woman is at the helm of the National Association of Magistrates, the feminization of the judiciary is far from being realized.

In most nations in criminal and administrative proceedings, district attorneys, public prosecutors and the like represent the public interest. Another unique characteristic of the Italian judiciary relates to the position of the public prosecutor, who is the accuser and investigator. Attached to each court is an office of the public prosecutor, which consists of officials responsible for initiating penal action in cases foreseen by law. A conscious effort was made to liken public prosecutors to judges. The former enjoy the same guarantees and powers as the latter. Even though prosecutors are not adjudicators, they were included in the judicial corps and given judicial status because of the need for impartiality and freedom from political and governmental pressure. Both prosecutors and judges share training and a career during which they often switch roles. This has encouraged a structural collusion between prosecutors and judges. Separation of the two careers is a major political issue. Italy is the only democratic nation in which the same corps of career magistrates perform both judicial and prosecuting functions in full independence (Guarnieri 1991b, 1997).

According to the Constitution, the initiation of criminal proceedings is a monopoly of the public prosecutor. Members of the Constituent Assembly believed that by making the institution of a penal action obligatory, arbitrary and capricious use of power would be avoided. However, theory differs from practice. In Italy, much discretion is exercised as far as the initiation of penal actions is concerned. At one time magistrates acted exclusively at the request of forces external to their ranks, such as the police, private citizens or public authorities. Recently they have increased their direct initiatives. With each prosecutor's office being autonomous, the discretionary character of this power has become clearer along with its use in a politically opportunistic manner. Di Federico writes:

> the judiciary, a bureaucratic body, ends up by exercising in full independence a discretionary power of the greatest importance, a power that places largely in magistrates' hands the definition and implementation of the country's criminal policy. This arbitrariness…is not accompanied by any form of accountability or responsibility. The scope of this discretion opens up much wider avenues to judicial activism than those existing in other countries where the judiciary operates only as a third party judge.
>
> (Di Federico 1989: 28–9)

As far as recruitment, advancement, socialization to and administration of their profession is concerned, Italian professionals of the law exercise a great deal of power. They are autonomous and independent which differentiates them from other Italian public officials, and from their counterparts in other nations.

Special legal units: administrative tribunals and the Constitutional Court

Italian tribunals, like those of other Continental nations, reflect a hierarchical organization, forming an integrated, single court system. The Italian judicial network consists of ordinary courts having both civil and criminal jurisdiction, administrative courts responsible for the activities of state institutions and their personnel, and a Constitutional Court for matters of constitutional import as well as a few specialized tribunals. Each component has its own judges and processes. In addition to being differentiated on the basis of subject matter, these courts may also be distinguished as to whether they hold original jurisdiction or serve as appeals courts having the power to overrule a lower court, or both, and whether they utilize a single judge or a panel of judges and include citizen participation. Administrative courts and the Constitutional Court will be discussed.

Administrative law, that law which regulates the rights and duties of the state, is formally recognized in Western Europe, unlike the Anglo-American experience. Those nations adhering to the civil law tradition have a complete hierarchy of administrative courts. The law which these courts administer relates to the organization and activities of the organs of the state and of minor public bodies exercising executive power. Administrative courts seek to protect the rights of citizens from the administration and to oversee the proper expenditure of public funds. The most prominent are the *Consiglio di Stato* (Council of State), and the *Corte dei Conti* (Court of Accounts).

The Italian Council of State is the oldest consultative organ of the government. Although the Constitution places greater emphasis on its consultative role, it is assigned judicial functions as well (Cattani 1962). It advises public bodies on a wide variety of issues. Typical ones are the legality of government bills, the issuing of regulations, the codification of legislation, and contracts and agreements to be entered into by the public administration. It is not possible to itemize all the subjects with which the court is concerned because whenever the public administration, especially the government, feels the need for advice on any topic, it turns to the Council of State. On certain issues the Council must be approached. The advice that it gives may not necessarily be followed. The opinion issued is rarely binding. In carrying out its judicial function, the Council of State settles disputes involving private individuals and the public administration as well as central and local governments. It handles cases which involve the legality of an administrative law or regulation, a challenge to the merits of an administrative act, thus necessitating a decision as to whether the act is in the interests of proper and constructive public administration; and subjects, within its own exclusive domain, such as public employment.

Members of the Council of State rotate back and forth between consultative and judicial assignments. Half of the members are chosen by the government and half selected on the basis of competitive examination. Political appointment as a method of selection has generated criticism. The traditional link between the Council of State and the public administration remains intact, meaning that a judge has ties with an apparatus whose work is to be judged (Rescigno 1984). Barile comments: 'the judges...lack those requisites of independence...which are considered essential' (Barile 1991: 121). They are not equidistant from both the citizen and the public administration.

Another check on administrative activities is the Court of Accounts. Of all the governmental organs having similar concerns, this is the most important. It is assigned responsibility for guaranteeing the legitimacy of government measures, undertaking a post-audit of the budget and supervising the financial management of entities to which the state contributes money. It reports directly to Parliament. Acting in a judicial capacity, it has jurisdiction over matters related to public accounts and other subjects specified by law. Its powers are wider than they appear, given the way in which the administrative and judicial functions combine (Cuocolo 1990). The Court is responsible for making sure that administrative decisions of the central government are in conformity with the law. Theoretically, an administrative decision cannot be implemented until it has been determined that it complies fully with existing laws. The Court is to monitor every governmental act. In reality, this control is exercised more in the case of decrees. Supervision exercised by the Court is not absolute.

According to a President of the Court, the most important facet of the control function is not that which concerns the legality of government acts, but that which focuses on finances (Carbone 1989). Increased public expenditures reflect an explosion in the state's activities. Hence, the court's financial control has grown in importance. Judicial duties are primarily concerned with fiscal issues. Jurisdiction encompasses issues related to the use of public monies, civil and military pensions paid by the public authorities, the personnel who actually manage public funds and the civil liability and accountability of public officials. The court enjoys unique decision-making powers, which illustrate the breadth of its authority. It is distinguished from other tribunals because it can venture beyond the original petition or issues raised by parties to a dispute. It is staffed by a special hierarchy of judges, which has been criticized for lack of independence.

As a negative reaction to fascism and in an effort to protect the new constitutional order, at the pinnacle of the judiciary, those who penned the Constitution provided for a Constitutional Court, a guarantor of civil liberties and an arbiter. It is primarily responsible for guaranteeing that the fundamental law is not violated and ensuring that the various authorities and institutions which it sanctions function in a proper and balanced manner. A prime task of the court is to judge the constitutionality of laws and acts having the force of law emanating from the national and regional governments. Thus, regional and national laws as well as decrees are subject to judicial review. Acting in this capacity, the Court is functioning as an advocate of civil liberties. Other types of controversies with which it deals places it in the role of an arbiter. It decides conflicts of attribution, disputes arising over the assignment of powers within the central government, between the central government and the regions and between the regions. The specific duties that the Constitution allots to each level and branch of government are open to interpretation. In addition, the Court is a participant in impeachment proceedings against the President of the Republic. Last, it determines the admissibility of proposals for referenda to decide upon abrogation of a law.

The Constitutional Court consists of fifteen judges, five of whom are nominated by the President of the Republic, five by Parliament sitting in joint session and five by the highest ordinary and administrative courts. In practice, the latter means that the Court of Cassation, the highest ordinary court, selects three appointees and the Council of State and the Court of Accounts, one each. The method of appointment clearly reflects the court's role as a referee for disputes involving various political structures and the desire to have an independent court. In spite of this, it has been labelled 'extremely dangerous' (Barile 1991: 248). Failure to come forth with nominees on time, as has happened in the case of the Parliament, can lead to paralysis of the court.

Parliamentary nominees must be selected with a two-thirds majority on the first three ballots and in the following ones a three-fifths majority. Given these requirements candidates need the support of disparate political forces. They are elected as a result of prior agreements between the major political parties, even though, in theory, the founding fathers envisioned that they would be 'above' and detached from them. In practice, the parties have divided up the available spots on the Court among themselves. By convention it is understood that when a judge's term has expired, the designation of a replacement belongs to the party of the retiring magistrate. This meant that in the early days of the Court the DC could claim two seats and the PCI, PSI and PLI one each. However, when the PLI lost some of its electoral strength the allocation was changed. The judgeship was then given to the strongest of the minor parties, excluding the MSI and other anti-system forces. Partisan influence also pervades presidential appointments. This scenario demonstrates once again the important role of political parties.

Although several practices of the Constitutional Court have as their purpose the insulation of members from political influence, evidence suggests that they are not totally successful. Giuseppe Branca, a former President of the Court, created a furore when at a professional conference he commented on the behaviour of members of the court during his presidency. He noted that twelve of the fifteen judges voted according to their political party orientations. As a result, the three 'independents' felt great pressure. Some people, such as Franco Bassanini, an eminent scholar and political figure, have no problem with this practice. Bassanini argues: 'Judges must exhibit a political sensitivity. To settle a constitutional controversy is different from applying the law in a border dispute between two farmers. A formalistic interpretation of the rule threatens a betrayal of its inner spirit' (cited in Folli 1993: 4). The Court has to pursue a very narrow path. It must be autonomous but not abstract, and political.

The Court ensures the orderly development of public life as well as observance of the constitutional rights of citizens. Although it is supposed to prevent the various organs of the state from treading on each other's toes beyond the limits established by the Constitution, it has been reluctant to intervene in conflicts among the various branches of the national government. This contrasts with its treatment of differences between the national government and regional units. The Court has been an important policy maker, and has left its mark on public policy as a promoter of significant reforms. On various occasions, it, rather than the Parliament, has taken the initiative in several policy sectors. It has been the vanguard in the areas of civil rights, taxation and communications. In striking down the charge that divorce was unconstitutional, in espousing equal rights for husband and wife and in enlarging social rights, among other activities, it has contributed to broadening the base of democracy. It has done a great deal, perhaps more than Parliament, to adapt old laws to the spirit of the postwar Constitution (Cheli 1994; Volcansek 1994). Due to legislative immobility, it was difficult to reform the existing codes of law and other norms which needed modification in order to meet the needs of Republican times. Thus the

Constitutional Court assumed a particular importance. It has represented an alternative to political stagnation. There is no doubt that the Court has been successful. It provoked a reaction from the establishment, which attempted to curb its influence by reducing the term of office of the constitutional judges, limiting somewhat the autonomy of the Court and scrutinizing meticulously candidates for its bench (Pizzorusso 1985b). Its success allayed fears that it was an American type of court grafted on to a civil law system.

The Constitutional Court has played a significant political role in the referendum process. This role has been described as 'one of mediation between the citizen's rights to promote referenda and the regime's need to preserve its stability' (Uleri 1989: 167). Moreover, prior to the vote, the Court has been the principal political voice of the promoters of the referendum. Not being limited to technical judgements concerning the admissibility of referenda, the Court's decisions have been invoked as a basis for redefining its own role. The criteria, which govern verdicts of admissibility, have been rewritten by the Constitutional Court, and often the Court has invited Parliament to amend the laws implementing referenda. The Court's dynamism contrasts sharply with the traditional conservative orientation of other parts of the judicial system. It is definitely a proactive body and will likely remain one.

Judicial independence and the High Council of the Judiciary

The founding fathers were anxious to guarantee all judges the possibility of performing their duties with a margin of both external and internal independence, meaning that they must be free from other organs of the state and must be able to make decisions without being bound to their superiors. Independence of the judiciary was recognized in the Constitution with provision for the governing body, the *Consiglio Superiore della Magistratura* (High Council of the Judiciary) (CSM). Established in 1958, when the necessary implementing legislation was passed, its purpose is to guarantee that justice is administered in an environment of maximum independence and without interference from other sources of public authority. Being responsible for all matters related to the appointment, assignment, transfer, promotion and discipline of judges, the CSM underwrites the professional and personal qualifications of the judiciary. It is this responsibility which represents a break with the past and a notable increase in the external independence of the judiciary, particularly as it relates to the Minister of Justice. In essence, the CSM deals with all affairs related to the judicial career. In addition, it nominates lay members of some courts and comments to the Minister of Justice on bills pertaining to the organization and functioning of the judicial system as well as general proposals relating to the subject area. Given the scope of its functions, it is generally acknowledged that the CSM is the autonomous, self-governing organ of the judiciary. Its independent nature is underscored by the fact that the Constitutional Court has ruled that the opinions, which its members express in carrying out their duties, are not censurable.

The role and functions of the CSM have served as a source of debate. One side emphasizes the intrinsically political nature of the body, claiming that its function of protecting the judiciary from every other public authority gives it, in addition to its expressed powers, a series of tacit ones which, nevertheless, are innate to its function. Put to good use, they allow the Council to exercise a substantial political role. The other camp asserts that the political nature of the CSM is an institutional result, meaning it emerges from the system used to elect its members as well as the history of the institution (Patrono 1989).

The CSM consists of thirty-three members, three of whom are *ex officio* and the remainder of whom are elected. Of the latter, two-thirds are selected by judges from the various levels of the court system and one-third by Parliament sitting in joint session from among professors of law and attorneys. The Constitution is silent as to the number of members and the method of election. These matters are left to the ordinary law. The method of electing the judicial contingent of the CSM has witnessed five reforms. The number of modifications reflects the intensity of debate. The biggest reform occurred when a majoritarian electoral system was abandoned for one of proportional representation. Since then, changes have mandated variations of this system. Parliament utilizes a different method to elect the lay contingent. A three-fifths majority of all the members of the assembly is required on the first ballot, and a three-fifths majority of those voting on subsequent ballots. Elected members of the CSM serve a four-year term and there are incompatibilities between this office and other activities, including those related to political parties.

The claim that the CSM is a self-governing organ is based on the fact that judges elect a majority of its members. This component, consisting of the so-called 'gowned members', is representative of the judicial power and is independent of other authorities. It symbolizes the autonomy of the judiciary. At the same time the inclusion of the President of the Republic (an *ex officio* member), who lends an aura of prestige to the body, and persons elected by the Parliament makes the CSM a liaison between the bench and other state organs. Lay participation helps to ensure that the CSM will not become a self-serving closed guild. It allows for the cultivation of relationships between the judges and other public powers so that the former will not be politically, culturally and psychologically isolated. In part, this allowed the CSM to become independent of the Minister of Justice (Patrono 1989; Pizzorusso 1985a).

The adoption of an electoral system based on proportional representation suited the realities of power within the magistracy more than its proclaimed objective of greater internal independence (Zannotti 1989). It institutionalized the various currents, which are affiliated with the judiciary. The judicial corps is divided into factions identified with all parts of the political spectrum. Proportional representation reinforces these groups and guarantees each one representation on the CSM. In the 1994 election of the 'gowned members', the first election of the Second Republic, the left-wing factions enjoyed an edge. In the election held in summer 1998, moderate factions advanced for the first time in several years. The anomaly is that when Berlusconi was at the helm of government, the left-wing factions won, while with the Prodi Government in power, forces to the right prevailed. This is understandable. The Berlusconi Government was anti-magistracy, and the results of the 1994 CSM elections were a reaction to this orientation. Now, magistrates of the left feel that the Olive Tree has not protected them sufficiently from attacks. In this last election, they punished the left-wing factions by assigning their votes elsewhere. While the centre-right forces lost support, moderates advanced and progressives declined. Originally these currents represented camps for debate of cultural issues related to the judiciary and society at large. They now focus less attention on cultural issues and more on the management of power within the magistracy.

The Constitution provided that Parliament elect part of the CSM membership in order to protect that body from charges of corporativism. However, as in the case of other institutions, the political parties, through Parliament, have perverted the constitutional mandate. Lay participants are selected on the basis of political party affiliation. Seats are allotted to the various political parties. According to the formula in vogue throughout the First Republic, the DC received four, the PCI three, the PSI two and one went to the minor parties. With the Berlusconi victory in 1994, members of the governing coalition each received two seats for a total of six, and the opposition four, one to the PPI and three to the PDS. In the 1998 election, over the adamant objection of Berlusconi, the distribution was the same one established by him. Six seats were allotted to the governing majority – two for the Democrats of the Left, and one each for Italian Renewal, PRC, the Greens and the PPI – and four to the opposition – one each for FI, AN, CCD and the UDR. Consequently, two interlocking divisions of power govern the CSM: the judges versus the lay members, and the judicial forces versus the diverse political parties. Each camp looks upon the other with a great deal of suspicion. Decisions require extensive negotiation resulting in the least demanding solutions.

The representative system of the CSM impacts on that body's decision-making process. Not only do the various groups have a negative impact internally, but they also serve as the instruments through which judges articulate their interests to the legislature and the government. The forces plus the decentralized structure of the judicial corps allow for excessive political manoeuvring. Their real significance cannot be captured without relating them to the career structure of the corps. When the traditional professional criteria for evaluation and advancement were abolished, they were informally replaced with affiliations with the judicial forces and/or political parties. Transfers and promotions and appointments to the main courts, when not based on seniority, are decided on the basis of agreements between the forces and the parties, which often stipulate a reciprocal exchange of favours. Everybody gets his or her due. Being composed of elected members who cannot be re-elected, but must save their seats for their force or political party, the CSM supports everybody and punishes nobody. Even though decision making is formally based on seniority, the exchange of favours among the political forces dominates the process (Guarnieri 1991b; Martinetti 1992). Participating in the appointment of CSM members, other actors external to the judiciary came to have considerable impact on the judicial corps. A change in the method of electing CSM members could temper the political nature of that body.

The President of the Republic serves as the presiding officer of the CSM. He convenes the gathering, oversees the election of its members, participates in its activities, but only votes in case of a tie and dissolves it, if it is unable to function. The President's role is to see that the Council does not exceed its authority and become entangled in politics. All of these powers are related to the head of state's role as guarantor of the Constitution. The vice-president is selected by the council from among the members elected by Parliament. This figure handles the daily operation of the Council. The Constitution envisioned that the CSM should not be completely separated from other state functions, nor from the life of the community at large. Thus, the president and vice-president of the Council are not judges. Throughout the First Republic, a Christian Democrat held the vice-presidency. Initially in the Second Republic, this post was filled by the PPI. It passed to the PDS on a temporary basis and in summer 1998 returned to the PPI. Even in the Second Republic, it seems a trend has been established.

A sensitive issue has been the relationship between the President of the Republic and the CSM. The head of state plays a dual role. As President of the CSM, his role is to protect the autonomy of the judiciary and specifically that of the CSM *vis-à-vis* other public authorities. As President of the Republic, he must serve as guarantor of the Constitution and assure respect for its principles on the part of all governing organs, including the judiciary. Behaviour appropriate to one of these roles is not necessarily appropriate to the other (Azzariti 1992). Relations between the CSM and its president became especially stormy during the tenure of Francesco Cossiga (1985–92). Intent on pursuing the mission of guaranteeing the performance of every branch of government in a very exacting manner, he openly engaged in bitter conflict with the CSM. It has been noted that 'in the period of a few years the transformation of the presidency was the most surprising and incisive event…in the Italian institutional experience…' (D'Orazio 1992: 254). Cossiga broke the myth of impartiality in his relations with the CSM. This body in particular, and the judiciary in general, charged that he compromised their autonomy. In several instances he struck items from the agenda of the CSM, which on one occasion caused the 'gowned members' to resign, although only temporarily.

Often Cossiga sent messages to the CSM, rather than explaining his position in person. These messages were issued in his capacity as head of state, not as President of the CSM. In this manner he explained the functions of the CSM and the role of the head of state as its president. Thus, he did not intervene internally as president of the body, but authoritatively from the outside as head of state (Ferrajoli 1990). In a similar vein, Cossiga issued instructions to the CSM via the vice-president just prior to sessions, which he himself failed to attend. Other irritants included the scheduling of meetings at such a time that it would not be possible to discuss the presiding officer's remarks. Also, upon becoming head of state and thus President of the CSM, Cossiga met with the leaders of the

Court of Cassation, the highest of the ordinary courts, before making contact with the CSM, indicating to some the pre-eminence of the Court of Cassation. These activities, along with others related to powers concerning the election of leadership positions within the judiciary and departures requested from the principle of the irremovability of magistrates, generated significant resentment against Cossiga. Scalfaro's behaviour as President of the CSM contrasts sharply with that of his predecessor.

The relationship between the Minister of Justice, the traditional head of the judicial service, and the CSM is politically sensitive. Basically, the minister executes the decisions of the CSM and offers support services to the judiciary. More specifically, the Constitution charges the minister with responsibility for taking disciplinary actions against judges and organizing and operating services related to the administration of justice. In terms of Ministry of Justice–CSM relations, it is generally acknowledged that the former is weaker and has difficulty in protecting itself. The major problem is that the spheres of the CSM and the ministry are not clearly defined (Nese 1992; Pizzorusso 1990). Difficult relations between the two bodies have culminated in a judges' strike.

Over the years the CSM has assumed a more potent role with the result that the traditional position enjoyed by the Court of Cassation as the apex of the judicial structure has been corroded. The Court of Cassation is still the court of last resort within the ordinary court system, but the CSM, because of the role it plays in managing their status, can have a major influence on the behaviour of judges. The declaration that the CSM is the self-governing organ of the judiciary is open to various interpretations (Pizzorusso 1989). Created to protect the independence of the judiciary and to guarantee the citizenry the professional qualifications of judges, the CSM has fallen short of its mark. There is a difference between theory and practice. In terms of function, the CSM is self-governing. However, its structure is not congruent with its mission. Given its identification with the political parties and judicial forces, the political game has another playground in the CSM.

Tangentopoli and the magistracy

The investigation into *Tangentopoli* began on a small scale and exploded into one of the most important developments in postwar Italy. It made public to an extent hitherto unknown the age-old practice of clientelism. Why then? Why not before? Simply put, the magistrates were in the right place at the right time. The institutional setting and political environment allowed a courageous group of prosecutors to step forth. Times of economic and political difficulty lend themselves to the exposure of corruption. In the early 1990s, Italy was undergoing a severe economic crisis and the citizenry was concerned with higher taxes and state inefficiency with respect to organized crime. Confidence in the hegemonic governing bloc, dominated by the DC and PSI, was eroding. With the fall of the Iron Curtain and the break-up of the PCI, part of the basic appeal of the anti-communist governing parties no longer existed. New actors, representing discontent among the people and addressing regional demands and specific socioeconomic issues, entered the political arena. These new forces reaped the benefits of revelations about *Tangentopoli* and aided the magistracy. Also important were the focused organization of political corruption and the decentralization of the judicial structure. The media had a decisive role in the *Tangentopoli* affair. In publicizing it, it configured the social construction of the scandal. Turning it into a moral crusade, the media captured the hostility of public opinion towards governmental forces. When it condemned the immorality and inefficiency of the political elite, the media struck a singular chord in public opinion (Giglioli 1996). The judiciary came to enjoy more support in the eyes of the public than political leaders. Political and economic uncertainties coupled with the media campaign afforded an appropriate working climate for the prosecutors and allowed judicial investigations to proceed.

The results of the prosecutors' efforts were widespread. It is one thing to search for incidents of corruption; it is another to approach them in systemic fashion. The prosecutors scrutinized the political, economic and administrative systems of the nation. The impact of their activism was cataclysmic. Corrupt practices were modified. The hazards affiliated with corruption increased and the public was sensitized against corruption. The old political equilibrium no longer held. Institutions were changed. The political system was drastically transformed and any continuity in political personnel was shattered. The executive and legislative branches of government were weakened to the advantage of the President of the Republic and the judiciary, both of whom garnered increased public support and confidence. The judges had a central role in the crisis of the regime (Morisi 1994; Pederzoli and Guarnieri 1997).

The magistrates' focus fell on Fininvest, a Berlusconi-owned enterprise, many of whose top executives were arrested. Berlusconi, as chief of government, and his Minister of Justice, Alfredo Biondi, presented a decree law granting a type of conditional amnesty to subjects of criminal investigations and making preventive custody for a number of offences, including corruption and extortion, more difficult. The prosecutors involved protested, asking for transfers to other jobs. Public outrage ensued. Not only did the political opposition exploit the issue, but the leaders of Berlusconi's two principal coalition partners rejected the decree, which was withdrawn. Berlusconi failed to understand the suspicion that surrounded his motives for issuing the decree. It was a political solution to corruption and a way of blocking judicial investigations. Rather than stopping, the investigations gained momentum. Features of the judiciary, such as the character of the CSM, the combination of the roles of prosecutor and judge, the promotion system, judicial autonomy and lack of responsibility to a specific entity, mandatory prosecution and the devolved and unpredictable nature of prosecution decision making, presented obstacles to stopping the judges (Nelken 1996a, 1996b).

Tangentopoli and judicial activism had systemic reverberations. They impacted judicial and investigative practices, the distribution of judicial power in government, relationships of the judiciary with other governmental institutions, and the operation of these units, particularly the public administration. Further effects remain to be seen.

The judiciary has progressed from an instrument of law and order to being a crusader for political change. This politicization is partly historical. After the war, many of the senior judges inherited from Fascism were very conservative. Reacting, the younger generation became radicalized in the 1960s and 1970s. The stage for the new role was set earlier with the creation of the CSM and its political divisions undertaking lobbying within the political system. Competing coalitions of magistrates and politicians resulted from a paradox: the independence of the judiciary, but its receptivity to pressures and influence from the political arena. Although judicial power expanded, until the 1990s it was counterbalanced by political parties and the political elite exploiting its internal divisions (Guarnieri 1992). The demise of these forces in the *Tangentopoli* era removed restraints.

Since 1992 there has been an intense conflict, which has become most acrimonious, between politicians and magistrates on the subject of justice. Accusing the government of mistakes and inertia, eminent prosecutors labelled working conditions 'intolerable', and justice 'paralysed'. They threatened to leave the corps. Several issues are involved. An important one is the prosecutors' power and resources, which have expanded along with judicial activism. The prosecutors' popularity, swelled by media attention, led to significant involvement in the policy-making process, modifying the face of the body politic (Righettini 1995). Political forces have exhibited different attitudes towards the prosecutors' actions and their powers. The right, especially FI and the Northern League, has severely criticized them. The left generally supported them until recently when it raised questions, causing alarm in their ranks.

From the prosecutors' perspective, the government is weakening their hand, thus neutralizing the fight against unlawfulness. According to them, no new laws have made it easier to uncover corruption. The window opened to fight political and administrative illegalities is, therefore, closing. With trials dragging on and claiming to have little to show for their efforts, they believe their impact on institutions and society is reduced and public trust, an essential element for obtaining information, has eroded. They feel betrayed by the public, which in their eyes is tired of the fight against corruption, as well as by the politicians trying to suffocate it. Being of the opinion that politicians are intolerant of judicial controls, magistrates have spoken of a conscious attempt to blackmail them and to weaken justice by stopping them.

Another issue in the conflict relates to the nature of justice as practised. Is it neutral or political? Who are the prosecutors' targets? Berlusconi, while head of government, attacked magistrates for interfering with the governing function. In opposition and convicted twice for bribery and once for fraud, with six more trials pending, one of which is in Spain, he continues to make the prosecutors the target of his wrath. Typical of his remarks is the following:

Certain prosecutors, after having eliminated all the representatives of democratic parties in '92 (I remember that they eliminated the PLI, the PRI, the
PSDI, all the men not on the left of the DC and not on the left of the PSI),
today continue such action utilizing justice as a weapon to eliminate the
opposition, to eliminate the leader of Forza Italia.

('Berlusconi, nuovo attacco' 1997: 2)

For Berlusconi, who argues that the Olive Tree only governs thanks to the
judiciary, and for some other politicians, justice is solely political and partisan.
He argues that the public prosecutors are investigating him because he is the
leader of the opposition. He equates these prosecutors with the Red Brigades.
Those who disagree with him indicate his legal problems relate to his activities in
the business world, not in political life. They believe that Berlusconi is politiciz-
ing what should be strictly legal issues.

Politicians and magistrates have diverse agendas. The former focus on
structural matters, such as the CSM, the need to separate judicial careers, and
the incompatibility of magistrates. The latter are more concerned with
operational issues, such as statutes of limitation, preventive custody and other
items related to speed and the efficiency of the judicial process. The battle
continues.

Conclusion

The present judicial system is the product of more than fifty years of experi-
mentation, based on a long tradition including a period of Fascism. The
experiment has yielded some interesting results. Legal arrangements, like other
components of the political system, remain polarized in the sense that they are
permeated by a continual clash between the old and the new and between form
and fact. This has resulted in a dysfunctional system. Some evaluations, arguing
it is undergoing a severe crisis, have placed it on the critical list. Prognosis is
guarded because internal and external political relationships protect these
dysfunctions in the administration of justice.

Within the judicial branch, there is much strife. Ministers of Justice, both
political appointees and technocrats, have attempted to leave their mark on the
judicial system. Functionaries in the ministry have claimed that they were used
for political purposes. The minister at the time fired two who rebelled, and
others resigned. Another facet of this conflict is reflected in the schism between
judges and attorneys. This hostility in part results from the antiquated recruitment process, which separates the bench from those who practise law. Understanding between the two camps is lacking. This is a severe problem because
lawyers and judges must interact daily. The judges, never having been practising
lawyers, cannot relate to the attorneys and their plight. Surveys reveal that
lawyers are suspicious of judges and believe their decisions are based on political
orientations (Fondazione Rosselli 1993). Often lawyers find it difficult to take the
public interest to heart. They regard judges as bureaucrats and resent being

barred from a judicial career. Attorneys have not been able to compete with judges because they lack a unitary professional association, which could advocate a collective view on the administration of justice, and professional needs and expectations.

Tensions between the judiciary and other parts of the political structure are particularly intense in the case of the CSM, which has accrued to itself authority which was not envisioned as being in its realm. Over time it has 'assumed an additional and prominent role as an authoritative interlocutor of the executive, the Parliament and the political elite regarding all questions relating to the administration of justice' (Di Federico 1989: 36). Such behaviour has generated acute conflict with Parliament, the Cabinet, especially its Minister of Justice; and the chief of state. Elements in the political environment have developed a close identification with the judiciary. The abandonment of traditional professional values, controls and procedures related to career patterns encouraged penetration of the judicial corps by political forces. The result has been that very often members of a judicial organ have close ties with centres of power. Often they seem to be an appendage of the executive or of political party factions, most notably in the First Republic those of the DC. Frequently, decisions seem to be the translation of political operations into judicial terms.

The magistracy and the political parties also have financial links. The parties, through public bodies, subsidize activities of the various judicial organizations, such as conventions, study centres and publications. Judges often solicit contributions from banks, public agencies or individuals to finance activities of their professional associations. People contribute for different reasons. Some feel they are buying an insurance policy against possible future judicial problems. Others view a request for funds as 'an intolerable form of procedure' (Di Federico 1989: 45) which cannot be ignored, especially if it comes from a magistrate who can initiate penal actions. Given the discretionary nature of the initiation of penal action, a contribution in this instance provides again a type of insurance policy. Although the political parties have a close relationship with the judiciary, it is interesting that none of the judicial currents have become in a formal sense ancillary organs of a political party, as in the case of trade unions and other labour and cultural organizations.

Political parties have also cultivated the judiciary with extra-judicial rewards, which increased by 80 per cent at the end of the First Republic (Zannotti and Sapignoli 1997). These include well-paid appointments as an arbitrator or as a consultant for various governmental departments, as well as nomination for a sub-national or national elected or appointive office. All magistrates serving in any of these capacities take leave from their professional posts, but have the right to return upon relinquishing their extra-judicial position. While on leave, their seniority in the judicial corps is not affected. There is also the problem of post-career activities of magistrates, especially those of the Constitutional Court. Legal experts are of the opinion that in all such cases, a mandatory waiting period prior to the assumption of post-career employment must be enacted. It is quite clear that there are strong links between judges and politicians.

In spite of popular myths to the contrary, courts are policy-making bodies. In performing judicial reviews, they declare the illegality or unconstitutionality of acts. They issue rules, which regulate the activities of the judicial organs themselves. These actions are related to policy making. From another perspective, the Italian courts are deeply involved in policy making because of the judiciary's extensive influence on the legislative process, particularly as it relates to judicial subjects. The magistracy is a very successful institutional interest group. It is distinguished from other groups of this type because of its monopoly of institutional power free of any counterweights.

At the executive level by law judges fill the senior administrative positions in the Ministry of Justice. Magistrates who hold these posts serve many years. They are able to develop expertise and to cultivate relationships within the ministry and without. They enjoy autonomy, especially from the minister, whose term in office is uncertain. Generally relationships between ordinary bureaucrats and magistrates are not equal. The latter hold the advantage. Bureaucrats are well aware that their autonomy and their power is conditioned by the judiciary. The administrative court system looms large over the heads of individual functionaries as well as the entire bureaucracy. Therefore, they have a propensity to identify with the interests of the magistrates (Zannotti 1989).

At the legislative level, the magistracy is well positioned to exercise influence. Many magistrates, while they are engaged in their judicial career, hold parliamentary seats. As Members of Parliament, their commission assignments are usually related to their professional interests. Thus they have an important podium from which to speak. Judicial professional interest groups enjoy privileged contacts within the executive and legislature. The other extra-judicial rewards conferred on magistrates by the political parties are also important in terms of influencing the policy-making process. The nature of this role is captured in the words of Di Federico.

> during the last twenty years, magistrates operating in the three branches of government and in other organizations…have been developing a tight, well-oiled network of informal ties to exchange information, coordinate strategies aimed at moving or supporting particular proposals and discouraging or preventing others.
>
> (Di Federico 1989: 38)

The magistracy has not been able to get what it wanted in all cases. However, being able to block what it considered undesirable, it has exercised its power successfully. Members of the judiciary are well situated throughout the political system. Their feet are in the political parties, the executive and the administration and the legislature. They know no institutional counterweights, and at the same time their wide prerogatives allow them to effectively balance the other public authorities. They arrogantly tread on the toes of others. Given this situation, it will be a difficult task to reform the judiciary.

The dysfunctions of the Italian judiciary restrict, distort and alter the proper functioning of the judicial structure. Italian legal arrangements, like many other things Italian, are paradoxical. The judiciary has at its disposal a high degree of institutional independence, but its power to act is in reality limited. The politicization of the judiciary has grave consequences not only for citizens' liberties, but also for the overall functioning of the system: 'A truly independent and professionally skilled judiciary in Italy is still an objective that is far from realization' (Guarnieri 1991a: 13).

10 The territorial distribution of power

The Italian regional state

Introduction

Critical to an understanding of any political system is knowledge of the distribution of political power across the national territory. Countries assign different values and functions to diverse units of government, designated as centre or periphery, depending on the unit's role within the political system. Centres representing the hub of a political system possess control. Peripheries are subordinate to the authority of the centre. Centre–periphery relationships are critical to a system's performance. They are influenced by many elements, such as the cleavage structure of the nation, history, constitutional arrangements, legal tradition, the economy, the political party system and the behaviour of political elites.

When Italy was created in the *Risorgimento*, leaders were deeply concerned about the maintenance of national unity. Historical experience and geography assured the development of sub-national identities. It was believed that a highly centralized administrative structure would provide the best vehicle for creating a cohesive state out of diverse regions. A unitary system with most power lodged in the centre, i.e. in the national government, was selected. This proved to be 'one of the most effective instruments of centralizing policies' (Pizzorusso 1988: 246). This arrangement was honest and reasonably efficient. While administrative integration of the peripheries occurred, regional animosities towards the central government did not decrease and regional identities increased. When taxes were imposed, open hostility towards the national government was evident. Any confidence which had developed in the efficiency of the new administrative system was dissipated when the prefects, liaisons between the centre and the peripheries, were used to engineer the outcome of parliamentary elections. In Italy's nation-building years, the hostility of many citizens towards the national government and the lack of a meaningful local governing experience hindered the development of a democratic tradition.

The Fascist regime further increased the role of the centre. Prefects were elevated in stature and authority. Elected local officers were eliminated and another representative of the national government, the *podestà*, was added to the system to replace the elected mayor. Peripheries became more dependent. A central issue addressed by the Constituent Assembly was that of centre–

periphery relationships. There was basic agreement that the extreme centralization of the Fascist period was a critical part of its anti-democratic character. However, political and ideological perspectives assured that there would be little consensus about decentralization in the assembly. Even among the supporters of devolution there was little agreement concerning what form it should take.

The leading party in the assembly, the DC, was committed to some form of regional government. A strong commitment to decentralization also came from the Republican and Action Parties. Having been in the forefront of the Resistance, they believed that democracy and efficiency would be furthered by devolution. Although divided on the subject, basically the Liberals wished to return to the old prefectoral system. Other parties on the right of the political spectrum joined them. The PCI and PSI had difficulty with the issue. They were committed to broadening participation and expanding the base of democracy. Obviously, devolution would encourage further development of citizens' public efforts. These parties were motivated by their important role in the Resistance movement, which was organized on a regional basis. Also, the Fascist model was odious to the Left. However, there was apprehension about the diffusion of power according to a regional plan. It was believed that decentralization would cause difficulties for the working-class parties in their quest for control of the government. It was feared that devolution might lead to divisiveness in the struggle for power. Expecting to win the early elections held under the new Constitution, the Communists were hoping to direct social and economic change from the centre. If regional governments were created, it was thought that the traditional political elite would lodge itself in these peripheries and sabotage any reform efforts.

Although arguments concerning the structure of the new state at the Constituent Assembly and in the nation were many, they can be summarized. Many who favoured decentralization did so as a reaction to the dictatorial era. Devolution of political power was to serve as a bulwark against the rise of another totalitarian regime. The need to recognize the historical, cultural and economic cleavages within the nation was also stressed. Arguing that unique problems existed at the regional level, it was believed that sub-national units of government could best handle them. Closely related was the argument that in many sectors national standards were not only unnecessary, but also cumbersome and costly. Many persons noted that a meaningful administrative apparatus close to the people would aid in developing a greater bond between them and their government, would encourage more citizen political participation, and would reduce the large-scale Roman bureaucracy. It was also argued that more local autonomy would provide the opportunity to groom a new political elite. Local governments were perceived as training grounds for future leaders. Some persons believed that a devolved system of government would enable the centre to more easily channel resources to the poorer peripheral areas of the country and work towards equalization of opportunity throughout the nation (Barile 1964, 1991). Arguments against devolution focused on the negative consequences decentralization would have for national unity. Critics were also apprehensive about creating another level of government because this would involve another bureaucracy in a country with an oversized and inefficient public administration. For some there was the fear that the leftist political parties would easily gain control of several regions.

The regional state: innovative devolution

Forces favouring some decentralization prevailed. The Constitution produced by the Constituent Assembly included provisions for new sub-national units of government, regional governments. Thus Italy is termed a regional state, which, with its devolution of power, is very different from a federal one. In spite of the historical and cultural experiences of the constituent parts of the regional state, the regions are not perceived as being original bodies with their own governing experience. Being creations of the centre, their powers are derived and not original. Unlike the member units of a federal state, the Italian regions are not competent to grant themselves a genuine constitution. In Italy the peripheries have fundamental laws called statutes, which are either formed by or approved by the centre. To make certain that there is no confusion about the possibility of a federal system being established, the Constitution refers to the republic as 'one and indivisible'. Moreover, the regional state lacks a second chamber in which representation is based on the federal principle with each component represented as a sub-national unit of government. In the regional state, the centre controls the activities of the component parts even to the point of being able to dismiss their representative organs under specified conditions. Although these parts have legislative powers, they are limited and they do not enjoy judicial or police powers (Cuocolo 1988). 'The existence of a real centre from which things are to be decentralised, and not only the existence of that centre but also its priority or supremacy...' is evident (Frenkel 1986: 66).

The rest of this chapter will focus on the distribution of power within the regional state. It will consider the principal reform that altered centre–periphery relations. Italy, like other Western European nations, faced the problem of 'overload', meaning that the political system was unable to adequately respond to cogent problems, leading to growing dissatisfaction within the populace. Decision makers faced two options, each one of which assigned a different role to the state. One choice was to 'roll back the state' and undertake a policy of privatization of many public services with a view to reducing costs. Another was to modify administrative structures and procedures with the objective of creating more efficient policy-making arrangements.

Although both approaches have been used in Western European nations, the second has been dominant. Great Britain is unique in that, when Margaret Thatcher was Prime Minister, a large number of reforms stressed the first option. Other Western European countries emphasized administrative reforms with privatization occupying a secondary position. Whereas in Great Britain the issue of reform was highly politicized, there was a consensus in the other Western European nations. Italy parts company from its colleagues because of the unsatisfactory outcome of the reform efforts which were embodied in Law Number 142, passed in 1990 (Capano 1991). This legislation is significant because it created new peripheral entities and new administrative relationships throughout the political system. It assigned specific administrative functions to the component parts of the regional state, hoping to concretize many constitutional provisions pertaining to centre–periphery relations. Basically these relations involve four governments moving from the periphery to the centre: the commune, the province, the region and the nation. The three units of sub-national government will be discussed.

The commune: a small unit with big responsibilities

The lowest level of the administrative hierarchy is occupied by the communes, which vary in population, size and other resource endowments. Legally, Italian administrative arrangements are highly centralized and uniform. However, in reality there is a great deal of fragmentation and heterogeneity. This is especially true at the communal level of government. According to the Constitution, these units are governed by general laws of the Republic, meaning that they are regulated by uniform norms regardless of their size and population. This fact has served as a source of concern. With the objective of streamlining local governmental arrangements and increasing efficiency after the Second World War, one of the first reforms in many European nations was a territorial one which reduced the number of fundamental units. Italy did not participate in this activity. Rationalization of the communal network was difficult. Tradition and the age of many communes created a bond between the locality and its populace that was not erasable. The parochialism of the political culture was too entrenched. Strength of local notables and party clientelism also accounted for hostility towards the consolidation effort, which would have meant a loss of political patronage for certain forces (Dente 1988).

The 1990 reform addressed the issue of the geographic and demographic characteristics of the communal map in hope of overcoming the existing excessive fragmentation. Recognizing the irrationality of the current network, the law forbids the establishment of communes with a population under a minimum number, but it did not establish a minimal area. It provides for a redrawing of the present boundaries, but on a voluntary basis at the initiative of the region, a superior level of government. Change is not controlled by the periphery, nor does the centre provide guidance and support. It only provides control. All depends on the desire of the individual region. To date, no serious attention has been given to the territorial dimension of the reform. Congruent with the notion of a unitary state, the Constitution notes that the functions of the communes are fixed by general laws. Their powers are not constitutionally guaranteed. They are expanded or decreased at the will of the centre. Mandated communal functions include the usual tasks of local government, such as the provision of police and fire services, the planning and management of many personal services (recreation, day care), public health, public lighting, road maintenance, cemeteries, local transportation services, the control and management of urban growth, and the provision of certain social services. Other responsibilities are optional.

In the First Republic, communal responsibilities increased tremendously and their mandates accumulated additional power resources to certain political parties (Cazzola 1991a). The commune no longer deals solely with problems of local interest. Rather it manages those of a general social nature, such as health and housing. Nanetti writes: 'Once an institution responsible for the management of sectorial policies the commune has become a general purpose government responsible for all policies within its territorial boundaries, aside from those higher level functions allocated the State and the region' (Nanetti 1988: 88). Communes have more formal than substantial powers. Many of these are mandated in such a way that communal control does not prevail. Local powers are shared with the centre and other public and semi-public bodies, such as government special agencies. The periphery's powers of decision making are limited and overshadowed by the centre. In spite of this, communes are an important employer (Caciagli 1991).

Governing organs of the commune consist of a legislative branch, the communal council and an executive, called the *Giunta comunale* which is composed of the mayor and the assessors, the heads of the various departments of government. In breaking the traditional principle of uniformity in local government, the 1990 reform law noted the need to accommodate these organs to the nature of the individual commune. Whereas in the past they were standardized, according to the reform, new communal statutes were to be formulated and determine their precise form. The council is the principal local decision-making body. Law 142 defines it as the organ which provides the basic orientation for local public policy and the direction for political and administrative controls. In other words, the council has been liberated from ordinary administrative functions and rather than ratifying every act of the *Giunta*, general oversight is stressed (Fernandez 1990). The council is presided over by the mayor.

The electoral reform of 1993 for the first time provided for the direct election of mayors. This change afforded these officers a popular mandate, and it also increased their powers. Since this reform, mayors from some of the most important cities have launched a campaign to address common problems. There is discussion of forming a mayors' political party. With their new electoral base, these officers have exerted greater influence on the national political scene. Previously they, as well as members of the *Giunta*, had been elected by the council. As part of the reform, the mayor now appoints the members of the *Giunta*. Not having to be members of the council as in the past, the *Giunta* can take advantage of the talents of persons not wanting to deal with electoral pressures. Collectively it is responsible for running local government, implementing policies of the council, supervising local employees, collaborating with the mayor, preparing the budget and presenting it to the council for its approval and taking action on behalf of the council, if it is deemed urgent and the council is not convened. Sometimes the *Giunta*, on the basis of urgency, exercises responsibilities belonging to the Council. The division of tasks is not always clear (Caretti and De Siervo 1994).

The assessors, singly and collectively, are seen as auxiliaries to the mayor. This official is their superior, having the power to delegate to them specific sectors of responsibility. Technically, assessors do not have their own powers, but only those delegated by the mayor. It is the latter who represents the commune in its entirety and serves as its chief administrator. Moreover, the mayor is an official of the centre whose office performs many state functions delegated to local governments, such as certain duties related to law and order. In addition to presiding over meetings of the council, the mayor has powers to convene it, establish its order of the day and direct its activities. The mayor also is the presiding officer of the *Giunta*. Moreover, this officer enjoys important appointment powers, which allow for the development of networks external to local government.

Throughout the First Republic, relationships between the council and the *Giunta* were often stormy, and the latter was extremely fragile because most executives were coalitions. Attitudes towards national political issues often influenced voting in administrative elections. Councils were often controlled by parties which, at the national level, were part of the opposition. This was true of the PCI, which at the national level was in the opposition or on the margins of government. At the local level, especially in the latter part of the First Republic, the party dominated almost all of the councils in the larger cities.

The formation of the executive in many communes, due to coalition politics, dragged on for an extended period. Often an executive was born after months of political intrigue. The reform, mandating the direct election of the mayor and the appointment of the *Giunta* by this official, was to remedy the situation and allow the mayor to enjoy a broader base of popular support. Throughout the First Republic the life of the *Giunta* was often short. Councils were known to bring them down with a vote of no confidence. Now these votes are exceptional. If successful, the council is automatically dissolved, necessitating new elections. With this practice, stability has been accorded to local government.

Traditionally, Italian local officials did not fully comprehend the actual extent of their powers because they had no constitutional guarantee against central involvement in local matters. As things developed, they often enjoyed a great deal of autonomy, even though they were subordinate to the centre. Local political leaders form a semi-separate political class. As local government has assumed more responsibility, these leaders control greater resources, financial and otherwise. They became more professional and their autonomy resulted from their expertise and specialization. Very often this experience is used to launch a national political career. In this sense, Italy is similar to France and Germany, but not Great Britain, where there is a definite separation between local and national elected officials.

Throughout the First Republic, power at the local level was concentrated in the hands of the assessors. It was so focused that the phrase 'the republic of the assessors' developed. Political parties exerted much less control over these officials than was believed (Bettin and Magnier 1991). In Italian local politics, political networks serve as crucial power resources. In the First Republic, the network that was important to an assessor differed from that of other local elected officials. That of the latter consisted of very circumscribed but strong ties, whereas that of the former was made up of much broader, but weaker, bonds (Recchi 1991). As officials moved into the executive of local administrations, their power became more personalized and more resistant to political party control. The new method for selecting these officials should temper the situation.

The pathway to a position in the executive branch of communal politics usually has passed through the Communal Council, which has provided an apprenticeship for the assessor. Also essential to the assumption of an executive position is experience in the public sector. In the First Republic there does not seem to have been a single pathway to the mayoralty. This office has been filled by Communal Councillors without any executive experience and, in some cases, it has been extensive party experience that is important. In the northern part of the nation there does appear to be an official route to this particular office: experience as assessors. Also in the First Republic, many mayors had national political experience (Cazzola 1991b). This might explain why clientelistic links have been so important to the relationship between central departments and local authorities.

As a result of *Tangentopoli*, assessors and some mayors and vice-mayors were forced to resign for having accepted bribes. All of the principal political parties were involved. Perhaps as a reaction to these scandals, the first class of mayors elected in the first local elections of the Second Republic feature a significant number of political neophytes. At the local level as well, a new conception of politics seems to be emerging with the significance assigned to the world of management (Lattes and Magnier 1995). Throughout most of the postwar period centre–periphery relations have been based on a clientelistic or patronage model, meaning that the primary function of local government is the distribution of favours and services to the electorate, with the scope of securing consensus and electoral support, in exchange for making sure that the community's interests are well represented and defended at the higher echelons of the governmental hierarchy (Dente 1985; Goldsmith 1991).

The answer to the question of 'who pays?' provides a clue to the nature of centre–periphery relations. The periphery is almost completely dependent on other governmental units, primarily the centre (Della Cananea 1997). Extreme financial centralization was intended to simplify the tax system and reinforce the instruments of macroeconomic policy. It was hoped that centralization would reduce abuses and inefficiency as well as redistribute public goods more equitably within the periphery. Basically, it was thought to be the solution to the serious economic imbalances that characterize the divided nation (Fraschini 1990). Problems were encountered because payment schedules were not met and there was a sharp rise in inflation.

The result was that peripheries were unable to guarantee the essential social services and local financial resources were in critical condition. Deficits by local governments grew dramatically, and were particularly severe in the South (Pola 1989). The state's policy on local finances is contradictory. The commune's ability to levy taxes is restricted by the state, yet the state has stepped in to cover the deficits of local government. Often communes have had to cut back on services, their financial resources not being commensurate with their responsibilities. The reform law addressed the negative consequences of this financial centralization by issuing a call to incorporate autonomy into the fiscal system. State transfers are to be adequate for the guarantee of essential services and for ensuring an equal distribution of resources. Local autonomy is based on the certainty of financial resources. However, the reform law did not adequately address the issue of local finance. It merely set forth a general outline for future action. Local finance remains characterized 'by legislation which is extremely fragmented, changeable and confusing' (Caretti and De Siervo 1994: 481–2).

The province: a unit which refuses to disappear

The level above the commune in the governmental hierarchy is occupied by the province. With the 1990 reform law, the province assumed a new role in terms of intergovernmental relations (Berti 1994). It performed only minor functions, and it was thought that when a major reform of local government was realized, this level would be eliminated. This did not occur; instead, its importance was enhanced. The province includes the territory of several communes, but in terms of functions it is of lesser significance, both quantitatively and qualitatively. As in the case of the communes, its powers are not constitutionally guaranteed. In an attempt to achieve a rational distribution of resources and orderly community development, the provinces, according to the 1990 reform, are given powers to promote the coordination and direction of the activities of the public agencies within their boundaries. They are assigned planning responsibilities. Many provinces were not able to take full advantage of the powers assigned to them by the reform. Higher levels of government, specifically that of some regions, were slow to recognize the new role of the provinces and tried to preserve the status quo which was advantageous to them. Some of these regions are in the South, and provincial leaders argued that if the spirit and meaning of the reform were not realized, the gap between the North and the South would only be enhanced (Di Giuseppantonio 1992). The pattern of governance at the provincial level is similar to that of the commune. The governing organs are the directly elected council, the executive or the *Giunta provinciale*, and the President. The President of the Province is directly elected and appoints, in turn, members of the *Giunta*.

In some cases, provincial geographic boundaries were not appropriate for the provision of services. The 1990 reform enriched local government with the creation of the metropolitan area, which encompasses a major commune and contiguous ones whose operations from a territorial, economic, social service and cultural perspective are interdependent. The law specifically established metropolitan areas for certain cities. In these instances the province became a metropolitan authority, responsible for managing services such as solid waste disposal, transportation, energy, and economic and commercial development. Acting in this capacity, it exercises its usual functions plus some, and the communes assume all functions not expressly attributed to the metropolitan authority. The 1990 reform law thus recognized the need to make local government arrangements more flexible. Relinquishing authority to a superior entity was a difficult pill for many communes to swallow (Rotelli 1991; Urbani 1990).

In line with the concept of the unitary state, the periphery is subject to a great deal of control by the centre. The prefect carried out this supervision until the regions were born in the 1970s. Prefectoral powers over the periphery were extensive, ranging from preservation of law and order to veto of any act of local government on the grounds of illegality and on its merit. With the creation of the regions, responsibility for controlling the legitimacy of the acts of the communes, provinces and other local bodies was transferred from the state to the regions as required by the Constitution. It was assumed by Regional Control Committees. The general merit of these acts is controlled by requesting deliberative bodies to re-examine their decisions. The purpose of this control is to prevent the implementation of unlawful measures and those contrary to the policy of the centre. Comparing the powers of the prefect in this area with those of the committees, it is to be noted that the latter are less powerful than the former. They can repeal only unlawful measures, and if they disapprove of a local act they can only ask the deliberative body involved to reconsider it. The system is not as restrictive as the previous one. Few decisions are repealed and other powers are not utilized. The structure of centre–periphery relations has contrasted sharply with the Constitution which provides that the republic 'adjusts the principles and the methods of its legislation to the requirements of autonomy and decentralization'.

The 1990 reform law addressed control over the organs of communal and provincial administrations (Staderini 1996). It provides that they can be dissolved under certain conditions by decree of the President of the Republic on the recommendation of the Minister of the Interior. A commissioner is appointed to govern for a specific period when elections to choose a new administration must be held. This extensive power must be used wisely due to the risk of political backlash. The 1990 reform traces the passage of the primary function of governments in the periphery from organs that guarantee respect for the rights of citizens to organs that deliver services to meet the needs of the collectivity. Financial resources are more important than ever. The financial picture of the provinces, which depend on financial transfers, is as dreary as that of the communes. Provincial tax powers are limited to a few areas, and regional payments to the provinces are irregular and insufficient. In looking at the relationship between the responsibilities delegated to the individual provinces and financial resources transferred by the regions, a geographical pattern, favouring the North, is evident once again. No unitary vision of local–regional financial relations has been developed (Petretto 1997).

The region: a continually developing unit

The regional governments called for in the fundamental law seem to be a logical recognition of long-standing socio-cultural development which had been disregarded in modern Italy. A careful examination of them demonstrates that basic systemic problems extended to the devolution process (Bartole and Mastragostino 1996). As opposed to the cases of the communes and the provinces, the powers of the regions are constitutionally guaranteed and cannot be retracted at the arbitrary whim of a political majority. The Constitution called for two kinds of regions: special and ordinary ones. Special regions are those which presented unique political and legal experiences and problems: Sicily, Sardinia, Val d'Aosta, Trentino Alto-Adige and Friuli Venezia-Giulia. The particularism of local cultures historically has been a main trait of European civilization and time has failed to eradicate it. Regional devolution hopefully is a means of confronting grievances in the periphery. Separatist movements, irridentist politics and international tensions contributed to making these regions special. The governments have more powers than those of the ordinary ones. The Constitution established fourteen ordinary regions, one of which divided into two. Although special regions began operating before the Constitution took effect, or soon after, this was not the case for the ordinary ones, which will be the focus of the ensuing discussion. Special enabling legislation was necessary to establish them, and Parliament did not pass it until 1970. In Western Europe, the regionalization process was considerably accelerated from the dawn of this decade, and Italy was the first Western European nation to adopt national arrangements for a regional state.

The regions are distinguished by the fact that they are autonomous bodies possessing their own powers and functions as stated by the fundamental law. Autonomy implies subordination to the sovereign power, which guarantees to the autonomous organ a particular sphere of liberty. Regional autonomy has several facets: political, legislative, financial, organizational and administrative. Politically, the regions can adopt a coalition, which differs from the national one. Their legislative autonomy is guaranteed by the Constitution, which sets forth certain areas of regional responsibility. Regions are granted financial autonomy, having the power of taxation among others. Organizational features may vary and regions have flexibility in terms of organizing their bureaucracy. Administrative autonomy is guaranteed by the Constitution. It must be underscored that this autonomy is limited and circumscribed by the sovereignty of the state. There is absolutely no equality between the state and the regions.

Having enumerated powers set forth by the Constitution, regions are distinguished from other peripheral units of government. Specific areas of responsibility include public charities, health and hospital assistance, museums and libraries of local bodies, urban matters, hunting and fishing, agriculture and forests. It was generally agreed that the list of enumerated subjects was not to be considered complete. In all of the areas in which the region legislates, the laws must be congruent with the interest of the nation or of other regions. Some of these powers had to be considered concurrent powers in which the national government would continue to have a role. There is a difference between the regional state and the federal state concerning concurrent powers. In the latter case, a sub-national unit of government may continue legislative activity in an area until the national government occupies the field. On the other hand, in Italy the regions were unable to commence legislative activity in areas enumerated by the Constitution until the national government defined and partitioned the field. Following the initiation of the regions, there were many areas of shared responsibility. This led to considerable overlap and inefficiency. In the concurrent exercise of powers, regions often had difficulty establishing independence of action.

Regions perform a participatory function as well. It was believed that they would afford an opportunity for greater participation in decision making at the sub-national and national levels of government. At the national level, regions relate to the legislative process in that they may introduce bills into the Parliament and they are represented in the electoral college which selects the President of the Republic. Regional officials participate in the meetings of the Council of Ministers with a consultative vote when the agenda item concerns them. Other channels of participation include an inter-regional commission within the Budget Ministry and the permanent State-Region Conference established for exchange of information and views between the centre and the periphery, and the development of a consensus pertaining to the thrust of intergovernmental relations.

The regional state was not implemented immediately. Its realization took place in three phases (Clauss 1983). In the first, between 1970 and 1971, the statutes which served as the basis of regional governance were adopted. The second phase (1972–5) involved the concretization of these statutes. Involving the transfer of administrative functions from the centre to the regions, this period is marked by conflicts, which were won primarily by the centre. Advocates of regionalism could scarcely consider the birth of the regions auspicious. The powers of these new governments were limited, and the centre was not prepared to entertain a significant devolution of functions. Persons who thought that a decentralization process would lead to a major reform of the overstaffed, top-heavy bureaucratic state were disappointed. In the last period of regional development, commencing in 1975, stellar legislation stressing major decentralization mechanisms provided for an enormous transfer of policy-making responsibility to the regions and created the instruments which were to institutionalize them as potent policy-making centres. Problems which emerged in the infancy of the regions were to be alleviated by this legislation, which was designed to coordinate the transfer of various functions from the centre to the periphery and to give implementing powers to regional administrations.

The hand of the regions has been further strengthened with the 1990 reform of local government. This provides that the regions may attribute functions to lesser sub-national entities and influence how they are performed with regional laws that discipline cooperation among these units and between them and the region. This reform views the region as a focal point for legislative, coordinative and planning activities as opposed to those concerned with simple administration (Barile 1991; Pica 1991).

The constitutionally mandated governing organs of the region are the Regional Council, a deliberative body, and an executive body called the *Giunta regionale* and its President. National laws determine the method of election, the composition of the Regional Councils and the criteria for eligibility and so on. Throughout the First Republic the list system of proportional representation was used to elect the Councils. This favoured the larger well-established national political parties rather than locally-oriented ones. Regions usually defended their interests by allying with a national political party, which acted as a link between the centre and the periphery. Rather than representing a challenge to the existing party system, the regions adapted to it (Meny 1986). The 1995 regional elections were governed by new legislation, which mandated complicated electoral arrangements, embodying proportional and majoritarian principles.

The President of the Region is directly elected. This official then appoints the other members of the *Giunta*, all of whom are responsible to the Regional Council, meaning that they govern for as long as they enjoy its confidence. Council–*Giunta* relations have been cemented by the new electoral law. It provides that if in the first two years of its life the council withdraws confidence from the *Giunta*, the term of the council is reduced from five to two years. Governmental stability is the scope of this mandate. Being an executive organ, the *Giunta* is supposed to implement programmes approved by the council and to propose measures for its consideration. In theory, it is a collegial organ. In practice, there is a tendency towards extensive individual activities on the part of members, allowing them to build their own self-serving networks and to articulate their particular interests at various levels of government. Frequently, they enter into agreement with national ministers in the same public policy area. The dichotomy between theory and practice may be attributed to *partitocrazia*.

The President of the *Giunta* serves a dual function: that of chief of government and that of a ceremonial chief executive. In the latter capacity, this official serves as President of the Region. Lacking an organ equal to the head of state at the regional level of government, the President of the *Giunta* combines ceremonial and governing roles. This figure performs three distinct functions involving regional and national governments: representation of the region, presiding over the *Giunta* and serving as chief of administration with responsibility for directing the administrative tasks mandated by the state conforming to instructions furnished by the national government. How these functions are carried out depends on the political party scene in the individual regions.

The presence of an official called a government commissioner illustrates the thrust of relations between the centre and the regions. Appointed by the national government, this official is its representative at the regional level. Something of a super-prefect, this person supervises the operation of the regional government and is assisted by the Regional Control Commission, a state organ. The commissioner and the Commission have a loosely defined veto over administrative

of relations with the state and many communes have dealt directly with Rome. The regions failed to provide the fulcrum for a sweeping reform of legislative and administrative principles and methods (Ferraresi 1991; Fossati 1990). It must be remembered that although the regions have not lived up to expectations, they have great potential. As Putnam writes: '*most institutional history moves slowly*' (Putnam 1993: 184). In the case of institution-building, decades are required.

Summary and conclusion

Around the world, local governments are experiencing difficult times. Those in Italy are no exception. Devolution in form has not meant devolution in fact. Throughout the First Republic, strong political parties and the clientelistic pattern ensured that uniformity and control would prevail. One may speak of uniformity and centralization. However, in contradictory fashion, new channels for communication of the needs and demands of the citizenry as well as the multiplication of local politico-administrative agencies have created new centres of power and new pressure groups, all of which have transformed, politicized, fragmented and complicated the power map. There are many relatively autonomous centres of power manifesting varied strengths at different times, creating tension throughout the intergovernmental system. The state is not the only centre of power in the regional state, although it is the dominant one. The birth of the various leagues with their stress on localism may be seen as a manifestation of anti-statism and a call for local autonomy. All of these local units of government interact in such a way that 'there is an everchanging movement through which power presents itself in an infinite number of ways varying in time and in space, at one time united and exclusive, at another, deeply divided and split up' (Rescigno 1984: 573).

This situation has created a myriad of problems, many of which have been addressed by the 1990 reform. Unfortunately, not all of its provisions have been implemented. The various actors responsible for implementation, principally the regions, have dragged their feet. This could mean that the gap between the northern and southern regions will be widened, with the former being more sensitive to relations with local entities and the latter more jealous of their functions. Given that regional legislators did not seriously re-evaluate local governmental units as required, the reform did not lead to new patterns of intergovernmental relations as hoped (D'Ignazio 1997).

The Prodi Government has confronted this problem with its 1998 announcement of a new devolution of power over a three-year period. The objective is to have a less weighty state and more powerful regions. The centre, being concerned with core business, will maintain powers of direction and control and relations with the EU. The rest are to be delegated to the periphery. There will be a massive transfer of funds and human resources with the new responsibilities. One must take a 'wait and see' attitude to these changes. The calls for federalism by the Northern League have had considerable resonance throughout the nation. Almost all of the parties in the Second Republic agree that some kind of federalism should be developed. However, as on most major reform issues, there is little consensus as to what form federalism should take.

11 Italy and the European Union

Contrasting behaviour

It has been noted that Italy is a land of contradictions. Nowhere is this more evident than in its relations with the EU. First known as the European Economic Community (EEC) with three component parts, the European Economic Community, the European Atomic Energy Community (Euratom) and the Coal and Steel Community, it later became known as the European Community (EC) and then the European Union (EU). Italy is a founding member of the EEC, and all Italian governments save one have been enthusiastic supporters of the organization. Even before the birth of the EEC, Article 11 of the Italian Constitution established limits on national sovereignty when necessary for ensuring peace and justice among nations. This article has been raised frequently in discussions of the EC-EU. No other major member-state of the organization has such a limitation and in some of these countries, notably Great Britain, the issue of giving up sovereignty has been a contentious one. For the last quarter of a century all major Italian political parties, with some variation in motives and attitudes, in their programmes have favoured the EC-EU or, at least, not opposed it. Until the impact of the Maastricht Treaty began to be felt, there were no large interest groups opposed to the organization (Chiti-Batelli 1995). The economic elites, through their most prominent spokesmen, such as Gianni Agnelli of Fiat, made it clear that they believed Italy's future rested with Europe.

The general public has clearly and frequently manifested its support for the EU. In polling carried out by the EU publication *Eurobarometer*, Italy has consistently ranked among the top member-states in terms of popular support for the EU and more European integration (*Eurobarometer* 1996). Of the big four member-states, France, Germany, Great Britain and Italy, the last had by far the most favourable image of the EU. Of the citizens of the major member-states, Italians felt the greatest trust in the EU (*Eurobarometer* 1997). Italian advocates for the EU point to a non-binding referendum held in Italy in 1989. In this election, 88 per cent of those voting supported the EU and indicated a positive attitude towards further integration. Parliamentarians for the European Federalist Movement initiated the referendum. They hoped it would give the Italian government and Italy's members of the European Parliament (EP) the opportunity to advocate further integration.

This support for the EU would lead one to believe that Italians are knowledgeable about it, but such is not the case. On several occasions, the public and its leaders have indicated in polls that they desire more information about the organization (Pragma 1994). In a poll carried out for *The European*, 80 per cent of the Italian members of the EP thought that the media in their country portrayed the development of the EU poorly or very poorly (Smart 1997). The problem is compounded by the fact that, with one or two exceptions among the elite newspapers, the press gives little coverage to the EU (Gramoglia 1998). There is general support for the regional organization, in spite of the superficial knowledge of its operation, which abounds. A small group in the government, Parliament and interest associations is very knowledgeable, but it is very limited.

In sharp contrast to the broad-based statements of support by Italians for the EU has been Italy's behaviour within the organization. Until recently words like 'non-compliance', 'evasion', 'inaction' or worse could be applied to Italy's reaction to the EU's rules and decisions. The nation has not been a good citizen of the organization. In spite of considerable improvement, it still holds most records for the number of proceedings undertaken by the European Commission against it for lack of implementation of Community directives (Agostini 1990). The Commission has issued more reasoned opinions against Italy than any other member-state. In the years leading to the 1992 programme and the initiation of the Single Market, Italy was notoriously behind other EU countries in converting almost 400 decrees from Brussels into national law. This situation prevailed in spite of a decision by the Italian Constitutional Court, which held that EU law is superior to national law. Even when directives were transposed into Italian law, often this was done very late. It is noteworthy that while other nations anticipate new developments in the EU and act before they need to, Italy rarely does so (Giuliani 1996).

Throughout the history of the European Court of Justice, Italy has had the highest number of procedures against it of any EU member-state. It also ranks first in terms of judgements not executed. In numerous cases Italy was brought back to the Court for a second condemnation for the same action. Unlike some of the other member-states, it has shown no ability to resolve legal controversies in pre-judicial phases (Cialdino 1989).

In an attempt to improve Italy's standing in the EU, in 1989 a law was passed by the Italian Parliament which was directed at some of the major problems the country experienced with the organization (Koff 1994). This law, known as the Community Law, requires among other things an annual omnibus measure, the purpose of which is to convert a large number of EU decrees into Italian law. Given the complex and slow procedure of law-making in the Italian Parliament, since the inception of the EEC most of its directives and other measures have been addressed in Italy by executive decree. The new approach taken by the Community Law has improved the situation, but it has not eliminated it. In spite of fixed dates for the annual legislation, it has been late every year. Furthermore, when the annual bill is being considered in Parliament, if there is other pressing business, it receives cursory treatment to get it out of the way. Since the law has brought some improvement, there is hope that things will continue to get better. According to the Community Law, every six months the government is supposed to provide the Parliament with a report on its EU programme for the following half year. These statements have often been late and superficial in their treatment of complex subjects. More often than not, they have described what has occurred rather than future activities. In addition, the government is supposed to furnish the Parliament with an annual report on the European Court of Justice's pronouncements regarding Italy. The focus should be on issues of compliance with EU obligations. Again these reports have not achieved their goals.

As might be expected, inefficient and self-serving bureaucrats cause problems for Italy in its relations with the EU. Many EU policies become lost in the vast bureaucracy. Often if extra work is involved, or if there is a perceived threat to doing things as they have always been done, bureaucrats do not implement EU measures. This situation has resulted in the loss of monies to which Italy was entitled from various structural fund programmes. These arrangements were created to help member-states develop economic parity among the various regions in their nations. Obviously, the poorest areas have been hurt the most by this situation. This plus the slow spending of monies awarded and thefts have contributed to Italy's poor reputation in Brussels. Italy's negotiating role has also been hurt.

Support for the EU

Given these problems, why do the Italian people and their elites support the EU? There are several reasons. Following its defeat in the Second World War, the leaders of the morally and materially weak country felt it was essential to immediately rejoin the community of nations in order to gain legitimacy in the eyes of the world. This was especially important in a nation that long had an inferiority complex in world affairs. Italy became an early member of the North Atlantic Treaty Organization (NATO). When the European Coal and Steel Community was proposed in 1951, Italy was one of the first nations to support the idea. Membership was perceived as a concrete manifestation of the country's acceptance by European nations. Italy took pride in the fact that the single most important meeting leading to the creation of the EEC and Euratom was held in Messina, Sicily in 1955. The founding document of the EEC was signed in 1957 in the Italian capital and this so-called Treaty of Rome with its amendments remains the basic document which governs the organization.

Italy's choice of Europe seems natural, given the three bases of Italian foreign policy. These are Europeanism, Atlanticism and a Mediterranean orientation. In spite of considerable internal stress, with Italy having the largest Communist Party in Western Europe, the country became a loyal member of NATO. For some observers, this meant too much subservience to the United States. Italy has been a strong defender of Mediterranean interests in both NATO and the EU. It was instrumental in bringing Spain and Portugal into the latter, and it advocated new security strategies for the Mediterranean nations. It was one of the major forces in the EU which brought forward an imaginative Mediterranean initiative involving Europe, North Africa and some Middle East nations. This initiative, incorporated in the Barcelona Treaty, was broad-based and involved economic development, social and cultural efforts and new security arrangements, among other things. Unfortunately, to date the initiative has had limited success, mainly because of economic recessions in Western Europe. Overall, Italy kept a low profile in international affairs throughout the 1960s and 1970s, but it became more assertive in the 1980s and 1990s.

Emphasis has been given to the economic miracle of the 1950s and 1960s and the major social changes which it wrought. In the minds of the economic and political elites and the public, these were associated with the EEC. Continued economic growth in subsequent years, in spite of some setbacks, was further identified, especially in the North, with membership in the EC-EU. Investment funds and help for the South as a poor area also added to the popularity of the organization. This created a strong pragmatic dimension to the support for Europe.

During the last years of the Fascist regime, many of the leaders of the Resistance were committed to limiting national sovereignty and developing an integrated Europe as a way to forestall future wars and to help build a democratic Italy. While democracy came to Western Europe, the performance of the government during the First Republic was a great disappointment to many Italians. For a long period, in spite of considerable discussion of reform, few concrete measures were realized. There was hope that meeting EU standards would necessitate widespread change. Economists, financiers and others hoped that the enormous public debt which was accrued in the First Republic and uncontrolled public spending could be reduced under pressure from the EU. This is exactly what happened during the period of the technocratic Dini and Ciampi Governments and during the Prodi Government.

Specific EC-EU goals have been attractive to Italy. From the time the organization started, Italy favoured the removal of barriers to the flow of workers across borders. It was thought this would help with unemployment problems, especially in the South. Several of the European countries developed what became known as the Schengen Agreement, and Italy adhered to it. The agreement called for the elimination of borders among signatory powers. It also aimed at limiting the movement of illegal immigrants. Once again Italy had difficulty meeting obligations (Roggero 1995). Thus, its formal entry into the agreement was delayed a few years. When in 1998 it finally became a full member, considerable fanfare marked the occasion. Although the Schengen Agreement is not a formal part of the EU structure, it operates alongside it.

Almost all members of the Italian Parliament would describe themselves as supporters of the EU. At the same time, most of them would concede that they possess little knowledge about it. This must be combined with the fact that they generally believe their constituents, while seeming to be supporters, were not really concerned about the workings of the organization in distant Brussels.

Among the parliamentarians, there are notable exceptions. The leadership group, including the heads and members of certain commissions, such as the foreign affairs commission in each chamber, is not only knowledgeable but also takes an active interest in the EU. Two special parliamentary units are concerned with European subject matter. The Senate has a council for European affairs, while in the Chamber of Deputies there is a special committee for European policy. While these have done some good work, not having the prestige and power of the standing commissions, their effectiveness has been limited.

In all member countries, national politicians criticize Brussels about specific policies and shift the blame to the EU for controversial decisions and norms. This has happened less frequently in Italy than in other member-states. Decisions in Brussels about subsidies to the steel industry and reductions in payments to milk farmers brought clamorous protests to Italy and even some violence. Politicians walked a tightrope between supporting national interests and adhering to European policy. When the intense moments of protest faded, no lasting criticism of the EU continued.

Institutional problems and leadership issues

The bureaucracy has also hurt Italy's relations with the EU. Even when European policies have been accepted at the political level in Rome, implementation is frequently delayed within the administrative structure. The bureaucracy's antagonism to innovation enters the picture. Frequent ministerial change and clientelistic politics have permitted bureaucrats to thwart the wishes of the policy makers. The bureaucracy has been significantly immune from pressures from outside its ranks, and the EU has been seen more as a disturbance than anything else (Giuliani 1992).

Italy has been less able to cope with Europe than other EU member-states. In part, this has occurred because the political system has had to face many crises and pressing problems. Equally important is its organization. The Ministry of Foreign Affairs has major responsibility for relations with the EU. It has been very protective of this role and at times it has been less than forthright with other parts of the government. With one exception, foreign affairs ministers have been enthusiastic pro-Europeans. However, given the turnover in this position, continuity in dealing with the EU has been lacking. The professional staff of the foreign service, most of whom have had worldwide experience, while not being sceptical of the EU, often are either indifferent to it or see it as a challenge to the traditional Italian foreign policy process.

Ministers, other than foreign secretaries, are involved in EU affairs if the subject matter relates to their responsibilities. However, they have generally been subservient to the Ministry of Foreign Affairs. Some keep offices in Brussels. Sometimes this has created confusion and contradictions between the foreign affairs staff and that of other ministries. There is also a Ministry for the Coordination of Community Policy. Being located in the Presidency of the

Council of Ministers, the executive office of the Prime Minister, it is not a full-fledged ministry. It has been understaffed and has not enjoyed strong leadership. Being loath to cede any of its responsibility, the foreign affairs ministry has not been helpful to it. Hence, it has been a disappointment to many observers, especially in its inability to fulfil its major responsibility, the coordination of European policy. Some coordination has been undertaken by the Interministerial Committee for Economic Planning. However, with all of its pressing responsibilities, this committee has not been able to devote much time to wide-ranging EU matters.

The Italian mission to the EU has been weaker than those of the other major member-states. Leadership at the highest level has been strong, but on the middle and lower levels the personnel have not been well-prepared (Noel 1993) and a traditional bureaucratic mentality has caused difficulties. In addition, Rome often offers poor support. Frequently the mission does not receive instructions, or when it does, they are late, unclear and sometimes contradictory. Given the relations with Rome, the mission probably has more independence than most of the others. This has not helped the development of a coordinated national policy towards the EU.

Compared to officials from other large member-states, Italians have held few leading positions in the EU organization. Frequently cited is the experience of the only Italian to hold the post of the President of the Commission. In the 1970s when it was Italy's turn to fill this position, most suitable candidates were reluctant to leave Rome. Finally, Franco Maria Malfatti was persuaded to accept the office. Complaining that he could not be away from Rome any longer, after less than two years, he resigned. He felt his career in the Christian Democratic Party was being damaged by his absence from the Italian capital. He had very little impact on the Commission, and no other Italian has been seriously considered for the presidency since that time. Other capable Italians have chosen not to leave Rome for work in Brussels.

In the case of Commissioners appointed by Italy, there have been several successful ones but, more often than not, they have been mediocre. Also, frequently there have been delays in Rome in making these appointments, and when they are finally made, the most important commission posts have been filled. Part of the problem results from the fact that coalition governments have made appointments and there have been difficult negotiations among the several parties in the coalitions. In 1994 this kind of internal conflict occurred within the centre-right government (Romano 1994). The appointment of Mario Monti, a highly respected conservative economist, caused no difficulty. He became the Commissioner for the Internal Market, Financial Services and Taxes, and he has been successful. The second position allotted to Italy became a political football within the government. The office went to Emma Bonino, a long-time activist in the small Radical Party. She was championed by Marco Panella, who with his personal electoral list supported the Freedom Pole. As Commissioner for Humanitarian Aid, Consumer Policies and Fisheries, she too has impressed people with her energy and work.

It would be incorrect to leave the impression that few, if any, Italian political leaders had an impact on the EU. As noted earlier, Alcides De Gasperi, the first Prime Minister of the First Republic, took Italy on the road to Europeanism. While he died before the birth of the EEC in 1957, he, along with Robert Schuman and Jean Monnet of France and Konrad Adenauer of Germany, was a central actor in the beginnings of Western European integration. If one person had to be identified as the most influential Italian in the history of the EC-EU, it would be Altiero Spinelli. While interned in a Fascist prison camp, with two others he authored a document entitled *The Manifesto of Ventotene* (Albertini 1982). This work became the clarion call of the Italian and European federalist movements. A good part of the Resistance was committed to a postwar unified Europe, and Spinelli was seen as its spokesman. During the early years of the first Republic Spinelli, as an advisor to De Gasperi and other leaders, advised them to pursue federal aims in Europe. His influence extended from DC leaders to Communists. His advice to the PCI leadership was an important factor in its accepting the EC and acknowledging European federalism as an appropriate road to pursue. Spinelli was a Communist in his younger years, but he left the party in order to work for his European federalist goals. Subsequently he was elected to the Chamber of Deputies and the European Parliament as an independent on the Communist ticket. He also served as an active Commissioner in Brussels.

In the 1980s, as a Member of the EP, Spinelli recommended that a European constitution be developed by a directly elected constituent assembly. While this did not happen, he did persuade the EP to move in that direction. In 1984 it approved the Draft Treaty on the European Union. Spinelli made a convincing attack on the Council of Ministers' arrogation of power. Among other things, the Draft Treaty called for a federal approach to economic and monetary affairs. It was a predecessor to the Single European Act, which was less ambitious and, therefore, more acceptable to most member-states. Article 1B of the act compelled member-states to accept 1992 as the date for completion of the internal market. Moreover, the EC was to be an 'area without internal frontiers in which the free movement of goods, persons, services and capital is ensured in accordance with the provisions of the Treaty'. Other important developments, such as the possibility of majority voting on some matters rather than uniform unanimous voting, resulted from the Act. Spinelli's commitment to federalism and his strong opposition to intergovernmentalism were central to many debates about the future of the regional organization.

There have been other leaders who have exerted influence on the EC-EU. However, they are better remembered for their role in domestic politics rather than European affairs. People such as Antonio Giolitti, Marco Panella and Filippo Maria Pandolfi, former prime ministers Emilio Colombo, Giuliano Andreotti and Bettino Craxi and former foreign minister De Michelis are often cited in the literature on the EU. The last three persons were found guilty or indicted for crimes not related to the EU. Their activities in European affairs do not seem to have enhanced their reputations in Italy.

The European Council, the executive of the EU, has a rotating presidency. Each member-state holds the position for six months on a rotating basis. While not a powerful position, it does focus attention on the occupant's nation during the six-month term. In contrast with some of its other activities, Italy has had five successful presidencies: 1975, 1980, 1985, 1990 and 1995. However, credit received for numerous achievements is not as great as the self-accolades presented in the Italian media. In its role as president, Italy has demonstrated considerable skill as mediator, negotiator and facilitator. During its tenure in 1975 the economic recession was addressed, budget reform launched and a decision to hold direct elections for the European Parliament was taken. In 1980 when Prime Minister Thatcher seemed intransigent about the British contribution to the EC budget and spending for the Common Agricultural Programme, Italian Foreign Minister Emilio Colombo was a key figure in negotiating a compromise. Also during this Italian presidency, a major new policy statement on the Middle East was adopted. Named the Declaration of Venice, it called for all states to recognize the legitimate rights of Palestinians. For the time, this was a major step.

In 1985, with Craxi as Prime Minister and Andreotti as Minister of Foreign Affairs, Italy introduced the issue of majority voting. This was essential for the development of the Maastricht Treaty. During this presidency, it was agreed to move to the Single Market by 1992. The Italians were instrumental in achieving agreement on an institutional reform, the Intergovernmental Conference. At the same time, Italy advocated and delicately negotiated the entry of Spain and Portugal into the EU. Five years later during the Italian presidency, the guidelines and timetable for the Euro were fixed and the decision to create a European Central Bank was taken. Also, Italy successfully engineered the convening of an Intergovernmental Conference on the European Monetary Union and Political Union. The 1995 presidency came at a very difficult time for Italy and Europe. The nation was experiencing another governmental crisis, and had a technocratic government during most of its European semester. Also, it faced parliamentary elections. The EU member-states were also deeply divided over the issue of mad cow disease, and it took all Italy's negotiating skill to achieve calm. This presidency also raised the need for a revision of the Maastricht Treaty (Ferraris 1996).

Another institution in which Italy has done well is the EP. Cynics argue that this has happened because the EP does not count for a great deal in the European system. A strong supporter of the Parliament, Italy has been a staunch advocate of increasing its powers. Although enhanced by the Single European Act, the EP for the most part has limited powers and is best known for its role as a forum on European and world issues. In addition to Spinelli, numerous top leaders have represented Italy in Strasbourg. Italy permits a double mandate whereby a person can be a member of the European and Italian Parliaments at the same time. This allows parties to include their top leaders in their delegations to the EP. This practice has had both positive and negative results. The leaders, as members of the EP, have become more knowledgeable about the EU and several have taken an active role in the representative body. However, frequently pressing business in Rome forces them to neglect their responsibilities in Strasbourg.

Italy was one of the nations which staunchly advocated the direct election of EP representatives. Italian leaders argued that this arrangement would enhance the role of that body and help with the EU's democratic image. Unfortunately, the elections proved to be a disappointment. As is the case in almost all member-states, in Italy the elections have been fought on national issues and have revolved around national politics. The parties prepare campaign programmes about Europe, but they receive meagre attention in the media or by leaders. The June 1994 European parliamentary election is a case at point. The campaign was a debate on the recently appointed Berlusconi Government. The Prime Minister, while mentioning some EU issues, used the election to ask the voters for a vote of confidence, after having been in office only a month.

In the four elections since the first in 1979, Italy has used a basic list system of proportional representation. Within the list system, the voters have the option of indicating preferences among the candidates. Citizens of other EU member-states can be candidates in Italy. For the purpose of this election, the country is divided into five large districts: Northeast, Northwest, Central, South and the Islands. As one of the big four members of the regional organization, the nation has 87 seats in the EP. The allocation of seats is divided among the electoral districts on the basis of population. Voter turnout, compared to other elections in Italy, has been low and it is clear voter interest has not been great (Koff 1995).

Italy's image in Europe

In spite of being a founding member and one of the big four nations in the EU, Italy has felt like a poor relative (Caracciolo 1997). In part as a result of the German–French axis, which dominated so many EU activities and Britain's keen sense of independence, Italy has often been isolated and appeared less than influential. There are several reasons for Italy's inferiority complex. First, in spite of the extensive rhetoric about its support for the EC-EU, its poor record in adhering to the organizations' rules, regulations and policies has made its commitment suspect. Second, Italy's internal problems, especially during the First Republic, appeared so serious that it was thought the country could not be a good EU citizen. The instability of its government meant there was frequent turnover in the ministers coming to Brussels. The problem of dealing with the Italian bureaucracy has already been emphasized. Italy's poor record in financial matters raised questions about its reliability. Its uncontrolled government spending and its huge public debt plus frequent periods of high inflation appeared almost insurmountable. The Prodi Government's successful efforts in financial matters brought some change in attitude among Italy's fellow member-states. Although a residue of doubt exists, there is a feeling that the Second Republic is going to be different from the First.

Other ills, such as the South of Italy, which was seen as one of the poorest regions in the EU, have caused concern to many in that organization. They thought the long-term costs of development in the South would be a considerable drain on the EU's financial resources. Highly visible problems such as illegal immigration, violence, crime and general social unrest were also considered. Dramatic activities by the Mafia and other terrorist organizations were widely reported throughout Europe. The murders of journalists, judges, police and government officials plus the kidnapping and murder of former Prime Minister Aldo Moro severely damaged Italy's reputation. Although the nation has made considerable progress in its war against violent crime and terrorism, occasional heinous acts make Europeans think the war has not been totally won.

General corruption, especially in the public sector, further damaged Italy's image. *Tangentopoli* seemed to confirm what Europeans had long believed about Italy. Theft of EU funds in record amounts at the regional and local levels injured Italy's credibility even more. It is estimated that for every 100 ECUs (the EU monetary unit) fraudulently used in Europe, 56 are used in Italy (Tropeano 1994). A European Commission annual report ranks Italy first or second among the member-states for actions regarding the misuse of structural funds (European Commission 1997). One famous case of theft involved an Archbishop in Palermo who was accused of defrauding Brussels of more than half a million dollars (Endean 1997).

In the last fifteen years, extensive immigration to Italy, both legal and illegal, has been seen as causing problems for the northern nations within the EU. Italy has had a large influx of people from the Developing World and Eastern Europe. It has made some efforts to slow the movement of these people to its shores, but it has had limited success. Having water on three sides has made it difficult to curb illegal immigration. This has been most evident in recent years with the arrival of clandestine Albanians and Kurds, who come during the night in small boats. The northern countries fear that the immigrants have as their goal moving from Italy to other EU member-states. Even Italy's adherence to the principle of the Schengen Agreement did not reassure them.

Efforts of the Prodi Government to qualify for the single European currency have been central to its programme. In some respects, Prodi gambled the success of his government on Italy's entrance into the Euro-club. He convinced the nation that, while there were heavy short-term costs, the long-term benefits would be substantial. The latter would include eliminating exchange costs, curbing inflation further, stabilizing exchange rate fluctuations and promoting a reduction in interest rates. All these should help stimulate the economy. EU parameters are a useful prod to achieve what should be the goal of all governments. Two former prime ministers, Dini and Ciampi, as members of the Prodi Government, carried much of the burden in the pursuit of membership in the single currency group.

In order to meet the Maastricht requirements, the Prodi Government reduced the budget deficit to under 3 per cent of the gross national product and imposed a one-time Euro-tax which it promises to return to the taxpayers. The sacrifices were sold to the public by saying that Italy had no real alternative and even a temporary delay in the nation's entry into the Euro-circle could, in effect, mean a relegation to a second division of member-states and inferior status. Italy, always conscious of its international status, wanted to avoid this at all costs. There has been some criticism of the government's actions, given the high rate of unemployment, especially in the South and among youth. Critics believe that remedying the unemployment situation should have precedence over all other policies. After Italy qualified for the single currency, certain foreign leaders, especially in the Netherlands and Germany, publicly questioned whether Italy could sustain its financial reforms over time. However, Italy was among the eleven that qualified for the Euro-club in 1998. There was extensive celebration and the stock market reacted very positively (Suseri 1998). Even the opposition parties, with the exception of a few leaders, joined the general approval of passing the Euro-test.

The achievements of the Prodi Government in considerably sanitizing the nation's financial situation could not have occurred in the First Republic. The nature of the parties and the political process was such that reform of pensions, cuts in social services and reductions of subsidies to sheltered government corporations were almost impossible to realize. The governing parties, especially the DC, which used government spending for electoral purposes, feared voter retaliation if they cut public spending. It should be recalled that in 1992 the value of the lire fell and the currency had to be deflated because of the high public debt, elevated interest rates and rampant inflation. Italy had to leave the exchange rate mechanism. This was a blow to the nation's economy and its standing in Europe. Although Great Britain, whose adherence to Europe was less than Italy's, also left the European Monetary System at the same time, it was Italy that felt most marginalized.

Regions and the EU

From the very beginning of the EEC, Italian leaders thought in terms of that organization helping the development of its poorest areas. Until some of the poorer Mediterranean countries joined the EC-EU, the Italian South was clearly the most needy region in the organization. It continues to be among the poorest. In its early years, the organization did little to benefit the South. Its agricultural policy aided the crops of northern Europe and northern Italy, which included grains, rice and similar items. The fruits and vegetables central to the economy of the Italian South received little assistance. The gap between the North and South widened. Thus Italy, in one of its most forceful efforts in the EEC, fought for a new regional policy which resulted in the European Regional Development Fund. This had a slow start in 1975 because of the severe impact of the oil embargo of 1973–4, but there was a steady increase in the funds committed to it. Accounting for 11 per cent of the EU budget in the middle 1990s, Italy was a beneficiary of a significant portion of these funds. There are other structural funds dedicated to poor regions. The Commissioner for Regional Policy in Brussels informed the Italian Budget Minister that the spending of structural funds for 1994–5 was abnormally low. For the period of 1994–9 only 2.5 per cent of the monies allocated for use in the South had been utilized by 1996. This figure should have been 30 per cent (Brusco 1997; Carli 1997).

Another problem, noted earlier, is that Italy has not applied for significant amounts of money available from the EU. This is particularly true of the regional governments, which complain that often they are not informed by their national counterpart of the availability of EU funds. In most cases this occurs because national bureaucrats do not bother to notify them. Things are improving, as some regions have opened offices in Brussels and are using consulting firms to aid them in obtaining EU monies.

Difficulties between regional and national governments go beyond the issue of structural funds. When the regional governments were born, the national government considered EEC policy to be part of the foreign policy domain of Rome. All contacts with Brussels from Italy had to be through the Ministry of Foreign Affairs. Even the implementation of EEC policy by the regions had strict limitations. A national law had to be passed before regions could act. Also, if the national government considered regional acts inappropriate, it could substitute for their actions. Subsequently, decisions by the Constitutional Court established very limited autonomy for the regions in dealing with Brussels. This did not change matters very much in practice.

A presidential decree in 1977 made the process less rigid, but it did not satisfy regional desires. Moreover, the national government did little to recognize the law's thrust. In 1988, Law Number 400 firmly established a legal distinction between foreign and EC affairs. This was followed by the Community Law of 1989, the La Pergola law, which mandated that the State–Region Conference hold special biannual sessions devoted to Community matters. The impact of these meetings has not been great, especially because their opinions are not binding. In spite of some changes, the national government continues to dominate the regions in EU matters. The sub-national units do not participate in the development of policies regarding the EU. This is very different than the situation in Germany and Austria. It is not surprising that the regions have been strong supporters of subsidiarity throughout the EU member-states. Since federalism is being seriously discussed in terms of reform in Italy, relations between the national and regional governments regarding the EU will likely change.

Conclusion

There is no doubt that the Europeanization of Italy has occurred. It is also clear that the rules and regulations of the EU have impacted on Italy, and will undoubtedly do so in a greater fashion in the future. This means changing behaviour and attitudes in several parts of the government, and such a process comes slowly. The rigid legalistic culture, the antediluvian bureaucratic system and the general institutional style impede the alterations required. Also, the long-standing Italian tendency to bend or bypass laws and regulations when possible will be difficult to overcome. When the achievements of the Prodi Government in bringing Italy into the Euro-club in less than two years are considered, Italy's future in the EU looks solid; but there remain problems which could become serious. Continued control of government spending and inflation are the most serious threats to Italy's position in Europe.

12 Italy

Difficulties in facing the millennium

The word 'crisis' has been used extensively by political leaders, scholars and journalists when discussing government and politics in Italy. All nations face crises from time to time, but the frequency and depth of the Italian crises have been greater than those in other Western democracies. In terms of depth, an exception to this would be the change from the Fourth to the Fifth Republic in France.

At one level, crises refer to the coming and going of governments. It should be recalled that there have been more than fifty since the birth of the First Republic. In the Second Republic, many hoped that stability would develop. Instead, however, there have been three governments in four years. Along with the governmental crises themselves, there have been innumerable threats of crises which have paralysed governments for significant periods. It often seems that Italy has constantly been either going into a crisis, is in a crisis or is just coming out of one.

However, the formal use of the word 'crisis' as related to the comings and goings of governments is only a part of the picture. Italy has had more than its share of economic crises as well. Some of these have resulted, at least in part, from the economic problems of the industrialized world. For example, there is the severe unemployment situation which Italy shares with Western Europe. However, parts of these crises and several others have been of the nation's own doing. Excessive government spending, a huge public debt and corrupt practices have often undermined the many achievements of the Italian economy. Furthermore, clientelistic behaviour, aside from real corruption by political leaders and parties in their relations with parts of the economy, has further damaged it. Although things have improved in the Second Republic, there continues to be fear that in some areas Italy could fall back to its mistaken ways.

It is not only governmental and economic crises that the nation has experienced. Some of these have been cited earlier in this volume. A series of threats to the entire system have sorely tested Italian democracy. By systemic standards, the First Republic had only a few years to plant its roots firmly before serious dangers to it emerged. In 1960, in response to a government which relied on support from the MSI, massive numbers of people took to the streets to protest the new role of the neo-fascists. There were deaths and injuries in several cities.

The government led by Fernando Tambroni, a DC leader, was forced to resign in face of the protests. In the middle of the 1960s, threats to the system coming from the secret service (in this case the military secret service, SIFAR) shocked the nation. Other secret service groups were subsequently involved in behaviour that seemed threatening.

In 1968, Italy, like other Western nations, faced militant protests by students who were joined by other radical groups. These protests were followed a year later by the Hot Autumn. Soon after, intense terrorism of the left and the right developed with the Red Brigades being most prominent. Many persons and considerable property fell victim to this terrorism. In spite of a great demonstration of solidarity with their democratic system, the confidence of the populace was further undermined. The P2 scandal emerged in the early 1980s. Still being debated in public is the undemocratic so-called Gladio super-secret defence plan against a potential communist threat. Moreover, the Mafia and its actions spread with impunity as well. The question became: could the democracy, which overcame each of these crises separately, survive an accumulation of them?

Usually in democracies, when a nation faces a crisis, its democratic nature does not come into question. That has not been the case in Italy. In other countries when crises occur, it is asked why the system is not working properly. In Italy the issue becomes the nature of democracy. There exists a vast literature devoted to the topic of the survival of Italian democracy. In addition, there are numerous works focusing on the related question of whether the nation is governable. By the standards of other Western democracies, it is understandable that both Italians and foreign observers question whether Italy is governable. However, this question cannot be asked in a vacuum. It avoids the fundamental point that the state, economy and society are intermingled and interdependent.

This is evident in the experience of the Prodi Government, which gained considerable popularity in its first two years. However, early in its third year its future was threatened. More than anything else, severe unemployment undercut both mass and elite confidence in the government. A general strike was threatened and many street demonstrations occurred. While it shares the problem of unemployment with most of Western Europe, a solution is more difficult in Italy. The issue of the costs of social benefits over and above salaries is a critical one. These costs are the highest in the industrialized world, and are estimated to range up to 90 per cent of salary. Further complicating the problem of unemployment is the dichotomy between the North and the South.

Since 1948, Italy has had one constitutional system. The number of formal amendments to the Constitution has been few, and the amendments themselves not of great significance. In practice, the Constitution has been flexible. It allowed an impoverished and defeated nation to accomplish enormous social and economic transformation. In spite of the lack of major change in the institutional structure, there have been new developments in political behaviour, not always for the better. *Partitocrazia* led to a blocked and overloaded system. In the 1980s and 1990s, elites and masses demanded changes in political arrangements. These demands focused on institutional reform.

Special legislative commissions were established, and these worked long and hard on the problem. Several major proposals were developed, but all came to naught because no agreement could be reached among the competing political forces. When, in 1997, a bicameral parliamentary commission was created, optimism was considerable. The major parties, with the exception of the Northern League, seemed committed to making reform work. This was another new development in the Second Republic. It was quickly agreed that Massimo D'Alema of the PDS should be President of the *Bicamerale*, as it was called. A clear agenda and a precise schedule for the commission's work were accepted. Its start was auspicious. The plan was for the commission to agree on proposals, which would be acted upon by the Parliament. When this assembly completed its work, the people would have their say in a referendum.

The major issues addressed were (1) strengthening the executive, (2) a revision of the electoral law, (3) federalism, (4) redesigning the Parliament and (5) judicial reform. The last was the most contentious subject. Two basic models for strengthening the executive were debated. The first called for semi-presidentialism similar to the French system. It involved a directly-elected President who would appoint the Prime Minister. The second was close to the German chancellor system. It differed because it called for a directly-elected Prime Minister who would not need parliamentary confidence. Opinion in the *Bicamerale* favoured the first model. The basic proposal regarding the electoral law called for an end to proportional representation. The mixed system was to be substituted with a single-member district run-off arrangement. Obviously, the small parties staunchly opposed this change.

Italy was to become a federal state. The regions were to have much more autonomy, including the all-important fiscal autonomy. This arrangement received support, in part, in order to lessen the threat of the Northern League. The League opposed the proposal, deeming it too moderate. As far as Parliament was concerned, it was to be smaller in size and the Senate was to become a federal body based on regional representation. Judicial reform was the most divisive issue. Berlusconi's legal situation was directly involved. Since he was under indictment, he strongly advocated that the judicial system be changed. More specifically, he demanded that prosecutors and judges have separate careers. D'Alema acquiesced to Berlusconi's proposal in order to get the total package of reform accepted. Members of the judicial system and others strongly criticized Berlusconi's position as an attack on the independence of the judiciary.

The *Bicamerale* finished its work in June 1997. Parliament immediately began to consider its proposals. Agreements that had been taken earlier were broken. The atmosphere became increasingly poisoned. Most of the major actors seemed to revert to roles of defending the interests of their parties. Berlusconi publicly stated that if his views on the judiciary were not accepted, he would scuttle all reform. When, in June 1998, the Parliament did not meet its deadline to finish the reform effort, the *Bicamerale* was declared dead. Its failure was a serious blow to the Second Republic, which at this point, did not look very different from the First. The reasons for the failure were many. The various parties had different agendas and diverse expectations related to outcome. Many reputations were tarnished, especially that of D'Alema, who hoped to use the *Bicamerale* to overcome his severe partisan reputation. However, in typical Italian fashion, whatever damage was done to D'Alema's image was not irreparable. How much damage the failure did to the Olive Tree Government is difficult to assess. During the proceedings of the *Bicamerale*, Prodi distanced himself from the commission. He seemed to believe that running the government was more important than taking a personal role in the reform effort. But with D'Alema as President of the *Bicamerale*, its failure reflected badly on the Olive Tree.

What is the future of reform in Italy? It will probably advance in separate pieces. Currently there is a referendum movement, led by Di Pietro and Segni, which is calling for a public vote on changing the electoral law by eliminating proportional representation. This referendum is very likely to succeed. However, both the Freedom Pole and the Olive Tree are divided on the issue. There is interest in convening a Constituent Assembly to rewrite the Constitution. This raises a few questions. Who can call the elections to select a new Constituent Assembly with a new electoral law? Who is authorized to pass the new law? Who can promulgate it? With the Constitution not providing answers to these questions, it means that if such occurred, from a juridical perspective it would represent a *coup d'état*. Complete sovereignty would be in the hands of a Constituent Assembly which would reorient the Constitution, according to which sovereignty resides with the people. And to whom is the remaking of the Constitution assigned? The fact of the matter is that this is not known (Barile 1995).

Consideration must be given to the spirit and the values represented by the fundamental law. It is these which make it significant and which must not be lost. Thus, it might not be wise to discard a document rooted in the Resistance to Fascism and based on a pact of groups representing the central subcultures. There is no guarantee that another such pact could be facilely concluded. Given the present environment, chances are it could not. On the one hand, the Republican Constitution has served the Italian people well and allowed for the multi-faceted development of the country. On the other hand, parties and the political class have manoeuvred the political system in a negative fashion. A new fundamental law cannot assure that appropriate respect for the spirit of democracy will be forthcoming. Moreover, many of the proposed institutional reforms can be undertaken within the framework of the existing document. It is true that the society for which it was written, as noted throughout this volume, has changed drastically. Political structures can be made congruent with these changes. Obviously some institutional reform is necessary. However, there is a danger of constitutional fetishism. The rules may change, but if the way they are applied is not modified, real reform cannot take place.

As described earlier, the Second Republic is something of a leadership state. Clearly, the mindset of the leaders must change. Many words are being exchanged about the Second Republic and the new political setting. The new political class must learn not only about the responsibility of government, but also about the responsibility of opposition. Constitutionalism or limited government is at the foundation of the Anglo-American democratic systems. It has several dimensions. First and foremost, a rule of law exists which, among other things, limits extreme behaviour by governments. In addition, opposition sees to it that governments operate in the open and in a responsible way. Furthermore, the opposition offers concrete alternatives to government programmes, and in testing the government usually compromises arise. Berlusconi and his colleagues have not offered well-developed policy alternatives, nor do they fully understand the spirit of compromise.

Unfortunately, the Second Republic started with a severe bitterness between the government and the opposition, and even within the governing coalition. Intemperate language was used frequently and continued through the periods of the Dini and Prodi Governments. It seems curious that with the decline of ideology and seemingly less depth in the divisions among the parties, the conflictual discourse has continued unabated. A sense of commitment to the nation instead of to parties will have to develop. This is what was lacking during the First Republic; so far, it has not been a feature of the Second Republic. It is essential for Italian democracy to work better. Although we use the phrase 'the Second Republic' throughout this volume, it is obvious that this Republic has not been consolidated. The transition from the First Republic to the Second is still ongoing, and many questions remain. The new major actors behave in a way similar to those of the First Republic. Much has been done, but a great deal remains to be done.

13 Postscript

On 9 October 1998 the Prodi Government, the second longest in post-Second World War Italian history, fell. This was not a total surprise, but for many it was unexpected when it happened. Until a few days before it lost a vote of confidence by only one vote in the Chamber of Deputies, it appeared that the government would carry on for at least several more months. As described earlier, it was a centre-left government which depended on the PRC for its majority. At best, the relationship with the PRC was an uneasy one. The issue which brought down the government was its finance bill. PRC leader Bertinotti was dissatisfied because it did not promise a thirty-five-hour working week aimed at reducing unemployment. Also, he felt that several social programmes, especially those related to health care, were not adequate. Besides these specific issues, it appeared to him that politically it was time to move his party into opposition.

Bertinotti's decision to withdraw support from the Prodi Government led to a schism in his own party. Twenty-one members led by party president Armando Cossutta left its ranks to form the Party of Italian Communists. As indicated above, Cossutta was a long-time leader of the PCI. In 1991, when it changed its name to the PDS and moderated its programme, he led the walkout from the convention, taking with him Communist militants. At the time he was recognized as the most prominent leader of the newly-created PRC. He and his followers, who left the PRC in 1998 because of its stance concerning support for the Prodi Government, contended that the time was wrong for causing its downfall. They foresaw the distinct possibility that an election might have to be called, and they realized there was a good chance that a centre-right government, led by Berlusconi, would be returned to power. Moreover, they feared that voters would punish the PRC for the fall of the centre-left government.

Since Prodi lost the vote of confidence by only one vote, it was logical that President Scalfaro invite him to try to form a new government. Initially, Prodi stated that he would only lead an Olive Tree coalition, the one the voters had supported in the 1996 election. It quickly became evident that he would not be able to form a new majority government. At a later date he modified his position on a broadened coalition, but by then it was too late. At this point the situation became very unclear. The opposition vociferously called for new elections. The outgoing government and the economic elites in the country were deeply concerned about a lengthy government crisis or an intense electoral campaign. They were particularly worried because the first phase of the Euro was scheduled to go into effect in January 1999. They believed that stability in government was especially critical in this moment. If an election was not to be called, the only alternative seemed to be another non-party technocratic government.

While speculation about who might head a technocratic government and the possibility of an election continued, behind the scenes negotiations aimed at the creation of a new and much broader coalition were taking place. The negotiators were Massimo D'Alema and Francesco Cossiga. The broad coalition headed by D'Alema which resulted from these meetings came as a surprise to the nation. Ranging from the far left of the political spectrum with the Italian Communists to the centre which included Cossiga's UDR, it was much broader than Prodi's Olive Tree coalition. For D'Alema and the Democrats of the Left, it meant that the party would not only be the largest in the government, as it had been in the Olive Tree coalition, but for the first time in Italian history a leader from the former Communist movement would serve as prime minister. It must be remembered that the PDS and the Democrats of the Left have been moving towards a social democratic position throughout the 1990s. The creation of the D'Alema Government was the culmination of a long march from the period of the Cold War, in which the PCI was isolated and excluded from the government, to the prime ministership.

For Cossiga, who had been an ally of the Freedom Pole, joining the government further legitimized his party and increased its prestige. Moreover, in terms of long-term goals, entering the governing coalition is another step towards the realization of his objective to recreate a Christian Democratic party which hopefully would dominate the centre of the political spectrum. As a power-broker for the new government, Cossiga is in the forefront of national political discourse. Many believe that if he is successful in creating a large centre party, in the future it could come into conflict with D'Alema's Democrats of the Left. But for the time being, working together suits both leaders.

The breadth of the government means that numerically it is strong. It enjoys a solid majority in the Parliament. It should have few difficulties passing considerable amounts of legislation which can be agreed upon. However, the breadth of the coalition is also its weakness. Satisfying the interests of several very diverse parties will be a difficult task. The Prodi Government was at times open to pressure, or, according to some people, blackmail, from the PRC. D'Alema will have to contend with the centrist UDR as well as the left-wing Italian Communists. If it can stay together, and that is a big 'if', the coalition should be able to confront many major issues.

The opposition, dominated by the parties of the Freedom Pole, felt considerable satisfaction when the Prodi Government fell. These parties believed that there was a good chance that an election would be called and if this occurred, they were optimistic that the results would bring them back to power. The surprise arrival of the D'Alema Government generated considerable and very vocal anger within the Pole, which referred to it as a clandestine government. For the most part this anger was aimed at Cossiga and his followers. The language of the Pole's complaints was very strong. Cossiga was repeatedly called a traitor. The Pole argued that UDR deputies were elected as centre to right representatives, and they should not have suddenly joined a government led by a former Communist leader and which included ministers who, until recently, had been members of the PRC. Their extreme language went far beyond normal political rhetoric. The attacks seemed to be more than a manifestation of frustration and disappointment. As stated earlier, a responsible opposition is one of the things which must develop along with a stable government, if the Second Republic is to mature and be more successful than the First. Unfortunately, the opposition has been long on attacks and criticism and short on alternative programmes. Among other things, this does not bode well for the kind of collaboration required for basic institutional reform.

The D'Alema Government has twenty-five ministers who come from eight political parties. Since these parties are of diverse political persuasions, the ministers are very different in attitudes. There are carryovers from the Prodi Government, some of whom occupy the same positions and others who have new roles. Dini has returned as Minister of Foreign Affairs and Ciampi once again is Minister for the Budget and Treasury. Their appointments were seen as an effort to reassure the international community and, more specifically, the allies of Italy in the EU that the country's foreign and economic policies would not change. With the Euro coming into effect in January 1999, this was considered very important.

As can be imagined, inclusion of new parties in the coalition, Cossiga's UDR and Cossutta's newly-formed Party of Italian Communists, made negotiations for their representation in the government very delicate. In spite of their great differences in politics, the new parties were given positions of considerable importance. A member of the Party of Italian Communists was appointed Minister of Justice. Only a short time before the fall of the Prodi Government, he had very harsh words to say about Cossiga. The UDR received the Ministers of Defence and Communications. Three former prime ministers were included in the government. In addition to Dini and Ciampi, Giuliano Amato, a highly respected professor of constitutional law, was appointed Minister for Institutional Reform. This appointment was seen as a way to demonstrate the significance the new government assigned to reform.

There are six women in D'Alema's Cabinet, the largest number in any Italian Government ever. Furthermore, they hold important positions. Rosa Russo Jervolino of the PPI is the Minister of the Interior. This has always been a powerful position in Italy, and no woman ever held the post before. It assumed added importance in the period in which the government was created and beyond because of the many problems with immigrants, both legal and illegal. Rosy Bindi, also of the PPI, continues to be Minister of Health. Of the remaining four female ministers, two represent the Democrats of the Left and one each the Greens and the Party of Italian Communists. There are fifty-six undersecretaries, the second largest number in the post-Second World War era. The large number was necessary to satisfy the eight parties which supported the coalition. Many delicate and difficult negotiations occurred before there was consensus as to who would get which of these positions. Not only were individual and party considerations important, but delicate balance had to be created in several key ministries. In this respect the Second Republic, which was supposed to be different, is reminiscent of the First.

The programme of the D'Alema Government is ambitious. In many ways it is an extension of Prodi's governmental platform. First, the international commitments, especially those regarding the EU, including the Euro obligations, are to be maintained. Second, reform of governmental institutions is to be emphasized. It should be recalled that D'Alema was the president of the failed *Bicamerale* which dealt with such reform. During his presentation to Parliament in which he requested a vote of confidence, he included a candid statement related to the need for reform. He admitted the method whereby he came to power demonstrated the difficulties of the Italian political system. He noted that he was not the head of an elected government, but rather was in his current position because of shifting alliances in Parliament. In the calls for reform, a change in the electoral law has top priority. Most proposals on this subject include the elimination of PR or a drastic limitation on it. On this issue, the government faces problems not only with the opposition, but also within its own ranks. The small parties in the coalition oppose the elimination of PR because it would do obvious harm to their electoral chances. There continues to be the possibility of a referendum on electoral change if Parliament fails to act. As for the unemployment problem which Italy is experiencing, the new government committed itself to confront the matter, especially in the South, with speed and intensity. D'Alema emphasized the need to help youth get work. Given that unemployment is a European-wide problem, the government asserted that it would work with its EU partners to resolve it. However, the severity of the situation is such that the government felt it had to undertake immediate actions and not wait for the EU to act. The very successful mayor of Naples, Antonio Bassolino, was appointed Minister of Labour. His major assignment is the rapid development of new programmes to generate employment.

It is difficult to speak of a honeymoon period for the D'Alema Government. Upon taking office, it encountered problems it had not anticipated. Strikes, called by the COBAS leaders, paralysed the transport system. The fact that the Prime Minister comes from the Democrats of the Left did not dissuade the strikers, nor were they concerned that some leaders of major unions, including the CGIL, condemned their actions. Illegal immigration intensified in the early days of the D'Alema regime. The Italian police could apprehend only a small portion of the persons who come in small ships and boats. Many of these vessels were not seaworthy and there have been several deaths caused by unsafe craft. One of the early acts of the D'Alema Government was a gesture to help some immigrants. Some of those with legal papers, work and a home will be offered permanent status in Italy. The response to this proposal was far greater than anticipated. Long lines developed in front of some governmental offices, and in several places violence erupted as a result of pushing and shoving among the applicants. The police intervened physically to maintain order. The situation was further complicated in the North because many immigrants living in Western European countries came to Italy in order to regularize their status.

As the difficulties with the immigrants were occurring, a major event took place which confused matters even more. Abdullah Ocalan, the leader of the Kurds in Turkey who had been fighting for independence, was arrested entering Rome with a false passport. Turkish officials, calling him one of the bloodiest terrorists in the world, immediately demanded his extradition. The Italian government refused because Italian law specifically states there shall be no extradition to countries which use the death penalty. This refusal infuriated the Turkish government and people. There were street riots and attacks on things Italian throughout Turkey and calls for boycotts of Italian goods. At the same time, Kurds from all over Western Europe converged on Rome to demonstrate on behalf of Ocalan and demand that he be given political asylum. The EU generally supported the Italian position, but it offered little help. Looking for a way out, Italy proposed that an international court be established in Europe to try the Kurdish leader and that an international conference explore the Kurdish issue.

One of the prices paid by the leaders of the Democrats of the Left for support of the D'Alema Government was a commitment to the Catholic parties in the coalition that the issue of financial aid to private schools, most of which are parochial, would be examined. The prospect of government finance for private schools has brought students and teachers from public institutions into the streets for numerous demonstrations. Also, some participants in the coalition, especially the Greens and the Italian Communists, strongly oppose the idea. To date, the matter has not been resolved.

With the creation of the D'Alema Government, politically things seem to have gone full circle. The Second Republic began with a centre-right government, gaining legitimacy for the AN. Now with the creation of the D'Alema coalition, militants from the far left have entered the cabinet and gained legitimacy. In the First Republic this never happened. In fact, the transition from the First to the Second Republic, to a considerable degree, seems to have been completed. Obviously, unforeseen events could change this evaluation. Although in terms of the parties and their policy orientations, the Second Republic looks very different from the First, it still embodies some of the same characteristics. The social democratic nature of the D'Alema coalition makes it appear to be pursuing the 'new politics' of the British, French and German governments led by Tony Blair, Lionel Jospin and Gerhard Schroder respectively. It avoids looking extreme in any manner.

In 1999, the term of President Scalfaro will end. The election of a new president may do damage to the governing coalition. Previous presidential elections have caused problems for governments. Catholics would like the outgoing President Scalfaro to have another term. Scalfaro has hinted that he may be agreeable to further service in this capacity. Many Catholics of all political persuasions seem to believe that since the Prime Minister has a laic identification, a Catholic should be elected President of the Republic. The centre-right groups want a president from the centre of the political spectrum, who should be almost anyone but Scalfaro. He is viewed by members of the Pole as having a central role in the creation of the D'Alema Government. Believing that an election should have been called when the Prodi Government fell and that this was their due, they are disgruntled. Also, Berlusconi and followers continue to perceive Scalfaro as going out of his way to show support for the prosecuting magistrates who pursue Berlusconi and his colleagues.

Prodi has also become a problem to the D'Alema coalition. He strongly believes that the secret negotiations involving D'Alema and Cossiga accounted for his government's defeat. He seems bitter, and has been taking a very independent line on several issues. The most prominent of these involves the elections for the European Parliament which are to be held in 1999. He has insisted he will head a list of candidates separate from the parties of the governing coalition. The parties in the government have offered to make him their candidate to succeed Jacques Santer as President of the European Commission. He has not been enthusiastic about his chances to be elected to this position.

A factor helping the new government is that in December 1998 Italy entered the 'white semester' (*semestre bianco*), the last six months of a president's term during which, according to the Constitution, no election can be held. This should help in passing controversial legislation. However, the tensions within the coalition are considerable and if it falls, another technocratic government will probably be appointed for at least the period of the 'white semester'.

Another thing to be observed is the new direction the Democrats of the Left will take under Walter Veltroni, D'Alema's successor as party secretary. Veltroni is seen as more moderate than D'Alema and more concerned with modernizing the party. He was an admirer of John F. Kennedy, and he sees the need to work closely with Blair, Jospin and Schroder. He is committed to changing the highly bureaucratized party organization and giving it his own stamp.

One of the characteristics of the First Republic was considerable uncertainty. It was hoped that the Second Republic would offer more stability and predictability. However, uncertainty still pervades the Italian political fabric.

Bibliography

Acciari, S. (1993) 'Politica e Massoni: ecco i documenti', *Corriere della Sera*, 16 July, p. 1.

'A crime wave hits southern Italy' (1990) *Italian Journal* 4, 6: 58.

Adams, J.C. (1970) *The Quest for Democratic Law: The Role of Parliament in the Legislative Process*, New York: Thomas Y. Crowell Company.

Agostini, M.V. (1990) 'Italy and its Community policy', *The International Spectator* 25, 4: 347–55.

Albertini, M. (1982) 'I principi d'azione del Manifesto di Ventotene', *Federalista* 24: 3–9.

Alexander, D. (1991) 'Pollution policies and politics: the Italian environment', in F. Sabetti and R. Catanzaro (eds), *Italian Politics: A Review*, London: Pinter.

Almond, G. and Powell, G.B., Jr (1966) *Comparative Politics: A Developmental Approach*, Boston: Little, Brown and Company.

Arabia, A.G. (1995) 'La riforma delle amministrazioni pubbliche negli studi del Dipartimento della Funzione Pubblica (1993–1994)', *Rivista trimestrale di diritto pubblico* 45, 1: 223–49.

Attanasio, R.M. (1994) 'Ai blocchi le commissioni "motore" del Parlamento', *Il Sole 24 Ore*, 16 May, p. 3.

Azzariti, G. (1992) 'Presidenza della Repubblica e Presidenza del Consiglio Superiore della Magistratura', *Politica del diritto* 23, 2: 307–27.

Baccaro, A. (1992) 'Quei giovani Peter Pan', *Corriere della Sera*, 5 December, p. 5.

Baget-Bozzo, G. (1991) 'La politica dei vescovi', *La Repubblica*, 28 November, p. 8.

Bagnasco, A. (1987) 'Borghesia e classe operaia', in U. Ascoli and R. Catanzaro (eds), *La società italiana degli anni ottanta*, Bari: Editore Laterza.

Baldassare, A. (1985) 'Le "performances" del parlamento italiano nell'ultimo quindicennio', in G. Pasquino (ed.), *Il sistema politico italiano*, Bari: Editori Laterza.

Baldassarri, M. (1993) *Industrial Policy in Italy: 1945–1990*, New York: St Martin's Press.

—— (1994) 'Introduction', in M. Baldassarri (ed.), *The Italian Economy: Heaven or Hell?*, New York: St Martin's Press.

Banfield, E.C. (1967) *The Moral Basis of a Backward Society*, New York: Free Press.

Barile, P. (1964) *Corso di diritto costituzionale*, Padova: Cedam.

—— (1991) *Istituzioni di diritto pubblico*, Padova: Cedam.

—— (1995) 'Dalla Resistenza alla costituzione', in Associazione G. Paolo Meucci (ed.), *Dialogo sulla costituzione*, Firenze: Fatatrac.

Barile, P., Cheli, E. and Grassi, S. (1995) *Istituzioni di diritto pubblico*, Padova: Cedam.

Bartole, S. and Mastragostino, F. (1996) *Le regioni*, Bologna: Il Mulino.

Baslini, A. and Vegas, G. (1984) *Decidere con il voto: una proposta per cambiare*, Milano: Sugar Co.

'Berlusconi, nuovo attacco' (1997) *La Repubblica*, 22 December, p. 2.

Berselli, E. (1997) 'Bertinotti preso sul serio', *Il Mulino* 46, 3: 452–60.

Berti, G. (1994) *Amministrazione comunale e provinciale*, Padova: Cedam.

Bettin, G. and Magnier, A. (1991) 'Il tempo dell'assessore', *Polis* 5, 2: 209–16.

Bettini, R. (1990) 'Il sommerso burocratico come sommerso organizzativo. Ricerche sulle burocrazie pubbliche in Italia', *Sociologia e ricerca sociale* 31: 125–44.

Bevilacqua, P. (1993) *Breve storia dell'Italia meridionale dall'ottocento a oggi*, Roma: Donzelli Editore.

Bianchi, G. (1994) 'L'identità dei Popolari', *La Repubblica*, 17 July, p. 12.

Bobbio, N. (1987) *Which Socialism? Marxism, Socialism and Democracy*, Minneapolis: University of Minnesota Press.

Boggs, C. and Plotke, D. (1980) *The Politics of Eurocommunism: Socialism in Transition*, London: Macmillan.

Bolzoni, A. and Viviano, F. (1995) 'Voti di Mafia', *La Repubblica*, 6 January, pp. 1, 7.

Bordogna, L. (1989) 'The COBAS: fragmentation of trade union representation and conflict', in R. Leonardi and P. Corbetta (eds), *Italian Politics: A Review*, London: Pinter Publishers.

Borrello, I. (1997) 'Il nuovo sistema dei controlli amministrativi', *Rivista trimestrale di diritto pubblico* 47, 3: 919–22.

Bozzi, A. (1985) *Istituzioni di diritto pubblico*, Milano: Giuffre.

Breda, M. (1995a) 'Scalfaro: non abusiamo dei referendum', *Corriere della Sera*, 27 May, p. 7.

—— (1995b) 'Scalfaro: la democrazia rispetta i vinti', *Corriere della Sera*, 4 September, p. 3.

Brusco, S. (1997) 'Fondi Ue, sprecati senza ragione', *La Repubblica*, 24 February, p. 10.

Bull, M.J. and Newell, J.L. (1993) 'Italian politics and the 1992 elections: from "stable instability" to instability and change', *Parliamentary Affairs* 46, 2: 203–7.

—— (1995) 'Italy changes course? The 1994 elections and the victory of the right', *Parliamentary Affairs* 48, 1: 72–99.

Burnham, W.D. (1970) *Critical Elections and the Mainsprings of American Politics*, New York: Norton.

Caciagli, M. (1988) 'Approssimazione alle culture politiche locali: problemi di analisi ed esperienze di ricerca', *Il Politico* 53, 2: 269–92.

—— (1990) 'Erosioni e mutamenti nell'elettorato democristiano', in M. Caciagli and A. Spreafico (eds), *Vent'anni di elezioni in Italia: 1968–1987*, Padova: Liviana Editrice.

—— (1991) 'Vita e opere di un ceto politico', *Polis* 5, 2: 209–16.

Cafagna, L. (1994) *Nord e Sud. Non fare a pezzi l'unità d'Italia*, Venezia: Marsilio Editori.

Calandra, P. (1986) *Il governo della Repubblica*, Bologna: Il Mulino.

Calise, M (1994) 'Il governo tra istituzione e politica', in M. Caciagli, F. Cazzola, L. Morlino and S. Passigli (eds), *L'Italia fra crisi e transizione*, Bari: Editori Laterza.

Campagno, G. (1994) 'Il governo Berlusconi ottiene la fiducia al Senato per due voti', *Corriere della Sera*, 19 May, pp. 1–2.

Capano, G. (1991) 'Tendenze recenti della riforma amministrativa in Italia: alcune riflessioni in chiave comparata', *Rivista trimestrale di scienza dell'amministrazione* 38, 4: 139–70.

Cappelletto, P. (1995) 'Il difficile percorso degli ombudsmen regionali: un bilancio di vent'anni di attività', *Polis* 9, 1: 113–31.

Caracciolo, L. (1997) 'Perchè l'Italia conta così poco', *La Repubblica*, 7 December, p. 13.

Carbone, G. (1989) 'Corte dei Conti: urgenze e diffidenze nella riforma dei controlli', *Quaderni costituzionali* 9, 3: 566–70.

Caretti, P. and De Siervo, U. (1994) *Istituzioni di diritto pubblico*, Torino: G. Giappichelli Editore.

—— (1996) *Istituzioni di diritto pubblico*, Torino: G. Giappichelli Editore.

Carli, S. (1997) 'UE in "fondo" c'è la guerra', *La Repubblica*, 30 June, p. 11.

Carrieri, M. (1996) 'Industrial relations and the labour movement', in S. Gundle and S. Parker (eds), *The New Italian Republic: From the Fall of the Berlin Wall to Berlusconi*, London: Routledge.

Cartocci, R. (1994) 'Il deficit integrazione in Italia: una lettura culturale della crisi di oggi', in M. Caciagli, F. Cazzola, L. Morlino and S. Passigli (eds), *L'Italia fra crisi e transizione*, Bari: Editori Laterza.

Caselli, G.C. and Della Porta, D. (1991) 'The history of the Red Brigades: organizational structures and strategies of action', in R. Catanzaro (ed.), *The Red Brigades and Left-Wing Terrorism in Italy*, London: Pinter Publishers.

Cassese, S. (1988) 'Italy', in D.C. Rowat (ed.), *Public Administration in Developed Democracies: A Comparative Study*, New York: Marcel Dekker.

—— (1993) 'Hypotheses on the Italian administrative system', *West European Politics* 16, 3: 316–28.

—— (1998a) 'Allarme lottizzazione', *La Repubblica*, 21 February, pp. 1, 18.

—— (1998b) *Lo stato introvabile*, Roma: Donzelli Editore.

Catanzaro, R. (1987) 'Mafia, economia e sistema politico', in U. Ascoli and R. Catanzaro (eds), *La società italiana degli anni ottanta*, Bari: Editori Laterza.

Cattani, L. (1962) *La costituzione della Repubblica italiana*, Milano: Edizioni CETIM.

Cazzola, F. (1991a) 'Le affinità elettive: partiti e potere municipale', *Polis* 5, 2: 267–97.

—— (1991b) 'I governanti di periferia', *Regione e governo locale* 12, 2: 269–302.

—— (1992a) 'La dissoluzione del sistema italiano', *Democrazia e diritto* 32, 3: 105–7.

—— (1992b) *L'Italia del pizzo. Fenomenologia della tangente quotidiana*, Torino: Einaudi.

Cecchini, M. (1995) 'Italia, un esercito di senza lavoro', *Corriere della Sera*, 13 May, p. 21.

Ceri, P. (1988) 'The nuclear power issue: a new political cleavage within Italian society?', in R.Y. Nanetti, R. Leonardi and P. Corbetta (eds), *Italian Politics: A Review*, London: Pinter Publishers.

Cheli, E. (1994) 'L'incidenza del sistema di giustizia costituzionale negli sviluppi della forma di governo italiano', in M. Caciagli, F. Cazzola, L. Morlino and S. Passigli (eds), *L'Italia fra crisi e transizione*, Bari: Editori Laterza.

Chimenti, C. (1989) *Organi costituzionali nella forma di governo italiano*, Torino: G. Giappichelli Editore.

Chiti-Batelli, A. (1995) *Letteratura pro e contro Maastricht*, Roma: Edizione Dimensione Europa.

Chubb, J. (1989) 'The Mafia and politics: the Italian state under siege', Western Societies Programme, Occasional paper n. 23. Center for International Studies, Cornell University.

Cialdino, C.C. (ed.) (1989) *Il contenzioso per inadempimento degli membri agli obblighi comunitari: il caso Italia*, Luxembourg: The Research Department of the Court of Justice.

Ciaurro, G.F. and Posteraro, F. (1980) 'La conversione in legge dei decreti d'urgenza', *Nuovi studi politici* 10, 2: 21–62.

Cipriani, G. (1994) *I mandanti: il patto strategico tra Massoneria, Mafia e poteri politici*, Roma: Editori Riuniti.

Clauss, J. (1983) 'Regional authorities and linguistic minorities in Italy', in Y. Meny (ed.), *Centres et périphéries: le partage du pouvoir*, Paris: Economica.

Coldagelli, L. (1992) 'Uno studio dell'ISPES', *Corriere della Sera*, 8 October, p. 3.

Compston, H. (1995) 'Union participation in economic policy-making in France, Italy, Germany and Britain, 1970–1993', *West European Politics* 18, 2: 314–39.

Contri, F. (1991) 'Donne in avvocatura e in magistratura', *Legalità e giustizia* 1: 25–31.

Coppola, F. (1994) 'L'ombudsman c'è ma non si vede', *La Repubblica*, 31 January, p. 20.

Coppola, P. (ed.) (1997) *Geografia politica delle regioni italiane*, Torino: Einaudi.

Corbetta, P. and Parisi, A.M.L. (1995) 'The referendum on the electoral law for the Senate: another momentous April', in C. Mershon and G. Pasquino (eds), *Italian Politics: Ending the First Republic*, Boulder: Westview Press.

Cotta, M. (1990) 'The "centrality" of parliament in a protracted democratic consolidation: the Italian case', in U. Liebert and M. Cotta (eds), *Parliament and Democratic Consolidation in Southern Europe: Greece, Italy, Portugal, Spain and Turkey*, London: Pinter Publishers.

Cuocolo, F. (1988) 'Diritto e politica nella giurisprudenza costituzionale in materia di regioni', in Consiglio Regionale della Liguria (ed.), *Corte Costituzionale e regioni*, Napoli: Edizioni Scientifiche Italiane.

—— (1990) *Istituzioni di diritto pubblico*, Milano: Giuffre.

D'Alimonte, R. and Bartolini, S. (1995) 'Il sistema partitico italiano: una transizione difficile', in S. Bartolini and R. D'Alimonte (eds), *Maggioritario ma non troppo*, Bologna: Il Mulino.

—— (1997) 'Come perdere una maggioranza: la competizione nei collegi uninominali', in R. D'Alimonte and S. Bartolini (eds), *Maggioritario per caso*, Bologna: Il Mulino.

Damato, F. (1987a) 'Esordio in un clima tossico', *La Nazione*, 2 July, p. 1.

—— (1987b) 'Ora il parlamento c'è. Quando un governo?', *La Nazione*, 2 July, p. 1.

D'Angelo, V. (1991) 'Chiesa o comune, il matrimonio trionfa', *Corriere della Sera*, 26 November, p. 11.

D'Antone, L. (ed.) (1996) *Radici storiche ed esperienza dell'intervento straordinario nel Mezzogiorno*, Napoli: Bibliopolis.

D'Antonio, M. (1993) 'The tortuous road of industry through the Mezzogiorno', in M. Baldassarri (ed.), *Industrial Policy in Italy: 1945–1990*, New York: St Martin's Press.

D'Auria, G. (1995) 'La "funzione legislativa" dell'amministrazione', *Rivista trimestrale di diritto pubblico* 45, 3: 697–728.

De Leo, G. (1986) 'Il procedimento legislativo redigente nel parlamento italiano', *Studi parlamentari e di politica costituzionale* 19, 74: 63–77.

Della Cananea, G. (1996) 'Reforming the state: the policy of administrative reform in Italy under the Ciampi Government', *West European Politics* 19, 2: 321–39.

—— (1997) 'The reform of finance and administration in Italy: contrasting achievements', *West European Politics* 20, 1: 194–209.

Della Porta, D. (1992) *Lo scambio occulto. Casi di corruzione politica in Italia*, Bologna: Il Mulino.

Della Porta, D. and Vannucci, A. (1995) 'Politics, the Mafia and the market for corrupt exchange', in C. Mershon and G. Pasquino (eds), *Italian Politics: Ending the First Republic*, Boulder: Westview Press.

Della Sala, V. (1988) 'The Italian budgetary process: political and institutional constraints', *West European Politics* 17: 110–25.

Del Vescovo, P. (1988) 'Il Consiglio di Gabinetto: un tentativo di rafforzamenti del governo', *Rivista trimestrale di diritto pubblico* 38, 4: 900–19.

De Micheli, C. (1997) 'L'attività legislativa dei governi al tramonto della Prima Repubblica', *Rivista italiana di scienza politica* 27, 1: 151–87.

Dente, B. (1985) 'Centre-local relations in Italy: the impact of the legal and political structures', in Y. Meny and V. Wright (eds), *Centre-Periphery Relations in Western Europe*, London: George Allen & Unwin.

—— (1988) 'Local government reform and legitimacy', in B. Dente and F. Kjellberg (eds), *The Dynamics of Institutional Change: Local Government Reorganization in Western Democracies*, Beverly Hills: Sage Publications.

Diamanti, I. (1993) *La Lega. Geografia, storia e sociologia di un nuovo soggetto politico*, Roma: Donzelli Editore.

Diani, M. (1990) 'The Italian ecology movement: from radicalism to moderation', in W. Rüdig (ed.), *Green Politics One 1990*, Carbondale: Southern Illinois University Press.

Dickmann, R. (1995) 'L'esercizio dell'iniziativa legislativa', *Rivista trimestrale di diritto pubblico* 45, 1: 3–64.

Di Federico, G. (1989) 'The crisis of the justice system and the referendum on the judiciary', in R. Leonardi and P. Corbetta (eds), *Italian Politics: A Review*, London: Pinter Publishers.

Di Giuseppantonio, E. (1992) 'Adesso paghiamo i ritardi delle regioni', *Le Autonomie* 84, 2: 20–1.

D'Ignazio, G. (1997) 'La legislazione regionale di attuazione della L. 142/1990: bilancio di un'esperienza e prospettive', Paper presented at the national conference of the Consiglio Regionale and Giunta Regionale of the Tuscan Region, 'Nuove funzioni e riforma delle autonomie locali nella prospettiva federalista', Florence, Italy.

Di Palma, G. (1976) 'Institutional rules and legislative outcomes in the Italian Parliament', *Legislative Studies Quarterly* 1:147–79.

—— (1987) 'Parlamento – arena o parlamento di trasformazione', *Rivista italiana di scienza politica* 17, 2:179–201.

Di Palma, G. and Cotta, M. (1986) 'Cadres, peones, and entrepreneurs: professional identities in a divided parliament', in E.N. Suleiman (ed.), *Parliaments and Parliamentarians in Democratic Politics*, New York: Holmes & Meier.

Di Virgilio, A. (1995) 'Dai partiti ai poli: la politica delle alleanze', in S. Bartolini and R. D'Alimonte (eds), *Maggioritario ma non troppo*, Bologna: Il Mulino.

Donovan, M. (1992) 'A party system in transformation: the April 1992 Italian election', *West European Politics* 15, 4: 170–7.

D'Orazio, G. (1992) 'La "doppia presidenza" e le sue crisi (il capo dello stato e il Consiglio Superiore della Magistratura)', *Quaderni costituzionali* 12, 2: 247–312.

D'Orta, C. (1990) 'Legge quadro sul pubblico impiego e qualifiche funzionali sette anni dopo: una riforma "strabica" ', *Rivista trimestrale di diritto pubblico* 40: 769–814.

Endean, C. (1997) 'Rome listens too late to turbulent priest', *The European*, 6–12 March, p. 4.

Eurobarometer (1996, 1997).

European Commission (1997) *Protecting the Community's Financial Interests. The Fight Against Fraud. Annual Report 1996*, Luxembourg: Office for Official Publications of the European Communities.

Farneti, P. (1985) *The Italian Party System*, London: Pinter Publishers.

Fernandez, A. (1990) 'Il nuovo ordinamento amministrativo', *Queste istituzioni* 18, 81–2: 12–35.

Ferrajoli, L. (1990) 'Un nuovo conflitto tra Presidente della Repubblica e Consiglio Superiore della Magistratura', *Questione giustizia* 9, 1: 1–17.

Ferraresi, F. (1991) 'Gli statuti comunali e provinciali: luce e ombre della legge 142/90', *Il nuovo governo locale* 9, 2: 127–45.

Ferraris, L.V. (1996) 'Il semestre italiano di Presidenza dell'Unione Europea', *La comunità internazionale* 51, 2: 179–85.

Ferrarotti, F. (1989) 'The Sicilian Mafia: 1860–1977', *Italian Journal* 3, 5: 17–28.

Fiammeri, B. (1998) 'Rischio di rottura tra Prodi e sindacato', *Il Sole 24 Ore*, 15 March, p. 7.

Fiori, G. (1995) *Il venditore: storia di Silvio Berlusconi e della Fininvest*, Milano: Garzanti.

Folli, S. (1993) 'La Consulta decide anche il proprio futuro', *Corriere della Sera*, 11 January, p. 4.

Follini, M. (1996) 'Perchè il Polo ha perso le elezioni', *Il Mulino* 45: 468–77.

Fondazione Rosselli (1993) *Primo rapporto sulle priorità nazionali*, Milano: Arnoldo Mondadori Editore.

'Forza Italia, rivolta dei club' (1994) *La Repubblica*, 21 May, p. 8.

Fossati, A. (1990) 'La "novità" della regione: una opportunità mancata?', *Aggiornamenti sociali* 41, 4: 307–18.

Fraschini, A. (1990) 'Il controllo degli enti locali: l'esperienza italiana', *Il nuovo governo locale* 8, 1: 57–73.

Freddi, G. (1992) 'La pubblica amministrazione: perchè funziona in modo così deludente', in G. Urbani (ed.), *Dentro la politica: come funzionano il governo e le istituzioni*, Milano: Il Sole 24 Ore Libri.

Frenkel, M. (1986) 'The distribution of legal powers in pluricentral systems', in R. Morgan (ed.), *Regionalism in European Politics*, London: Policy Studies Institute.

Furlong, P. (1990) 'Parliament in Italian politics', *West European Politics* 13: 52–7.

Galli, G. (1966) *Il bipartitismo imperfetto*, Bologna: Il Mulino.

—— (1983) *L'Italia sotterranea: storia, politica e scandali*, Bari: Laterza.

Gambino, S. and Urbani, P. (1991) 'La delega di funzioni regionali agli enti locali di fronte all'attuazione della l. n. 142/90', *Regione e governo locale* 12, 3–4: 371–83.

Garruto, R. (1965) 'Le commissioni parlamentari', *La funzione amministrativa* 14: 744–68.

Gasperoni, G. (1997) 'Genere e condizioni di lavoro nella magistratura italiana', *Polis* 11, 2: 231–51.

Gibbins, J.R. (1989) 'Contemporary political culture: an introduction', in J.R. Gibbins (ed.), *Contemporary Political Culture: Politics in a Postmodern Age*, London: Sage Publications.

Giglioli, P.P. (1996) 'Political corruption and the media: the Tangentopoli affair', *International Social Science Journal* 48, 149: 381–94.

Gilbert, M. (1995) *The Italian Revolution: The End of Politics, Italian Style?*, Boulder: Westview Press.

Ginsborg, P. (1990) *A History of Contemporary Italy: Society and Politics: 1943–1988*, London: Penguin.

—— (1994) *Le virtù della Repubblica*, Milano: Il Saggiatore.

Giovagnoli, A. (1996) *Il partito italiano. La Democrazia Cristiana dal 1942 al 1994*, Bari: Laterza.

Giuglia, G. (1988) 'La figura dei ministri senza portfoglio dopo la legge n. 400 del 1988', *Giurisprudenza costituzionale* 2: 1420–40.

—— (1989) 'La figura del Vice Presidente del Consiglio dopo legge n. 400 del 1988: prime riflessioni', *Quaderni costituzionali* 9: 187–93.

Giuliani, M. (1992) 'Il processo decisionale italiano e le politiche comunitarie', *Polis* 6, 2: 307–42.

—— (1996) 'Italy', in W. Wessels and D. Rometsch (eds), *The European Union and Member States*, Manchester: Manchester University Press.

—— (1997) 'Measures of consensual law-making: Italian "consociativismo" ', *Southern European Society and Politics* 2, 12: 66–96.

Golden, M. (1986) 'Interest representation, party systems and the state: Italy in comparative perspective', *Comparative Politics* 18, 3: 279–301.

Goldsmith, M. (1991) 'Il governo locale: teoria e pratica', *Rivista trimestrale di scienza dell'amministrazione* 38, 4: 17–41.

Graldi, P. (1986) 'La giustizia come azienda', *Corriere della Sera*, 17 July, p. 7.

Gramoglia, G. (1998) Interview, 20 March, Florence, Italy.

Grisalia, M.C. (1986) *Poteri di messaggio ed esternazione presidenziale*, Milano: Giuffre.

Guadagnini, M. (1983) 'Partiti e classe parlamentare negli anni settanta', *Rivista italiana di scienza politica* 13, 2: 261–94.

—— (1984) 'Il personale politico parlamentare degli anni '70 agli anni '80: problemi di ricerca e di analisi e alcuni dati empirici', in Centro Studi di Scienza Politica 'Paolo Farneti' (ed.), *Il sistema politico italiano tra crisi e innovazione*, Milano: Franco Angeli Editore.

Gualmini, E. (1997) 'L'evoluzione degli assetti concertativi in Italia e in Germania', *Rivista italiana di scienza politica* 27, 1: 101–50.

Guarnieri, C. (1991a) 'Checks without balances: judicial powers and politics in Italy', *Italian Journal* 5, 3–4: 8–13.

—— (1991b) 'Magistratura e politica: il caso italiano', *Rivista italiana di scienza politica* 21, 1: 3–32.

—— (1992) *Magistratura e politica in Italia*, Bologna: Il Mulino.

—— (1997) 'The judiciary in the Italian political crisis', *West European Politics* 20, 1: 157–75.

Guidorossi, G. and Weber, M. (1988) 'Immagine dei partiti e antagonismo politico in Italia, Spagna, Portogallo e Grecia', *Il Politico* 53, 2: 225–59.

Gusso, M. (1982) *Il Partito Radicale: organizzazione e leadership*, Padova: Cleup.

Guyon, J. (1993) 'No longer business as usual', *The Wall Street Journal Europe*, 10 March, pp. 1, 7.

Hallenstein, D. (1994a) 'Token leftist falls foul of hardliners', *The European*, 20–26 May, p. 2.

—— (1994b) 'Ambitiousness pulls out all the stops', *The European*, 7–13 October, p. 11.

Hanson, A.H. (1964) 'The purpose of parliament', *Parliamentary Affairs* 17: 279–95.

Hebblethwaite, P. (1987) 'The Italian church post-1968: responses to secularisation', *Newsletter: Association for the Study of Modern Italy*, 11: 25–9.

Hernes, G. and Selvik, A. (1981) 'Local corporatism', in S. Berger (ed.), *Organizing Interests in Western Europe: Pluralism, Corporatism, and the Transformation of Politics*, New York: Cambridge University Press.

Honorati, M.L.M. (1995) *Lezioni di diritto parlamentare*, Torino: G. Giappichelli Editore.

Ignazi, P. (1998a) 'Forza Italia alle prove d'opposizione dura', *Il Sole 24 Ore*, 19 April, pp. 1–2.

—— (1998b) *Il polo escluso: profilo storico del Movimento Sociale Italiano*, Bologna: Il Mulino.

Indrio, U. (1971) *La presidenza di Saragat*, Milano: Arnoldo Mondadori Editore.

Inglehart, R. (1989) 'Observations on cultural change and postmodernism', in J.R. Gibbins (ed.), *Contemporary Political Change: Politics in a Postmodern Age*, London: Sage Publications.

Istituto Nazionale dell'Informazione (1996) *I deputati e senatori del tredicesimo parlamento repubblicano*, Roma: Editoriale Italiana.

'Italy: now for a party' (1998) *The Economist*, 4 April, p. 42.

'Italy: Roman power' (1988) *The Economist*, 26 March, pp. 44–5.

Katz, R.S. (1995) 'The 1993 parliamentary electoral reform', in C. Mershon and G. Pasquino (eds), *Italian Politics: Ending the First Republic*, Boulder: Westview Press.

Kelly, R.J. (1991) 'Terrorism and intrigue: the Red Brigades – Aldo Moro's Murder – and the Gladio affair', *Italian Journal* 5, 1: 14–21.

Kirchheimer, O. (1966) 'The transformation of Western European party systems', in J. LaPalombara and M. Weiner (eds), *Political Parties and Political Development*, Princeton: Princeton University Press.

Kitschelt, H. (1989) *The Logic of Party Formation: Ecological Politics in Belgium and West Germany*, Ithaca: Cornell University Press.

—— (1995) *The Radical Right in Western Europe: A Comparative Analysis*, Ann Arbor: The University of Michigan Press.

Koff, H. (1993) 'The impact of non-European Community immigration on Italian society and politics', unpublished B.A. Honors Thesis, State University of New York at Binghamton.

Koff, S. (1982) 'The Italian presidency: constitutional role and political practice', *Presidential Studies Quarterly* 12: 44–58.

—— (1994) 'The European Union and the Italian Parliament', paper delivered at the 1994 international conference on national parliaments and the European Union, Wroxton, England.

—— (1995) 'Great Britain and Italy "polls apart": the 1994 election campaigns', paper presented at the meeting of the Fifth International Congress, 'European Parliament Elections 1979–1994', Pavia, Italy.

Kreppel, A. (1997) 'The impact of parties in government on legislative output in Italy', *European Journal of Political Research* 31, 3: 327–50.

Kurth, J. (1993) 'A tale of four countries: parallel politics in southern Europe, 1815–1990', in J. Kurth, J. Petras with D. Maquire and R. Chilcote (eds), *Mediterranean Paradoxes: The Politics and Social Structure of Southern Europe*, Providence: Berg.

Labriola, S. (1989) *Il governo della Repubblica: origini e poteri: commento alla legge 23 Agosto 1988, n. 400*, Rimini: Maggioli Editore.

La Malfa, U. (1971) 'Il processo legislativo', in Centro di Ricerca e Documentazione 'Luigi Einaudi' (ed.), *Processo allo stato: la democrazia non può permettersi il lusso di non funzionare*, Firenze: Sansoni Editore.

Lampugnani, R. (1998) 'Con la Lega vinceremo', *L'Unità*, 5 April, p. 5.

Lanzalaco, L. (1990) 'Pininfarina, President of the Confederation of Industry and the problems of business interest associations', in R. Nanetti and R. Catanzaro (eds), *Italian Politics: A Review*, London: Pinter Publishers.

LaPalombara, J. (1964) *Interest Groups in Italian Politics*, Princeton: Princeton University Press.

—— (1987) *Democracy Italian Style*, New Haven: Yale University Press.

—— (1994) ' "Clientela e parentela" rivisitato', in M. Caciagli, F. Cazzola, L. Morlino and S. Passigli (eds), *L'Italia fra crisi e transizione*, Bari: Editori Laterza.

Latella, M. (1994) 'Berlusconi: Forza Italia sono io', *Corriere della Sera*, 22 November, p. 5.

Lattes, G.B. and Magnier, A. (1995) 'I nuovi sindaci: come cambia una carriera politica', *Rivista italiana di scienza politica* 25, 1: 91–118.

Leonardi, R. (1995) *Convergence, Cohesion and Integration in the European Union*, New York: St Martin's Press.

Leonardi, R., Nanetti, R. and Pasquino, G. (1978) 'Institutionalization of parliament and parliamentarization of parties in Italy', *Legislative Studies Quarterly* 3: 161–86.

Lepri, S. (1992) 'Settore pubblico sotto tiro', *La Stampa*, 22 July, p. 28.

Lerner, G. (1994) 'Ma davvero ha vinto la TV?', *La Stampa*, 2 April, pp. 1, 6.

Locke, R.M. (1990) 'The resurgence of the local union: industrial restructuring and industrial relations in Italy', *Politics and Society* 18, 3: 347–75.

Lombardo, A. (1984) *La grande riforma: governo, istituzioni, partiti*, Milano: Sugar Co.

Luccioli, G. (1991) 'Un'associazione per le donne giudici', *Legalità e giustizia* 1: 11–17.

Luzi, G. (1998) 'Giù le mani da De Gasperi', *La Repubblica*, 12 April, p. 6.

Magatti, M. (1996) 'Tangentopoli, una questione sociale', *Il Mulino* 45, 368: 1058–69.

Manca, D. (1995) 'Italia malata di disoccupazione', *Corriere della Sera*, 30 March, p. 19.

Mannheimer, R. (1990) 'Vecchi e nuovi caratteri del voto comunista', in M. Caciagli and A. Spreafico (eds), *Vent'anni di elezioni in Italia: 1968–1987*, Padova: Liviana Editrice.

Mannheimer, R. and Sani, G. (1987) *Il mercato elettorale: identikit dell'elettore italiano*, Bologna: Il Mulino.

Manzella, A. (1996) 'The first majoritarian parliament', in R.S. Katz and P. Ignazi (eds), *Italian Politics: The Year of the Tycoon*, Boulder: Westview Press.

Marchi, T. (1950) 'Il capo dello stato', in P. Calamandrei and A. Levi (eds), *Commentario sistematico alla costituzione italiana*, Firenze: G. Barbera.

Marro, E. (1992) 'Rapporto Svimez', *Corriere della Sera*, 3 July, p. 6.

Martinelli, A. (1980) 'Organised business and Italian politics: Confindustria and the Christian Democrats in the postwar period', in P. Lange and S. Tarrow (eds), *Italy in Transition: Conflict and Consensus*, London: Frank Cass & Company.

Martines, T. (1990) *Diritto pubblico*, Milano: Giuffre.

Martinetti, C. (1992) 'Il CSM, tempio di battaglie e veleni', *La Stampa*, 26 July, p. 4.

Mattina, L. (1993) 'Abete's Confindustria: from alliance with the DC to multiparty appeal', in S. Hellman and G. Pasquino (eds), *Italian Politics: A Review*, London: Pinter Publishers.

—— (1995) 'I candidati', in S. Bartolini and R. D'Alimonte (eds), *Maggioritario ma non troppo*, Bologna: Il Mulino.

Meletti, G. (1992) 'Il partito dei precari', *Corriere della Sera*, 25 March, p. 3.

Mennitti, D. (ed.) (1997) *Forza Italia: radiografia di un evento*, Roma: Ideazione Editrice.

Meny, Y. (1986) 'The political dynamics of regionalism: Italy, France, Spain', in R. Morgan (ed.), *Regionalism in European Politics*, London: Policy Studies Institute.

Merkel, W. (1987) *Prima e dopo Craxi: le trasformazioni del PSI*, Padova: Liviana Editrice.

Messina, S. (1995) 'Il MSI non serve più', *La Repubblica*, 26 January, p. 6.

'Montecitorio' (1992) *Il Messaggero*, 10 April, p. 6.

Morisi, M. (1992) *Le leggi del consenso*, Messina: Rubbettino.

—— (1994) 'La giurisdizione come "lavoro politico": vecchi e nuovi interrogativi', in M. Caciagli, F. Cazzola, L. Morlino and S. Passigli (eds), *L'Italia fra crisi e transizione*, Bari: Editori Laterza.

Morlino, L. (1986) 'Solo un'occasione di più per la guerra tra partiti', *Corriere della Sera*, 3 November, p. 7.

Musso, E.S. (1986) *Diritto costituzionale*, Padova: Cedam.

Mutti, A. (1996) 'Programmi per il Mezzogiorno', *Il Mulino*, 45, 364: 309–19.

N.A. (1997) 'A (slightly) new Italian establishment', *The Economist*, 12 July, p. 26.

—— (1998a) 'Prc, son passati sette anni', *Liberazione*, 8 February, p. 15.

—— (1998b) 'Berlusconi, un partito sotto il segno della DC', *La Repubblica*, 12 April, p. 6.

Nanetti, R.Y. (1988) *Growth and Territorial Policies: The Italian Model of Social Capitalism*, London: Pinter Publishers.

Nanetti, R.Y., Leonardi, R. and Corbetta, P. (1988) 'Introduction', in R.Y. Nanetti, R. Leonardi and P. Corbetta (eds), *Italian Politics: A Review*, London: Pinter Publishers.

Negri, N. and Sciolla, L. (eds) (1997) *Il paese dei paradossi. Le basi sociali della politica in Italia*, Roma: Nuova Italia Scientifica.

Nelken, D. (1996a) 'A legal revolution? the judges and *Tangentopoli*', in S. Gundle and S. Parker (eds), *The New Italian Republic: From the Fall of the Berlin Wall to Berlusconi*, London: Routledge.

—— (1996b) 'Stopping the judges', in M. Caciagli and D. Kertzer (eds), *Italian Politics: The Stalled Transition*, Boulder: Westview Press.

Nese, M. (1992) 'Ecco perchè Martelli non sbaglia', *Corriere della Sera*, 10 July, p. 15.

—— (1993) 'Le darò la lista dei carabinieri Massoni', *Corriere della Sera*, 14 July, p. 11.

'The New Left' (1989) *The Economist*, 9 December, pp. 51–2.

Noel, E. (1993) Interview, 9 December, San Domenico (Fiesole), Italy.

Nuvoli, P. and Spreafico, A. (1990) 'Il partito del non voto', in M. Caciagli and A. Spreafico (eds), *Vent'anni di elezioni in Italia: 1968–1987*, Padova: Liviana Editrice.

Occhiocupo, N. (1973) *Il Segretariato Generale della Presidenza della Repubblica*, Milano: Giuffre.

Offe, C. (1981) 'The attribution of public status to interest groups: observations on the West German case', in S. Berger (ed.), *Organizing Interests in Western Europe: Pluralism, Corporatism and the Transformation of Politics*, New York: Cambridge University Press.

Orefice, P. (1992) 'Anselmi: per le donne la strada è sempre in salita', *Il Messaggero*, 13 April, p. 5.

Palombelli, B. (1994) 'Berlusconi prende il largo', *La Repubblica*, 19 May, pp. 2–3.

Pappalardo, A. (1995) 'La nuova legge elettorale in parlamento: chi, come e perchè', in S. Bartolini and R. D'Alimonte (eds), *Maggioritario ma non troppo*, Bologna: Il Mulino.

Pasquino, G. (1992) 'La classe politica e la sua cultura di governo', in G. Urbani (ed.), *Dentro la politica: come funzionano il governo e le istituzioni*, Milano: Il Sole 24 Ore.

Pastori, G. (1991) 'La pubblica amministrazione', in G. Amato and A. Barbera (eds), *Manuale di diritto costituzionale*, Bologna: Il Mulino.

Patrono, M. (1989) 'Scenari per una riforma del Consiglio Superiore della Magistratura', *Quaderni costituzionali* 9, 3: 447–69.

PDC (1995) 'Come evitare i trabocchetti al seggio', *Corriere della Sera*, 23 April, p. 2.

Pederzoli, P. and Guarnieri, C. (1997) 'The judicialization of politics: Italian style', *Journal of Modern Italian Studies* 2, 3: 321–36.

Pescosolido, G. (1998) *Unità nazionale e sviluppo economico*, Bari: Laterza.

Petretto, A. (1997) 'La redistribuzione delle funzioni: profili finanziari', paper presented at the national conference of the Consiglio Regionale and the Giunta Regionale of the Tuscan Region 'Nuove funzioni e riforma delle autonomie locali nella prospettiva federalista', Florence, Italy.

Pica, F. (1991) 'Gli adempimenti della l. 142/90 per la contabilità e la finanza locale', *Il nuovo governo locale* 7, 2: 45–64.

Pizzorusso, A. (1981) *Lezioni di diritto costituzionale*, Roma: Il Foro Italiano

—— (1984) *Lezioni di diritto costituzionale*, Roma: Il Foro Italiano.

—— (1985a) 'The Italian Constitution', *Jahrbuch des offentlichen Rechts der Gegenwart* 34: 105–21.

—— (1985b) *L'organizzazione della giustizia in Italia: la magistratura nel sistema politico e istituzionale*, Torino: Einaudi.

—— (1988) *Law in the Making: A Comparative Survey*, London: Springer-Verlag.

—— (1989) 'Problemi definitori e prospettive di riforma del C.S.M.', *Quaderni costituzionali* 9, 3: 471–87.

—— (1990) 'L'incerto ruolo costituzionale del Ministero della Giustizia', *Il Politico* 55, 2: 313–22.

—— (1997) *Manuale di istituzioni di diritto pubblico*, Napoli: Jovene Editore.

Pola, G. (1989) 'Dissesto dei bilanci comunali e crisi della finanza locale', *Il nuovo governo locale* 7, 2: 45–64.

Pragma (1994) 'Quantità e qualità dell'informazione ad pubblico', in Pragma (ed.), *L'Europa degli italiani. Risultati della ricerca e contributi interpretativi*, Commissione delle Comunità Europee, Ufficio per l'Italia.

Puledda, V. (1993) 'Lo stato che vorrei', *La Repubblica*, 17 September, p. 43.

Putnam, R.D. (1993) *Making Democracy Work: Civic Traditions in Modern Italy*, Princeton: Princeton University Press.

'Il Quirinale scrive' (1994) *La Repubblica*, 11 May, p. 3.

Rebuffa, G. (1995) *La costituzione impossibile: cultura politica e sistema parlamentare in Italia*, Bologna: Il Mulino.

Recchi, E. (1991) 'Il network politico dell'amministratore comunale italiano', *Polis* 5, 2: 243–65.

—— (1996) 'Fishing from the same schools: parliamentary recruitment and consociationalism in the First and Second Italian Republics', *West European Politics* 19, 2: 340–59.

Regalia, I. and Regini, M. (1987) 'I sindacati nel sistema politico e amministrativo', in U. Ascoli and R. Catanzaro (eds), *La società italiana degli anni ottanta*, Bari: Editori Laterza.

Regini, M. (1980) 'Labour unions, industrial action and politics', in P. Lange and S. Tarrow (eds), *Italy in Transition: Conflict and Consensus*, London: Frank Cass.

Regini, M. and Regalia, I. (1997) 'Employers, unions and the state: the resurgence of concertation in Italy?', in M. Bull and M. Rhodes (eds), *Crisis and Transition in Italian Politics*, London: Frank Cass.

Rescigno, G.U. (1984) *Corso di diritto pubblico*, Bologna: Zanichelli.

—— (1990) *Corso di diritto pubblico*, Bologna: Zanichelli.

—— (1994) 'A proposito di Prima e Seconda Repubblica', *Studi parlamentari e di politica costituzionale* 27, 103: 5–26.

Rhodes, M. (1995a) 'Italian Greens: struggles for survival', *Environmental Politics* 4, 2: 305–12.

—— (1995b) 'Reinventing the left: the origins of Italy's Progressive Alliance', in C. Mershon and G. Pasquino (eds), *Italian Politics: Ending the First Republic*, Boulder: Westview Press.

Richardson, J. (1995) 'The market for political activism: interest groups as a challenge to political parties', *West European Politics* 18, 1: 116–39.

Righettini, S. (1995) 'La politicizzazione di un potere neutrale. Magistratura e crisi italiana', *Rivista italiana di scienza politica* 25, 2: 227–65.

Roggero, F. (1995) 'Schengen a passo di lumaca', *Il Sole 24 Ore*, 17 July, p. 25.

Romano, S. (1994) 'Così, Roma trascura l'Europa', *La Stampa*, 27 October, p. 2.

Rotelli, E. (1991) 'L'assetto istituzionale delle aree metropolitane', *Il nuovo governo locale* 9, 1: 91–103.

Sabel, C.F. (1981) 'The internal politics of trade unions', in S. Berger (ed.), *Organizing Interests in Western Europe: Pluralism, Corporatism and the Transformation of Politics*, New York: Cambridge University Press.

Salerno, G. (1992) *Il referendum*, Padova: Cedam.

Salvati, M. (1981) 'May 1968 and the Hot Autumn of 1969: the responses of two ruling classes', in S. Berger (ed.), *Organizing Interests in Western Europe: Pluralism, Corporatism and the Transformation of Politics*, New York: Cambridge University Press.

—— (1995) 'Crisi politica, risanamento finanziario e ruolo della concertazione', *Il Mulino* 45: 431–36.

Salvemini, G. (1936) *Under the Axe of Fascism*, London: Victor Gollancz.

Sani, G. (1980) 'The political culture of Italy: continuity and change', in G.A. Almond and S. Verba (eds), *The Civic Culture Revisited*, Boston: Little, Brown.

—— (1992) 'L'influenza della cultura politica: cosa i cittadini chiedono ai partiti e perchè li votano', in G. Urbani (ed.), *Dentro la politica: come funzionano il governo e le istituzioni*, Milano: Il Sole 24 Ore.

Saracena, G. (1995) 'I principi azzurri', *Corriere della Sera*, 27 March, p. 18.

Sartori, G. (ed.) (1973) *Correnti, frazioni e fazioni nei partiti politici italiani*, Bologna: Il Mulino.

Schiavone, A. (1998) *Italiani senza Italia: storia e identità*, Torino: Einaudi.

Schlesinger, P. (1990) 'The Berlusconi phenomenon', in Z. Baranski and R.Lumley (eds), *Culture and Conflict in Postwar Italy*, London: Macmillan.

Scudiero, M. (1988) 'La Corte Costituzionale e l'identificazione dei principi fondamentali della legislazione statale', in Consiglio Regionale della Liguria (ed.), *Corte Costituzionale e regioni*, Napoli: Edizioni Scientifiche Italiane.

Sechi, G. (1992) 'Delegificazione del rapporto di pubblico impiego', *L'amministrazione italiana* 47, 2: 191–211.

Seisselberg, J. (1996) 'Conditions of success and political problems of a "media-mediated personality-party": the case of Forza Italia', *West European Politics* 19, 4: 715–43.

Siniscalco, D. (1996) 'Parola chiave concertazione', *Il Mulino* 45, 365: 502–7.

Sivo, V. (1994) 'Trentin: CGIL addio', *La Repubblica*, 25 January, p. 40.

—— (1998) 'Lavoro nero, radiografia-choc. Fuorilegge un'azienda su due', *La Repubblica*, 16 July, p. 6.

Smart, V. (1997) 'How our MEPs view the state of the union', *The European*, 10–16 April, p. 15.

Smith, D.M. (1959) *Italy: A Modern History*, Ann Arbor: The University of Michigan Press.

Solazzo, A. (1992) 'Onorevoli nei guai salvati dal Parlamento', *Corriere della Sera*, 19 June, p. 6.

'Sondaggio Fini leader della destra' (1995) *La Repubblica*, 28 January, p. 3.

Spadaro, A. (1985) 'Riflessioni sul mandato imperativo di partito', *Studi parlamentari e di politica costituzionale* 18, 67: 21–54.

Speroni, D. (1993) 'I bei tempi di Cirino', *Corriere della Sera*, 26 May, p. 22.

Staderini, F. (1996) *Diritto degli enti locali*, Padova: Cedam.

Stille, A. (1995) *Excellent Cadavers: The Mafia and the Death of the First Italian Republic*, New York: Pantheon Books.

Suseri, N. (1998) 'Le borse festeggiano gli undici', *La Repubblica*, 5 May, p. 2.

Tamburrano, G. (1971) *Storia e cronaca del centrosinistra*, Milano: Feltrinelli.

—— (1974) *L'iceberg democristiano: il potere in Italia oggi e domani*, Milano: Feltrinelli.

Tarchi, M. (1997) *Dal Msi ad An*, Bologna: Il Mulino.

Taylor, J. (1995) 'Paper monuments to Fascism', *The European Magazine*, 14–20 April, pp. 4–5.

Testa, V. (1994) 'Il partito d'un solo uomo', *La Repubblica*, 8 July, p. 8.

Tropeano, M. (1994) 'Comino: una task-force anti-truffa', *La Stampa*, 28 August, p. 27.

Truman, D.B. (1951) *The Governmental Process*, New York: Alfred A. Knopf.

Turani, G. (1993) 'Storia di una mangiatoia', *La Repubblica*, 12 March, p. 4.

Uleri, P.V. (1989) 'The 1987 referenda', in R. Leonardi and P. Corbetta (eds), *Italian Politics: A Review*, London: Pinter Publishers.

U.R. (1995) 'La Cdu di Buttiglione', *La Repubblica*, 24 July, p. 8.

Urbani, P. (1990) 'La legge di riforma delle autonomie locali: riflessioni sui profili funzionali', *Studi parlamentari e di politica costituzionale* 23, 89–90: 13–25.

Vanwelkenhuysen, A. (1986) 'Arbitration in conflicts between regions or between a region and the federal or national authorities', in R. Morgan (ed.), *Regionalism in European Politics*, London: Policy Studies Institute.

Verzichelli, L. (1995) 'Gli eletti', in S. Bartolini and R. D'Alimonte (eds), *Maggioritario ma non troppo*, Bologna: Il Mulino.

—— (1996) 'I gruppi parlamentari dopo il 1994: fluidità e riaggregazioni', *Rivista italiana di scienza politica* 26, 2: 391–413.

—— (1997) 'La classe politica della transizione', in R. D'Alimonte and S. Bartolini (eds), *Maggioritario per caso*, Bologna: Il Mulino.

Volcansek, M.L. (1994) 'Political power and judicial review in Italy', *Comparative Political Studies* 26, 4: 492–509.

Woods, D. (1995) 'The crisis of center–periphery integration in Italy and the rise of regional populism: the Lombard League', *Comparative Politics* 27, 2: 187–203.

Zannotti, F. (1989) *La magistratura. Un gruppo di pressione istituzionale. L'autodeterminazione delle retribuzioni*, Padova: Cedam.

Zannotti, F. and Sapignoli, M. (1997) 'L'incremento degli incarichi extra-giudiziari dei magistrati italiani: una ricerca sugli anni 1992, 1993, 1994', *Polis* 11, 2: 213–29.

Zuccolini, R. (1991) 'Però sul voto i cattolici vogliono decidere da soli', *Corriere della Sera*, 1 October, p. 7.

Index

incivismo 26–7; *see also* political culture
initiatives 56
Institute for Industrial Reconstruction
    (*Istituto per la Ricostruzione Industriale*) *see*
    IRI
interest groups 78–109; access channels
    102–8; agricultural groups 90–1;
    anomic groups 81; associational groups
    82–100; business groups 82–5;
    environmental groups 85–91;
    institutional groups 100–2; labour
    groups 85–91; non-associational groups
    81–2; opposition to EU 198; and
    political culture 18; 'politico-Mafia
    lobby' 99
IRI (*Istituto per la Ricostruzione Industriale* –
    Institute for Industrial Reconstruction)
    101–2
Israel 67
Istituto per la Ricostruzione Industriale (Institute
    for Industrial Reconstruction) *see* IRI
Italia Nostra (Our Italy) 92
Italian Catholic Action (*Azione Cattolica
    Italiana*) *see* ACI
Italian Communist Party *see* PCI
Italian Confederation of Workers' Unions
    (*Confederazione Italiana Sindacati Lavoratori*)
    see CISL
Italian General Confederation of Labour
    (*Confederazione Generale Italiana di Lavoro*)
    see CGIL
Italian Liberal Party *see* PLI
Italian Popular Party *see* PPI
Italian Renewal 54, 173
Italian Republican Party *see* PRI
Italian Social Democratic Party *see* PSDI
Italian Social Movement *see* MSI
Italian Social Movement – Tri-Colour
    Flame *see* MSFT
Italian Socialist Party *see* PSI
Italian Union of Labour (*Unione Italiana del
    Lavoro*) *see* UIL

Jemolo, Arturo Carlo 144
Jervolino, Rosa Russo 218
John XXIII, Pope 21, 22
John Paul II, Pope 19, 22–3
Jospin, Lionel 220, 221
justice system 164–81; administrative
    tribunals 167–9; career for women 166;

Constitutional Court 169–71; CSM
    171–5; interest group activity 107;
    judicial independence 164, 165, 166,
    171; legal careers 164–7; recruitment of
    judges 165; and *Tangentopoli* 175–8

Kennedy, Jack 221
Kickback City *see* Tangentopoli
Kinnock, Neil 50
Kirchheimer, Otto 35

La Malfa, Giorgio 39
La Malfa, Ugo 39, 120
LaPalombara, Joseph 15, 104, 106
Lateran Pacts 20
Law Number 142 (1990): and communes
    185, 186; implementation 196; and
    provinces 189, 190; and regions 192–3
Law Number 400 (1988) 133; change in
    undersecretaries' role 138; distinction
    between foreign and EU affairs 209;
    increase in prime ministerial powers
    135, 136; provisions concerning decree
    laws 140; vigilance of Cabinet
    committees 139
League of Nations 13
Leagues 26, 28; *see also* Northern League
Lega per l'Ambiente (League for the
    Environment) 92
Leone, Giovanni 141, 147
Life Senators 111, 146
Lotta Continua (Continuous Struggle) 94

Maastricht Treaty 88, 89, 198, 205
Mafia 97–100; activities in the South 6, 64;
    compared to BR 99, 100; contribution
    to Italy's European image 207; growth
    3, 212; impact on Scalfaro election 141;
    influence in FI organization 44; and the
    judiciary 107, 165; P2 ties 96;
    prosecutions 49; pursuit by the *Rete* 53
Malfatti, Franco Maria 203
Mani Pulite 2, 75; *see also* Tangentopoli
The Manifesto of Ventotene 204
Mannheimer, R. 61, 62
Mater et Magistra (Mother and Teacher) 21
Mattei, Enrico 102
Mazzini, Giuseppe 9–10
Middle East 94, 205
Miglio, Gianfranco 144